MUSIC
PATTERNS AND STYLE

MUSIC
PATTERNS AND STYLE

Richard P. DeLone
Indiana University

Addison-Wesley Publishing Company
Reading, Massachusetts · Menlo Park, California · London · Don Mills, Ontario

This book is in the
ADDISON-WESLEY SERIES IN MUSIC

 Printed in the United States of America. Published simultaneously in Canada. Library of Congress Catalog Card No. 78-100859.

To my loving father and mother,
Louis and Helena DeLone

PREFACE

In the traditional music curriculum there has been a separation between courses in music theory and courses in music literature and history. Many students and teachers have mentioned the need for a book in which the materials, structure, and literature of music are dealt with in tandem, rather than only as discrete subjects. The present book is the result of an attempt to fill this need. It is designed to provide the basis for a year's program which will give the student a grasp of basic musical materials and formal structures and of some of their manifestations in music literature in various periods of history. Although most emphasis is placed on materials, particularly as a point of departure, the importance of establishing connections between musical materials and the structural and other aspects of music literature of different stylistic periods is paramount throughout the book.

The approach taken in this book involves considerable participation and activity by the student beyond the assimilation of a certain amount of information. This participation involves the completion of a number of exercises at the end of each chapter. Most of the exercise sets require both analytical and written (inventive) work. The ear is regarded as the main referent for analysis. A variety of musical styles, forms, and materials is found in the exercises. Those exercises marked *optional* might be omitted by classes limited to one semester's duration or by students in music appreciation classes having less need than music students for practical mastery of the materials. Mastery of the exercises, although desirable, is not the primary reason for their inclusion. They are important because they supplement the musical examples within each chapter in exposing the student to a variety of materials, styles, and organizational procedures.

The chapters dealing with musical styles and historical periods (Chapters 14 and 15) are cursory, providing only sketches for whatever in-depth study is deemed appropriate by the teacher. Such in-depth work could take the form of analytical studies of selected complete works, stylistic comparisons, or chronological studies of composers' representative works. Other approaches to comprehensive study of the literature could be interpolated as the teacher desires and as the needs of particular classes might suggest. Those students or teachers so inclined will find extensive supplementation on a more advanced level in the two volumes entitled *The Materials and Structure of Music,* by William Christ, Peter DeLone, Diane Kliewer, Lewis Rowell, and William Thomson.

In general, this book is intended for use by those who have not yet achieved a thorough understanding of musical materials or their formal articulation in past and current music. It should be especially useful to college freshmen, musically oriented high school students, and those anticipating careers as teachers, charged with the responsibility of communicating about music on different levels and from different standpoints.

It is hoped that one dominant point of view will be clear during study of the various topics dealt with in this book—namely, that a sympathetic understanding of music (on any level) must come primarily from active involvement with music, rather than passive acceptance of it.

I wish to thank the staff of Addison-Wesley, who through their knowledge and editorial skills have played a major role in the revisions and preparation for publication of the manuscript. I am also indebted to Diane Kliewer for her knowledgeable assistance in proofreading and indexing; and to many of my colleagues, especially Dr. Allen Winold of Indiana University for his suggestions and encouragement. As usual, my family has endured with understanding many fatherless hours.

Bloomington, Indiana R. P. D.
June 1970

CONTENTS

Chapter 15 **The Twentieth Century in Brief Perspective**

Chapter 1

TONE AND NOTATION OF PITCH

Music is organized sound. Our ability to participate in music as comprehending listeners and performers depends to a great extent on our capacity to perceive the organization of the sounds we hear. There are, of course, various levels of musical understanding, corresponding to different musical backgrounds and training (or lack of it). However, little real *comprehension* of music is possible without a grasp of the interplaying factors that constitute its organization. These factors are grasped through both hearing and reading music. They may be perceived directly by the ear, as patterns of sound, or indirectly by the eye, as a collection of written signs which denote sound patterns.

Musical sound embodies both *pitch* (the high-low characteristic) and *rhythm* (the long-short characteristic). Pitch may be described psychologically as the spatial element of music, while rhythm represents musical time, or *duration.*

Musical pitch results from controlled vibration of a string, air column, or membrane. For example, we sing by forcing air through the larynx. Wind instruments are played by blowing air through reeds (in oboes and clarinets) or metal cups (in trumpets, horns, and trombones) into conical or cylindrical bores or tubes, made of metal or wood, of varying lengths. The length of this tubing determines the pitch range of the instrument. In the case of stringed instruments, such as the violin, guitar, or harp, one or more of the stretched strings are bowed, plucked, or struck, producing a pitch that varies with the length of the vibrating string—the longer the string, the lower the pitch, and vice versa. Pitch on stringed instruments is also affected by the thickness and tension of the strings.

Musical sounds have other properties which also contribute to the organization of a piece of music. These include *intensity,* or relative loudness, and *timbre,* or tone color or tone quality—that is, the particular characteristics of the sound of an oboe as opposed to a saxophone or tuba, or the "color" of the sound produced by a section of stringed instruments as contrasted with that produced by a group of winds. Obviously the number of colors obtainable from the various human voices and different types of instruments, alone, in groups such as choruses and orchestras, or in smaller combinations, is immense.

There are many other factors of vital importance to musical organization with which we shall deal later. For the time being, let us turn to the subject of musical space—that is, pitch—and the means of representing it in what is perhaps the most apparent and most easily appreciated aspect of music, melody.

PITCH CONTOUR AND PITCH NOTATION

As a form of communication, the language of music is diverse and flexible, having a vocabulary of sounds as varied as the resources of composers' imaginations. Much of this diversity and flexibility is beyond the reach of any means of encoding it that has yet been devised. However, music can be pictured in writing by a set of conventional signs which make a kind of musical code called *notation.* Still, music is alive only when it exists in the form of sound. Whereas much of the meaning of a written language can be obtained by reading the written symbols, music takes on meaning only through *hearing.* Musical notation is a shorthand means of recording the tones which have been organized by a composer into a musical composition. It is only with the performance, that is, with the translation of the composer's instructions from written code to live sound, that music actually happens and communicates. Although such a statement seems obvious, it warrants careful consideration. Far too often, music has been treated as a kind of graphic art, rather than a heard or auditory one.

Example 1-1 shows a notational representation of the pitches of a familiar melody. Even though the rhythm of the melody is not revealed in such a representation of pitch alone, we immediately recognize the melody by listening to a performance of its pitches. After the pitch series has been played, with all the notes held for an equal length of time, sing it.

That one can easily identify the melody (without hearing its precise rhythms) as a portion of *America* can be attributed to an important aspect of

Example 1-1 America (pitches only)

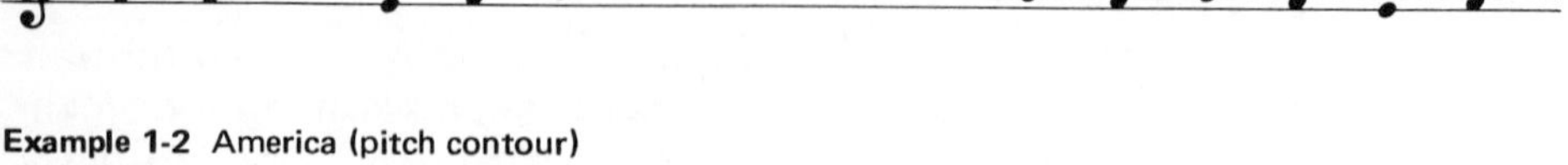

Example 1-2 America (pitch contour)

its pitch organization, melodic *contour.* Contour is the rise and fall, both general and detailed, of a melody. A distinct melodic contour, or *melodic curve,* is a feature of most, but by no means all, melodies.

Melodic contour can be pictured graphically without recourse to the conventions of musical notation. For example, the rise and fall of the preceding melody can be shown as in Example 1-2. The contour line of this example is actually a rudimentary means of notating—that is, giving a visual impression of—the melody's spatial profile. The limitations of this means of notation are obvious, since many melodies have similar pitch profiles. Note that the contour of the melody in Example 1-3 is similar to that of *America,* although the precise pitch materials are quite different. Thus, graphing melodic contours can be useful for recalling general features of pitch organization; it is also employed by some current composers as a sketch for improvization. However, the precise rendering of pitches, not just contour, necessitates a more accurate coding system.

Example 1-3 French folk song (pitches only)

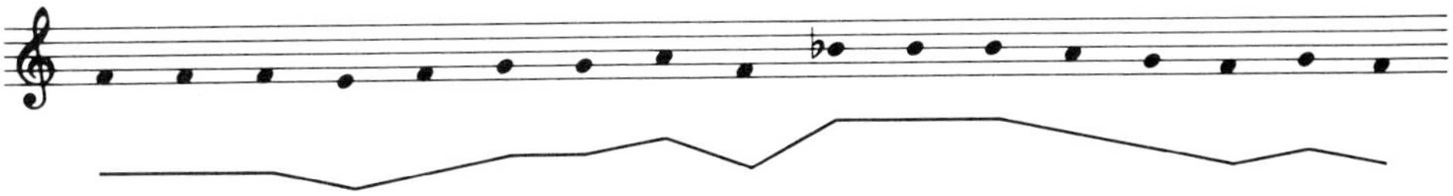

The piano keyboard may serve as a useful reference for a brief discussion of pitch notation. A sketch of a keyboard is shown in Example 1-4. The piano keyboard spans 88 keys, 52 of which are white and the remaining 36 black. For the moment we shall refer only to the white keys. If one faces the keyboard and depresses the keys in succession from left to right, the tones produced by the keys will be found to progress from low to high.

Each key's pitch is represented in notation by a strategically placed note head (○ or ●). The differences between the pitches of various notes are represented graphically by means of a *staff,* a ladder-like assemblage of five lines and intervening spaces:

Note heads are written on both lines and spaces, as shown here:

Each note can be made to represent a distinct musical pitch. Notes sounded by adjacent keys—remember that we are talking only about the white keys—are written on adjacent lines and spaces. For example, in this version the first

Example 1-4 Piano keyboard

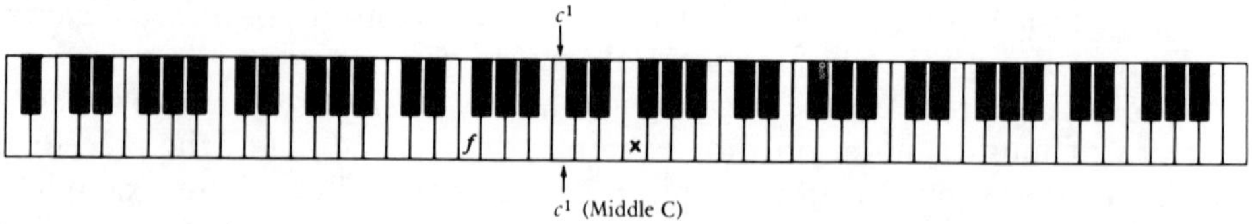

note of *America* (Example 1-1) is written on the first space of the staff (counting up from the bottom). Let us suppose that this space represents the key marked x in Example 1-4. The second note has the same pitch and consequently the same position on the staff; it is also produced by depressing the same key on the piano. The third note, which is slightly higher in pitch, is written on the next higher position on the staff, which is the second line. This note may be produced on the keyboard by sounding the white key immediately to the right of the one used to sound the first two notes of *America.* The fourth note, represented on the first line of the staff, is produced by sounding the key to the left of the one used for the first two notes of *America.* Disregard the ninth note for the moment; we shall explain the symbol to the left of it later in this chapter.

BASS AND TREBLE CLEFS

It is obvious that we are not going to be able to depict all 52 white keys on only five lines and four spaces. The staff, clearly, can represent only a small portion of the keyboard. In order to pinpoint the part of the keyboard that is represented by the staff, we use a sign called a *clef.* By indicating that a certain line of the staff represents a specific pitch, the clef sign gives us a reference point for measuring the distance between various pitches. It also allows us to name the pitches, using a simple alphabetical nomenclature involving only the letters A through G.

The two clefs most commonly used to specify pitches are the bass clef and the treble clef. The *bass clef,* also called the F clef, pinpoints *f* on the fourth line of the staff (the line enclosed by the two dots in the clef sign:

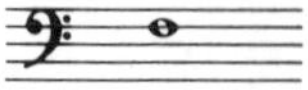

See Example 1-4. This note occurs on the keyboard seven white keys below the pitch notated as the first note of *America.*

The white-key notes most often depicted in the bass clef are shown in Example 1-5, with their respective letter names. As we shall see shortly, the various upper- and lower-case letters, the former in single, double, and triple forms, and the numbers used as superscripts, indicate precise locations in the pitch gamut.

Example 1-5 The bass clef gamut

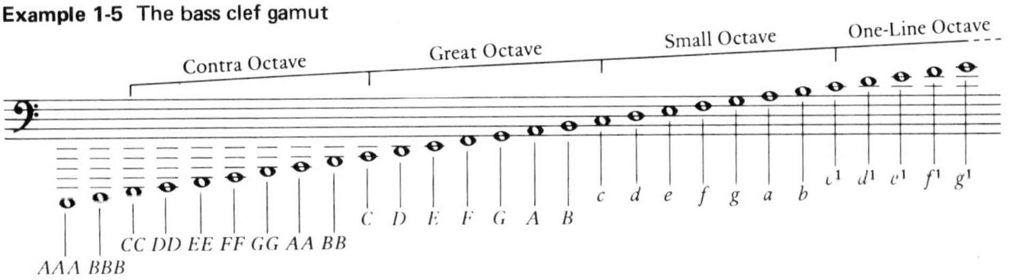

Note that the range of pitches that can be represented on the staff is not limited to the five lines and four spaces. In Example 1-5 there are numerous notes written on lines and spaces above and below the staff. The short lines used for depicting such notes are called *ledger lines.* We refer to *C,* for example, as being "on the second ledger line below the staff," to *D* as being "in the second space below the staff," to g^1 as being "on the third ledger line above the staff," and so on.

The *treble clef,* also called the G clef, pinpoints the note g^1 on the second line:

The treble clef gamut is shown in Example 1-6. Note that the gamuts of the bass and treble clefs overlap. This overlap is possible because there are no specific upper limits for writing in the bass clef, or lower limits for writing in the treble clef—or, for that matter, lower limits for the bass clef or upper limits for the treble clef.

Example 1-6 The treble clef gamut

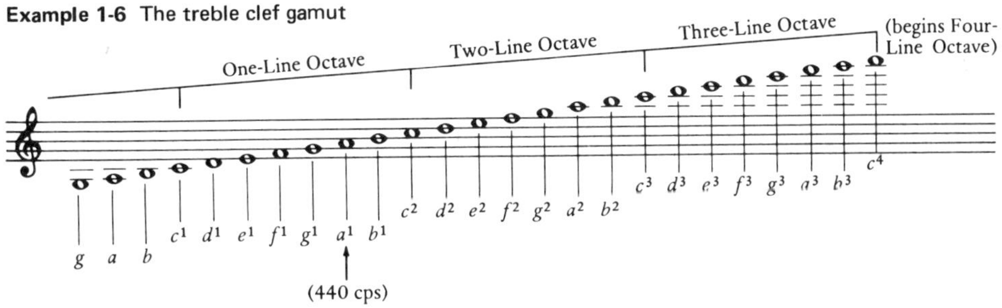

A composer's decision to notate a passage in any particular clef is made more on the basis of context and practical considerations than of notational "rules." One important consideration is the range of the instrument or voice for which the music is to be notated. Another is musical tradition. For example, piano music is usually written on two staffs, treble for the upper parts (or right hand) and bass for the lower parts (or left hand). In general, high parts (either vocal or instrumental) are written in the treble clef and low parts are

Example 1-7

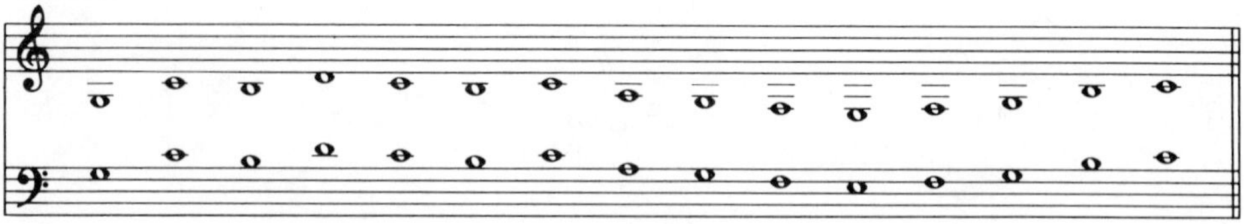

notated in the bass clef. There are several important exceptions to this rule of thumb which we shall note later. Example 1-7 shows a note series written in both the treble and the bass clefs. From the appearance of the example, it would seem more convenient to write the series in the bass clef, since doing so requires fewer ledger lines.

One may logically ask why so many notes require only seven different letter names. The answer may be suggested by listening to the patterns of tones in (a) and (b) of Example 1-8. Note that in each of these two groups of tones, the highest and lowest pitches seem to produce a sameness or duplication that is not apparent with any of the other notes in these two groups. Now play all of the note pairs joined by curved lines in (c), (d), and (e). All of these pairs produce the unique musical *interval,* or pitch distance, of an *octave.** Listen to the opening of the first movement of Mozart's *Haffner*

Example 1-8 Tone groups exemplifying octaves

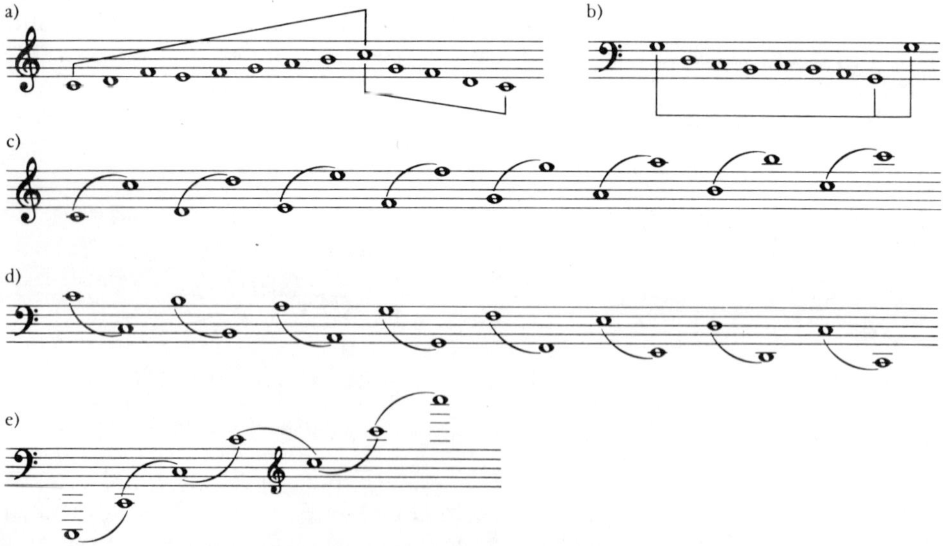

*In acoustical terms, the frequencies of any two notes separated by the distance of an octave have the simple ratio of 2:1. For example, when the note marked a^1 in Example 1-6 is played on the piano, the piano string vibrates at the rate of 440 vibrations (or cycles) per second. The note marked *a,* therefore, vibrates at 220 cps, and a^2 at 880 cps.

Example 1-9

Mozart

Symphony (reproduced in Example 1-9) and note the use of octaves there.

The octave (or eight-note span) is an essential element of Western music and its notation. Octave duplication is reflected in notation by the recurrence of identical letter names, as a glance at the pitch gamuts shown in Examples 1-5 and 1-6 will show. Every eighth note in these examples has the same letter name. However, pitches of different *register*—that is, pitches which have the same letter name but are at different locations on the staff—must be distinguished in some way. All the notes in Example 1-10 are C's, but they are all in different registers; we have to modify our simple alphabetical labeling system to take account of these differences.

Example 1-10

To do this, we divide the gamut of pitches into segments, each segment, in this case, beginning on a C. Each segment thus consists of seven consecutive notes, which we label, in ascending order, C, D, E, F, G, A, and B. We call each set of seven consecutive notes an *octave,** and give it a more specific name such as "Great Octave," "Small Octave," "One-Line Octave," etc. We also modify our alphabetical labeling system by representing all tones in the Great Octave by upper-case letters, all tones in the Small Octave by lower-case letters, all tones in the One-Line Octave by lower-case letters with super-

Example 1-11 The nomenclature for the various octaves

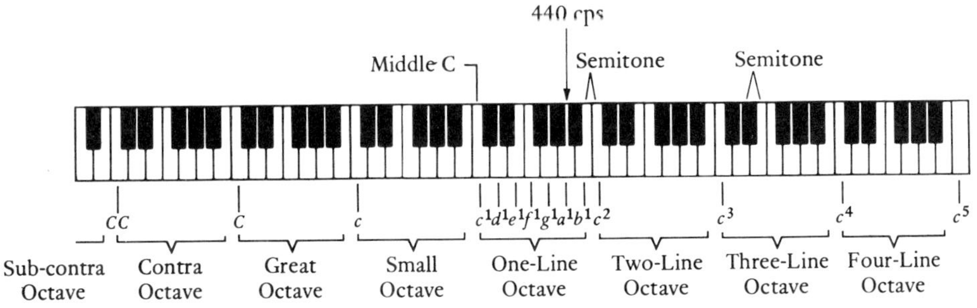

*Note that the term *octave* refers both to the interval, or distance separating two pitches, and to the entire gamut of pitches between them.

script 1's, and so on.* Examples 1-5 and 1-6 deserve careful study at this point. Example 1-11 shows the various octaves of the piano keyboard.

C CLEFS

All keyboard music is written in the treble and bass clefs, as are most vocal and instrumental compositions. However, music written for the viola, bassoon, cello, and some other instruments and voices is often written in clefs whose signs are oriented to middle C (c^1). The most frequently used C clefs are known as the alto and tenor clefs. The *alto clef* sign affixes middle C to the third line of the staff:

The *tenor clef* places middle C on the fourth line of the staff:

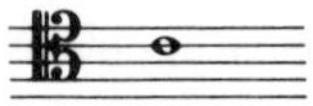

Viola parts are notated most often in the alto clef (sometimes called the viola clef), and some of the notes in the cello's playing range are commonly written in the tenor clef. Obviously, anyone who cannot identify notes written in C clefs will have little success in reading orchestral scores.

The string part shown in Example 1-12 has been notated in four clefs: treble, bass, alto, and tenor. Careful study of this example will facilitate your grasp of the C clefs. The key to easy reading of the C clefs is to remember that the position of middle C (c^1) on the staff is indicated by the two converging lines of the clef sign.

Example 1-12

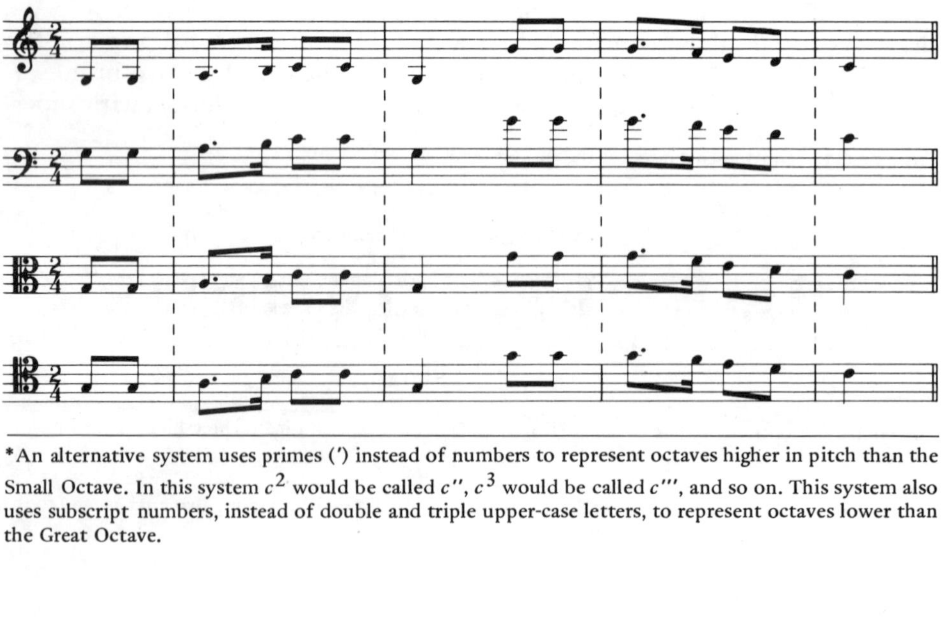

*An alternative system uses primes (′) instead of numbers to represent octaves higher in pitch than the Small Octave. In this system c^2 would be called c'', c^3 would be called c''', and so on. This system also uses subscript numbers, instead of double and triple upper-case letters, to represent octaves lower than the Great Octave.

The C clefs were in existence long before the treble and bass clefs, having originally been devised for the notation of parts for men's voices. In addition to the alto and tenor clefs, two other C clefs were available. In the *mezzo-soprano clef,* the second line of the staff was used to pinpoint c^1:

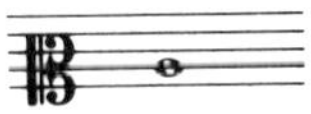

In the *soprano clef,* c^1 was located on the first line of the staff:

These two clefs are seldom used now except in connection with the technique of transposition, a technique which we shall consider later.

Although some musicians have challenged the practicality of the continued use of C clefs, it should be pointed out that notational traditions, the frequent use of C clefs in early music,* and the fact that C clefs minimize the number of ledger lines needed in the parts for which they are used constitute sufficient reasons for their study. Most professional musicians acquire proficiency in reading C clefs; and, of course, those who play instruments whose parts are notated in C clefs must master them.

Remember that, although we have discussed pitch notation in terms of the piano keyboard, the system of notation that we have described is used for most instruments and voices. Our system of pitch notation is based on relationships, that is, relative pitch distances, called intervals. If the notational system is to have any real usefulness, there must be a generally agreed upon reference point. At the present time the reference point is the note a^1, which is generally agreed to represent a pitch of 440 cps (cycles, or vibrations, per second), or a pitch within four or five cycles of this. Without such a reference point, ensemble music as we know it could not exist.

WHOLE STEPS AND HALF-STEPS

So far we have been disregarding the black keys of the piano keyboard. Note in Example 1-4 that the black keys occur between the white keys, but that not every pair of white keys has an intervening black key. The piano is tuned in such a way that the interval (pitch distance) from one key to the next, whether black or white, is the same throughout the keyboard.† Consequently,

---

*In order to read the scores of much music written during the Renaissance (about 1450 to 1600) and Baroque (about 1600 to 1750) periods, one must have a thorough understanding of C clefs.

†This system of tuning is called *equal temperament,* and was invented during the lifetime of J. S. Bach (1685-1750). Previously, the pitch of each note was determined by a more complicated system, known as *just intonation,* based on the ratios between the frequencies of various pitches.

the interval between c^1 and d^1 is twice as large as the interval between e^1 and f^1 or between b^1 and c^1. Note that this pattern of intervals is the same in each octave of the keyboard. We call the larger interval (between *c* and *d,* for example) a *whole step,* and the smaller one a *half-step,* or *semitone.* Play various pairs of adjacent white keys on the piano and notice the difference in sound between a whole step and a half-step.

If all the adjacent white keys of any octave are played successively in ascending or descending step motion, the resulting pattern is called a *scale.* Most scales consist of patterns of whole steps and half-steps deployed in various arrangements.

Play or sing, in a comfortable register, each of the scales shown in Example 1-13. Note carefully the location of whole steps and half-steps in each and the resulting uniqueness of each pattern. We shall discuss some types of scales in Chapters 4 and 5.

Example 1-13 Scales

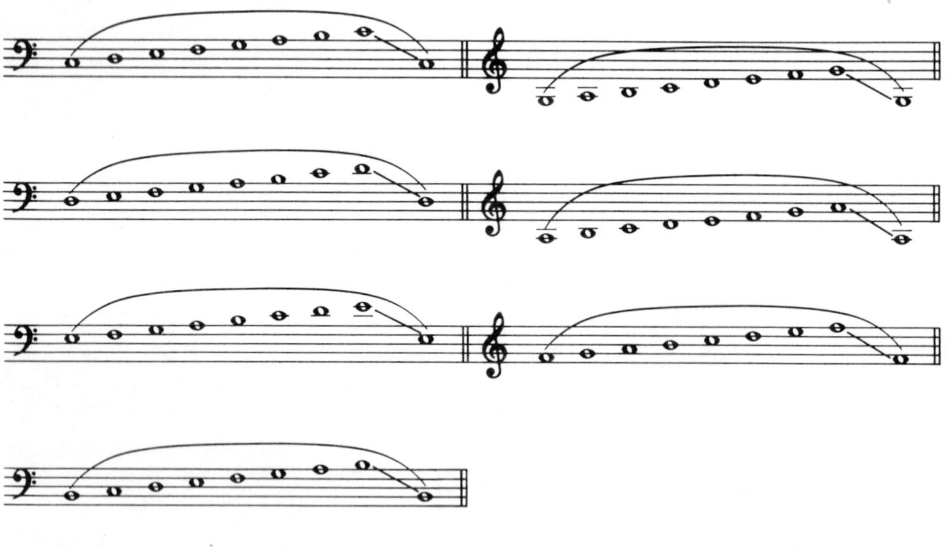

ACCIDENTALS

The notes produced by sounding the 52 white keys of the piano keyboard are referred to as "natural" notes. There are seven of them in each octave, and each one has a separate line or space on the staff allotted to it. The 36 black keys allow half-step gradations in pitch between the white keys where such gradations do not already exist in the "natural" scale. The black keys, in effect, raise or lower the pitch of a "natural" note by a semitone. Obviously, the pitch distance between two adjacent black keys separated by one white key will be a whole step—the same as the distance between two white keys separated by a black key. This fact can easily be confirmed by playing various pairs of white and black notes and listening to or singing the resulting intervals.

Locate c^1 on the keyboard. Play it. Now depress the black key immediately adjacent to c^1 and above it. The pitch produced is called *c*♯ (*c* sharp), and the distance between it and c^1 is a half-step identical in size to the half-step between two adjacent white keys (for example, e^1 and f^1). Now locate d^1 on the keyboard and play it. Then depress the black key immediately adjacent to d^1 and *below* it. The pitch produced is called *d*♭ (*d* flat), and the distance between it and d^1 is a half-step. This is, of course, the same black key that you depressed to produce *c*♯. It is a peculiarity of our system of tuning, equal temperament, that the same black key is used to produce both the pitch a half-step *above* the immediately adjacent white key to the left and the pitch a half-step *below* the adjacent white key to the right. As a rule, a raised half-step modification of a "natural" note is called a *sharp* (♯), and a lowered half-step modification is called a *flat* (♭). The notational signs for sharps and flats are written immediately to the left of the note head, as shown in Example 1-14. These signs are called *accidentals.*

Example 1-14

The effect of an accidental continues throughout the measure in which it is introduced, unless some other sign is used to cancel its effect. Thus in measure 2, the third note, on the third line of the staff, is *b*♭, even though there is no flat sign immediately in front of it—the flat sign before the first note of the measure affects any following note in that measure which falls on the same line or space. Note that an accidental applies only to a specific line or space—that is, only to a specific register. If the second *b*♭ in measure 3 had fallen on the second space above the staff, it would have required a flat sign of its own:

The effect of an accidental does not extend across a barline. That is why, in measure 3, a sharp sign had to be placed before the second note in order to produce the same pitch as was produced by the last note of measure 2.

There is another important accidental besides the sharp and the flat. The *natural sign* (♮), which appears in the third and fifth measures of Example 1-14, is used to cancel the effect of a previous sharp or flat, thus restoring the note's "natural" form. In measure 3, the natural sign on f^1 cancels the effect of the previous sharp sign in the same space. Therefore, although these two notes are written on the same space of the staff, their pitches differ by a semitone.

Two other accidentals, the *double sharp* (𝄪) and the *double flat* (𝄫), are less commonly used. As their names imply, they raise or lower the pitch of a note by two half-steps, i.e., one whole step.

KEY SIGNATURES

A *key signature* is an accidental or a group of accidentals affixed at the beginning of a composition, immediately after the clef sign. A key signature may contain as many as seven accidentals. It signifies the predominant use of a particular pitch set throughout a composition.

The key signature signifies to the performer the application of specific half-step alterations *throughout* the composition and in *all* octaves. Thus the two sharp signs at the beginning of Example 1-15(a) tell the performer to play all *f*'s as *f*♯ and all *c*'s as *c*♯, unless otherwise instructed by natural signs. The key signature in Example 1-15(b) indicates that all *b*'s, *e*'s, *a*'s, and *d*'s are to be played or sung as *b*♭, *e*♭, *a*♭, and *d*♭, respectively.

The specific location on the staff of the accidentals in a key signature is conventional. In the treble clef, the sharp sign indicating that all *f*'s are to be played as *f*♯ is conventionally placed on the top line of the staff, but it applies equally to *f*'s in the first space and to *f*'s in the fourth space above the staff.

Example 1-15

a)

b)

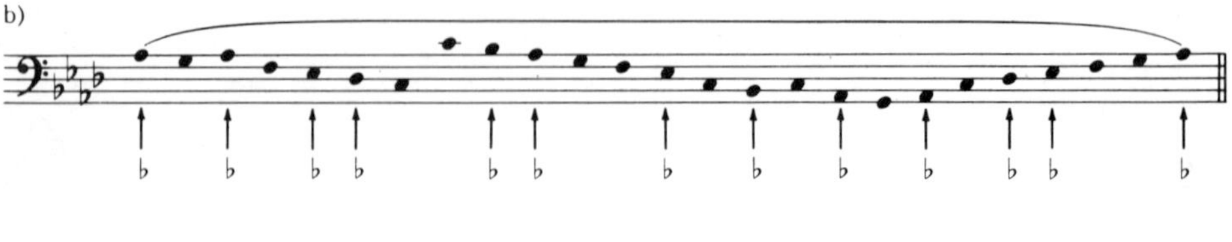

EXERCISES

1. Locate each of the items listed below in the following musical example. Write the letter denoting the item at the point of its occurrence in the example.

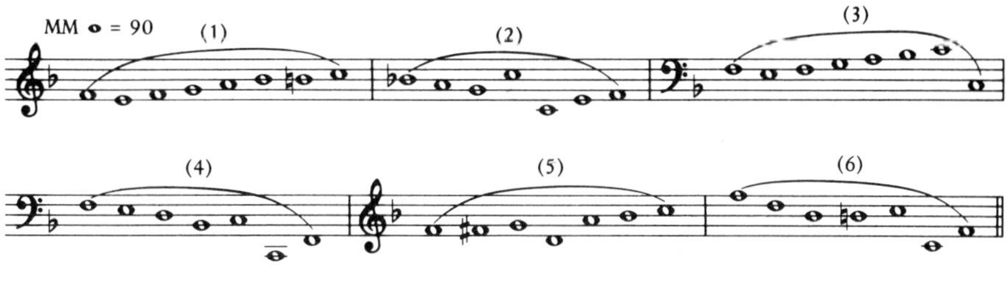

a) a half-step | b) a key signature
c) a treble clef sign | d) f^1, c^2, d^1, c, and C
e) a bass clef sign | f) the interval of an octave
g) sharp, flat, and natural signs | h) a whole step
i) a staff | j) a ledger line

If possible, play the example on the piano, at a comfortable tempo (speed, or pace), giving each note about the same length.

2. Draw the melodic profile or contour of each of the phrases [numbered from (1) to (6)] of the musical example in Exercise 1. Play the first pitch of each phrase and then sing the phrase in a comfortable vocal register. Compare the phrase contour with the physical effort involved in articulating the pitch profile.

1) 2)

3) 4)

5) 6)

3. Locate and play each of the following pitches on the piano. Then write the letter name for each pitch in the space provided.

a)

b)
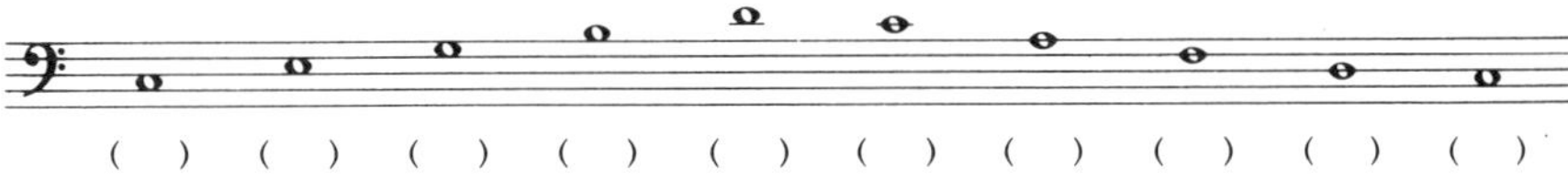

c) 

d) 

e) 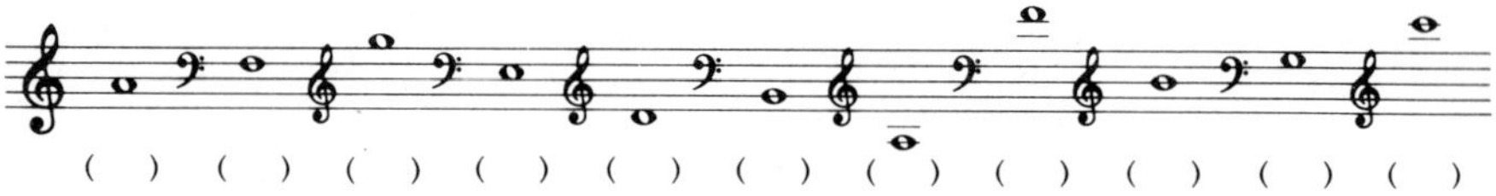

4. Write the pitches called for in the octave segment indicated. Use the most appropriate clef for each part (a, b, and c).

   a) One-Line Octave: *c, e, b*♭, *f*♯, *e*♭, *d, c*

   b) Small Octave: *a, b, d*♭, *c, g*♯, *d*♯, *e*

   c) Great Octave: *g, e, b, a*♭, *e*♭, *f, d*

5. Write each of the following pitches in the bass clef so that the sounds represented will be identical to those represented by the treble clef notes.

(Sample)

(optional)

6. Each of the following patterns is for use in practicing vocal reading. Play the first (blackened) note, and then sing the remainder of the pattern in a comfortable vocal register and at a comfortable tempo. Do not use the piano to reinforce your vocal reading. Check your performance with the piano *after* singing the pattern. If you make mistakes, go on to the next pattern and return later to the patterns that you missed.

a)

b)

c)

d)

e)

f)
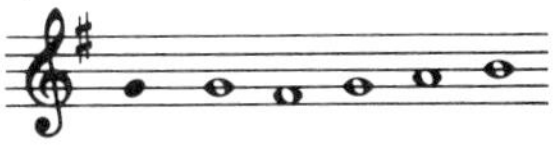

g)
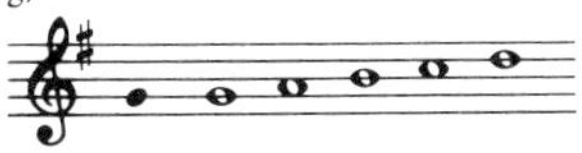

h)
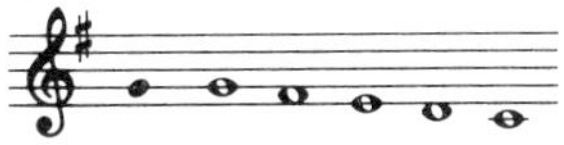

i)

j)

k)
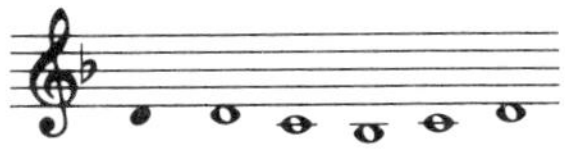

l)
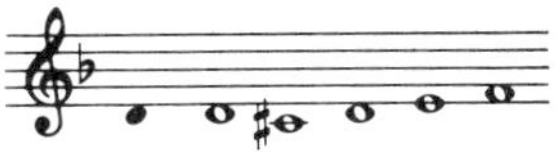

m)
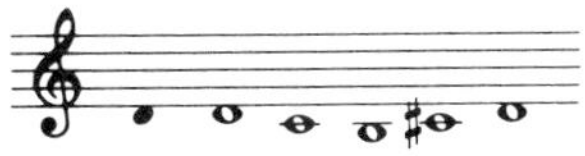

n)

o)

p)
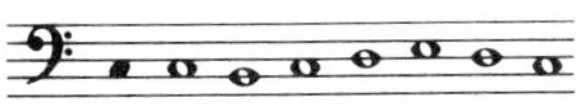

q)
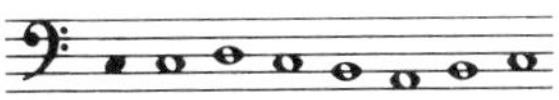

r)

s)

t)
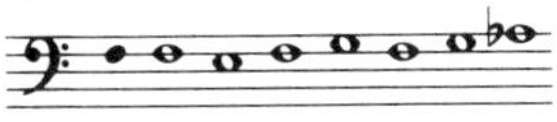

u)
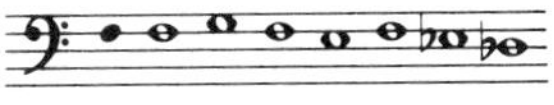

v)

w)
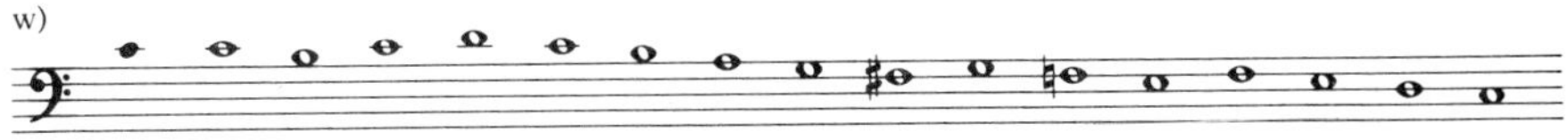

Chapter 2

DURATION OF TONE AND ITS NOTATION

One way in which music differs from the graphic arts is that its articulation and perception involve the passing of time. This temporal aspect of music, which is manifested in musical *rhythm,* operates in a number of ways. In this chapter we shall attempt to account for some of the factors which seem most important in determining musical rhythm and its notation. Later we shall show ways in which rhythm constitutes an integral part of musical design.

METER

Using *c* as a starting pitch, sing the pitches of *America* at a comfortable pace, giving each note the same duration, as in Chapter 1. The annoyance experienced in such an experiment is mainly due to the fact that the various pitches are given no clear rhythmic definition; that is, the melodic pitches are not differentiated by either duration or rhythmic grouping.

Now sing or hum the repeated opening phrase (verse) of *Aura Lee,* the pitches of which are shown in Example 2-1 as note heads without stems. The first six notes of the tune establish a *pulse,* which consists of regularly recurring stimuli or articulations like the ticking of a watch. This pulse is due to the equal duration (short) of the six notes, which we infer here on the basis of familiarity with the song, not on the basis of its partial notation in Example 2-1. The seventh note (a^1), marked "long," should last twice as long as each of those preceding it. Its precise duration can be measured by mentally

Example 2-1 Aura Lee (verse)

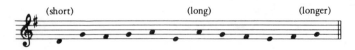

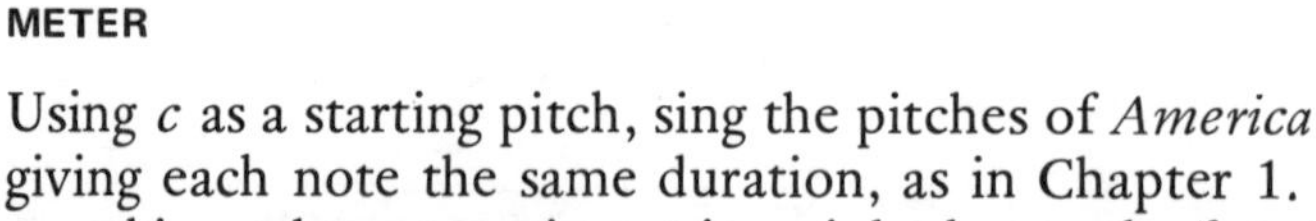

continuing the previously established pulse and sustaining the note through two pulses. The final note of the example (marked "longer") actually lasts through four pulses.

We see from this example that pulse acts as a constant frame of reference against which the various durations that give a composition its rhythm and rhythmic variety can be measured. But more important than pulse alone is *pulse grouping.* A stream of pulses, grouped by twos or threes (or some other number), produces *meter.* Metered pulses are usually called *beats,* and may be either strong or weak according to their position within the group. Note the distinction between pulse and beat. It is convenient to think of pulse as a sort of "ticking" or recurring throbbing having no sustained quality. Musical beats, however, which we have described as metered pulses, are considered as lasting until a new pulse occurs. For that reason each beat is given a precise temporal span, or length, which is only begun, not ended, by an audible or a mentally supplied tick.

Meter is created by means of *accent,* or stress. Accent denotes simply the process of "marking off" or emphasizing those beats which are most important in establishing the metrical pattern. Accented (stressed) beats are called strong beats; unaccented (unstressed) beats are called weak beats. If we group beats in pairs, each pair consisting of a strong beat followed by a weak beat, the result is a *duple meter.* We can produce the duple meter of *Aura Lee* by stressing the first, third, fifth, etc., pulses, as shown in Example 2-2. In this example the symbol > represents an accent, and the vertical lines beneath the notes indicate beats. Note the use of the curved line, or *tie,* joining the seventh and eighth notes; a tie indicates that the tone is held through two or more notes.

Example 2-2 Aura Lee (pictured in duple meter)

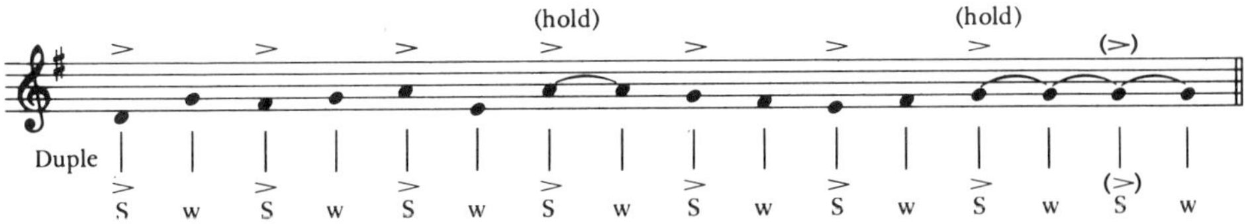

If beats are grouped by threes, a *triple meter* results. Example 2-3 shows *Aura Lee* written in triple meter. Sing the example, observing the ties, and compare its rhythmic effect with that of Example 2-2. Note that the rhythm

Example 2-3 Aura Lee (pictured in triple meter)

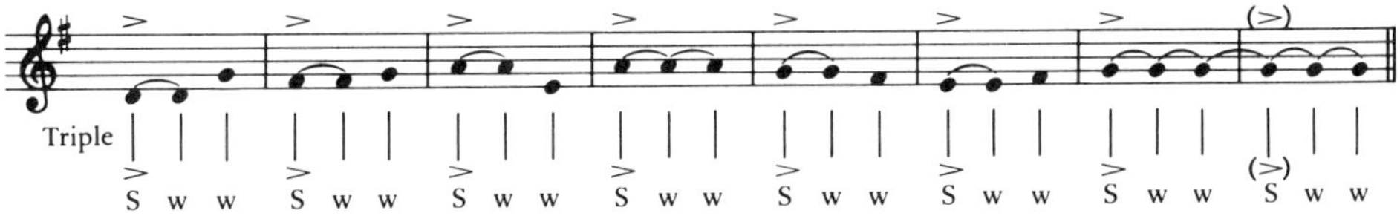

of Example 2-3 is based on a long-short pattern consisting of a note held for two beats followed by a note held for only one beat. In such an arrangement the strong beat is given additional emphasis by its coinciding with the longer of the two notes in each metric group. The vertical lines inserted in Example 2-3 after each metric group are called barlines. Barlines help to delineate visually the relation between rhythmic patterns and the pattern of strong and weak beats which constitutes the meter. The distance from one barline to the next, measured in terms of beats, is called a *measure.*

As the product of pulse and pulse grouping, meter provides a framework which enables several melodies with diverse rhythmic characteristics to coexist in time. By providing a uniform frame of reference, metered pulse facilitates precise relationships between different instruments or voices. The rhythmic organization of the simultaneously heard melodies in Example 2-4 is dependent on a common pulse or beat. Although adherence to a basic pulse typifies most traditional rhythmic organization, some recent composers have on occasion abandoned such bases in favor of more complex or more flexible patterns.

Example 2-4

J. S. Bach, *A Musical Offering*

TEMPO

Tempo means *pulse rate.* The tempo of a musical composition is the speed at which beat articulations occur. Tempo markings appear at the upper left of the first stave of a composition. Word indications such as *Allegro* ("Quickly"), *Lento* ("Slowly"), or *Lebhaft* ("Lively"), chosen from Italian, French, German, or English, provide general guides to the tempo desired by the composer.

However, word indications for tempos often prove insufficient. For that reason, musicians often assign a metronome marking to a work, or to a section of a work, to afford greater accuracy in specifying the tempo. A metronome marking indicates the number of beats per minute that should occur during the work. For example, MM = 60* indicates that the composition should proceed at the rate of 60 beats per minute (or one every second). The higher the metronomic marking, the quicker the pulse rate of the composition. Most tempo indications fall between 60 and 120 beats per minute. Maximum accuracy is obtained by the use of an appropriate word followed by a metronome marking, e.g., "Allegro, MM (♩) = 110."†

NOTE VALUES

The beat is represented in notation by a system of durational signs called *note values,* any one of which may be taken as the notational equivalent for a musical beat. The following are the most frequently used note values**:

breve (double whole note)	𝅜
whole note	𝅝
half note	𝅗𝅥
quarter note	𝅘𝅥
eighth note	𝅘𝅥𝅮
sixteenth note	𝅘𝅥𝅯
thirty-second note	𝅘𝅥𝅰
sixty-fourth note	𝅘𝅥𝅱

As the names whole, half, quarter, eighth, etc., imply, the various note values have a hierarchical relation based on the beat unit and the tempo. For example, if the quarter note is chosen as the beat unit and a tempo is determined, all other durational signs denote a precise length as multiples (the half and whole notes) or divisions (the eighth, sixteenth, thirty-second, and sixty-fourth notes) of the length of the beat unit at the chosen tempo.

---

*MM stands for "Mälzel's Metronome." The metronome was invented by J. N. Mälzel in 1816.

†Here the sign (♩) represents the notational equivalent of a beat.

**In practice the half, quarter, and eighth notes appear most often as beat equivalents.

Read the rhythm of the passages in Example 2-5 by intoning on the syllable *ta.* Establish the meter first by tapping several beats at the desired tempo. Continue to tap beats while reading the note values of the example.

Example 2-5

a)

b)

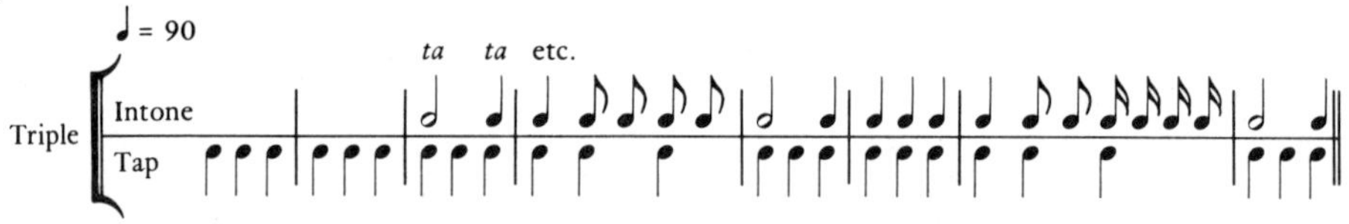

c)

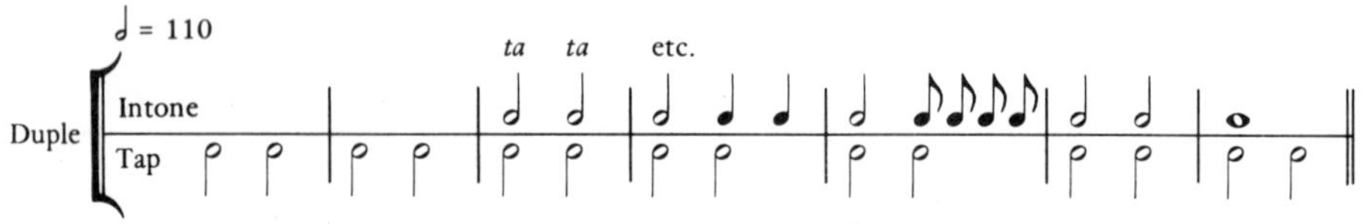

d)

METER SIGNATURES

Together with the tempo indication, the meter signature provides a further indication of the rhythmic organization of a composition. A meter signature consists of two superposed numerals. The upper number generally denotes the pattern of accentuation, that is, the number of beats per metric group or measure. The lower number of the signature indicates the note value that represents the beat; that is, it specifies the basic unit of duration used in the composition. The chart on page 21 shows the most common meter signatures and what they signify.

The metrical patterns represented by these signatures are known as *simple meters.* In simple meters, the upper number of the meter signature is always 2, 3, or 4; we shall discuss complex meters later in this chapter. Note that the familiar signature for quadruple time, 4/4 (so-called *common time*), consists of two pairs of beats arranged in the pattern SwSw (Strong, weak, Strong, weak). In effect, quadruple meter is *duple.*

Simple Meters

Signature	*Number of Beats*	*Accentuation Pattern*	*Basic Duration (Beat)*
$\frac{2}{4}, \frac{3}{4}, \frac{4}{4}$	2, 3, 4	Sw, Sww, SwSw	♩
$\frac{2}{8}, \frac{3}{8}, \frac{4}{8}$	2, 3, 4	Sw, Sww, SwSw	♪
$\frac{2}{2}, \frac{3}{2}, \frac{4}{2}$	2, 3, 4	Sw, Sww, SwSw	𝅗𝅥
C	4	SwSw	same as $\frac{4}{4}$
¢	2	Sw	same as $\frac{2}{2}$

Note the two special meter signatures, **C** and **¢**. These are a shorthand notation for 4/4 (common time) and 2/2 ("cut" time). The latter is called "cut" time because, although each measure contains durations equivalent to those of a measure of common time, the number of beats is cut in half, from four to two.

The accentual basis for a meter, as noted earlier, is visually clarified through the use of barlines. These occur, as in Example 2-6, immediately before the first (strong) beat of each measure.

MELODIC RHYTHM

The durations that constitute a piece of music are by no means limited to the basic duration or beat. One can imagine how tedious music would be if the rhythm of a melody were confined to a tandem-like duplication of the meter. On the contrary, most melodies employ a variety of durations which may be equal to, longer than, or shorter than the basic unit. See Example 2-6, in which the beat is equal to a quarter note. Note how the beat is firmly established by the succession of four quarter notes in the third measure. However, other durations—half notes, eighths, and sixteenths—vary the melody's rhythm. Dotted notes also occur in this melody; these will be discussed in the following section.

Note that an accurate rendition of the rhythm of the melody in Example 2-6—that is, the *melodic rhythm*—necessitates a clearly established pulse, maintained as a background for precise articulation of the half note (exactly

Example 2-6

Mozart

twice the span of one beat) that begins the example, the eighth notes, falling in pairs or longer groups, that divide the beat into equal halves, and the sixteenths, similarly occurring in groups, that effect a subdivision of the beat into parts equal to exactly one-fourth of the basic duration. It is the interplay of various *levels* of rhythmic activity that provides rhythmic interest. The mere reinforcement of the meter itself, though necessary to establish the pulse grouping or rhythmic organization of the composition, acts only as a backdrop to the rhythmic play of the melody.

TIES, DOTS, SLURS, AND RESTS

In the discussion of pitch notation in Chapter 1, it was noted that some flexibility exists in clef usage. Similarly, considerable latitude exists in the choice of signs used for rhythmic notation. For example, a melody may be rewritten using a different beat unit. So long as the metric pattern (i.e., the number of beats per measure) and the tempo (i.e., the number of beats per minute) remain the same, the two differently notated versions of the melody will produce identical results in performance. This is illustrated in Example 2-7. A

Example 2-7

Brahms

composer's choice of notation is often based largely on considerations of readability. Most performers would find it easier to pick out the rhythmic patterns at a glance in part (a) of Example 2-7 than in either part (b) or part (c).

There are also certain symbols that allow a composer some choice in notating rhythms. For example, a *dot* placed immediately after a note head indicates that the duration of the note is extended by one-half its normal value or length. A dot thus has the effect of prolonging the sound in the same way as a tie drawn to connect two note heads:

Any note value may be prolonged by means of a dot. However, a dot is used only to prolong a note *within* the measure in which it occurs. A tie must be used if one wishes to prolong a note into the following measure:

Note the use of dots and ties in Example 2-7.

It is important to distinguish between a tie and a *slur.* Though a slur is a curved line like a tie, it usually joins notes of different pitches, and it indicates that the notes are to be connected smoothly in performance:

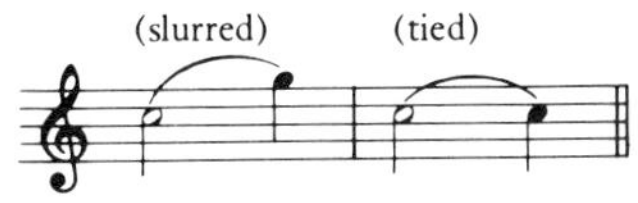

This style of performance—i.e., connecting the successive notes of a melody smoothly—is called *legato. Staccato,* which is the opposite of legato, means short, separate articulations. Staccato articulation is indicated by a dot placed above or below a note head. Note the use of legato and staccato in Example 2-4.

As suggested by the term itself, *rest* denotes silence. All note values have rest equivalents. On page 24, rest equivalents for both plain and dotted notes (shown also in their alternative notational form as tied notes) are given.

SUGGESTIONS FOR NOTATING RHYTHM

All the signs and symbols mentioned so far, and numerous others, are used in notation like a kind of musical shorthand. Having affixed a clef sign, a key signature, and a meter signature, the composer then writes out the melody, spacing the notes within the measure in a manner that is consistent, neat in appearance, and readable.

Plain Note | *Rest Equivalent* | *Dotted Note* | *Tied Note* | *Rest Equivalent*

Note stems usually hang down from the note head when the note head (pitch indication) is placed on or above the third line of the staff; stems point upward when the note head falls below the third line, regardless of what clef is being used. Stems hang from the left side of the note head, and point upward from the right side. Example 2-8 illustrates these rules. Note that when two or more notes are connected by a *beam,* the stems of all the notes within the beam point in the same direction. The direction in which they point is determined by the note farthest from the third line of the staff. If the highest and lowest notes in the group are equally distant from the third line, then the stems normally fall.

Example 2-8

French Folk Song

The use of beams to group time values in notating instrumental or keyboard music avoids the necessity for placing separate flags under or above each note. This procedure applies, of course, only to note durations smaller than the quarter note. In general, the grouping of notes by means of beams acts as an aid to grasping the composition's rhythms in relation to the beat structure. Note the use of beams and separately flagged notes in the three melodies in Example 2-9. The notation in the examples reveals a clear picture of the rhythmic patterns of the composition.

Example 2-9

a) J. S. Bach

b) A. Scarlatti

c) Mozart

Separately flagged notes are sometimes used in vocal music to show the occurrence of a new word or syllable, as in Example 2-10. This practice, however, is becoming obsolete.

Example 2-10

Mendelssohn

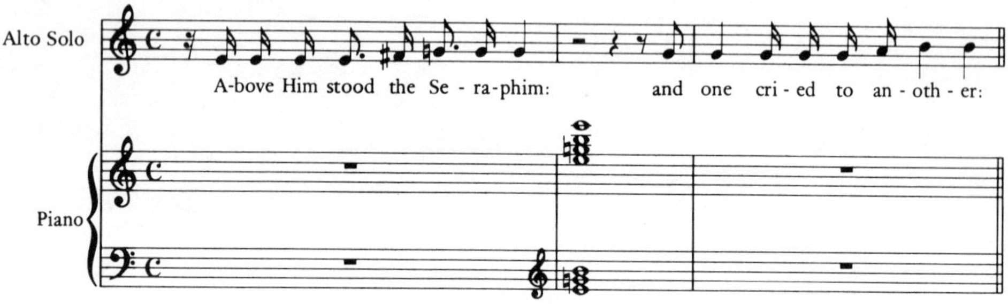
Alto Solo
A-bove Him stood the Se - ra-phim:
and one cri - ed to an - oth - er:
Piano

The following are a few general rules of thumb for rhythmic notation:

1. Whole rests may be used to indicate silence during a complete measure in any meter.
2. The use of rests should clarify, not obscure, the beat structure within the measure; thus

is preferable to:

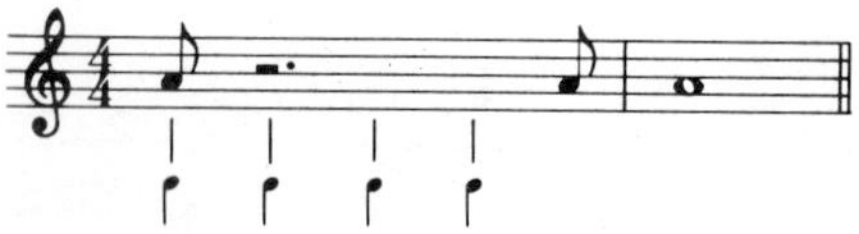

3. Ties join note heads on the side *away from* the note stem, thus:

rather than:

4. A rest for two consecutive beats in a 3/4 measure is shown as:

rather than as:

5. When the beat is subdivided into fourths or smaller subdivisions, a beam should not extend beyond one beat; thus

is preferable to:

However, when the beat is divided into halves, it is permissible to extend a beam through a half-measure (see Example 2-4, measure 4). In simple meter, if the beat is a note value that *can* be beamed, such as an eighth note or a sixteenth note, the beam may extend over the entire measure (see Examples 2-8 and 2-9b).

IRREGULAR DIVISIONS OF THE BEAT

As was mentioned earlier in this chapter, a *simple* meter is one which has a signature whose upper number is 2, 3, or 4. Simple meters have two basic characteristics: first, their plan of accentuation involves no more than four beats per measure; second, the durations that normally occur in simple meters

Example 2-11

Schubert

constitute multiples or divisions of the basic duration by two, four, eight, etc. (the *duple series*). Such is the case in Example 2-11, where the beat is a quarter note.

Divisions of the beat by numbers other than two or multiples of two are common enough in simple meters, but they are classed as *irregular* divisions. Triple divisions (or subdivisions) may be indicated by the use of the triplet sign: ⌐3¬. Examine the regular (duple) and irregular (triple) beat divisions that occur in Example 2-12. Note that the bracket enclosing the number 3 is optional when the three notes comprising the beat are joined by a beam. The bracket is used in Example 2-13, but not in Example 2-12.

Example 2-12

Schumann

It is obvious from Example 2-12 that, when irregular triple divisions of the beat are used, the note values do not have the same meaning that they do for duple divisions of the beat. The eighth notes in measure 5 are somewhat shorter in duration than the eighth notes in measure 1. The following general rule for notation may be applied: When dividing a beat into three equal parts by the use of a triplet sign, use the same note value that would be used for a duple division of the beat. The same principle applies to subdivisions of the beat. Thus measure 3 of Example 2-12 might be revised as follows:

Example 2-13 shows considerable use both of irregular divisions of the beat (measures 5, 6, 7, and 8) and of irregular divisions of a complete measure (measures 1, 2, and 3). Only measure 4 contains normal duple beat divisions. Patterns such as those illustrated here allow a freedom of rhythm and spontaneity of interpretation not implicit in normal divisions.

Example 2-13

Schumann

The vertically aligned dots, followed by a double barline, indicate the immediate repetition of the section preceding. The sign *D. C.* (which stands for the Italian phrase *da capo,* meaning literally "from the head") indicates that the performer is to return to the beginning of the passage and start playing through the piece again. The phrase *al fine* ("to the end") indicates that the piece is not to be repeated in its entirety, but only to the point marked *fine* ("end").

COMPOUND METER

The triplet sign indicates a triple division or subdivision of the basic duration in a meter whose normal beat division involves a duple series. In contrast to simple meter, *compound meter* denotes the *regular* division of two, three, or four beats *by three.* The method of notating compound meter, as we shall demonstrate shortly, eliminates the need for the triplet sign to show the triple patterns.

Establish a moderate tempo by tapping your finger or a pencil at about MM = 80. Intone two equal notes against each beat; then repeat the experiment, but this time intone three even pulses against each beat. Think of each tap as marking a beat unit consisting of *three* equal parts. In notating compound meter a dotted note is used to represent the beat. The triple division of the beat may be represented by three simple note values, as follows:

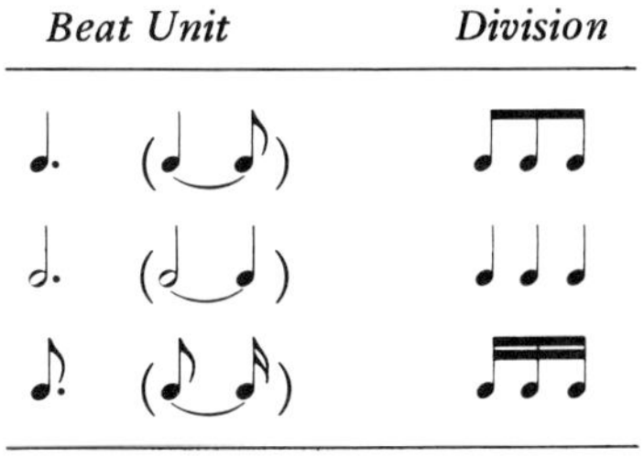

Note that the eighth note remains equal to exactly one-half the duration of a quarter note. Hence the common note values may be used without any special notational sign, such as the triplet sign, to indicate triple division of the beat.

Example 2-14

Irish Folk Song

The melody in Example 2-14 is written in compound meter. In this example two beats (Sw) occur in each measure, and each beat is made up of three equal eighth notes or their equivalent. The basic duration in the example is represented by the dotted quarter note. Establish a moderate tempo, MM = 80 per ♩., and tap the rhythm of the melody. As you tap the basic duration (♩.), *think* its primary division:

This melody begins with an *upbeat,* that is, an unaccented duration which leads to or introduces a note falling on a strong beat. Upbeats are characteristically (but not always) shorter than the accented note which succeeds them.

The meter signature of Example 2-14 is 6/8, suggesting six eighth-note beats per measure. In effect, however, the example consists (like most music notated in compound meter) of a broader basic pulse, or basic duration, than that appearing in the meter signature. Clearly the eighth notes of Example 2-14 are grasped as *divisions* (triple) of the main pulse, rather than as beat units. In such an example one would not mark time or count rhythm using the eighth note as the basic unit. Only in extremely slow passages would musicians generally count measures at the rate of six beats per measure. The same statement applies to other compound meters such as 9/8 and 12/8, which, if taken literally, would imply nine and twelve beats per measure. Such large numbers of beats are obviously impractical.

It should be clear from this discussion that compound meter signatures actually describe the number of durations, and their level (eighths, quarters, etc.), that occur as primary beat *divisions.* This is in contrast to simple meters, whose meter signatures indicate the number of *main pulses* per measure.

That musicians continue to notate compound time, as in Example 2-14, is one of the many shortcomings of our system of notation. Perhaps a more meaningful way to indicate a typical compound meter such as 6/8 would be to write $\frac{2}{\text{♩.}}$. In this case the upper number would literally denote the number of beats per measure and the lower note value would indicate precisely the basic duration.

CONDUCTORS' BEAT PATTERNS

A thorough grasp of the relation between rhythmic patterns and pulse grouping, i.e., meter, can come from physical participation in both. The beat patterns employed by conductors for picturing meter can serve as a useful basis for experiencing rhythm. Study the various beat patterns shown below and learn to execute them. The upper diagrams show a simplified representation of conductors' beat patterns. The lower diagrams more nearly approximate the actual movements of the conductor's baton.

Duple (simple or compound)	*Triple (simple or compound)*	*Quadruple (simple or compound)*

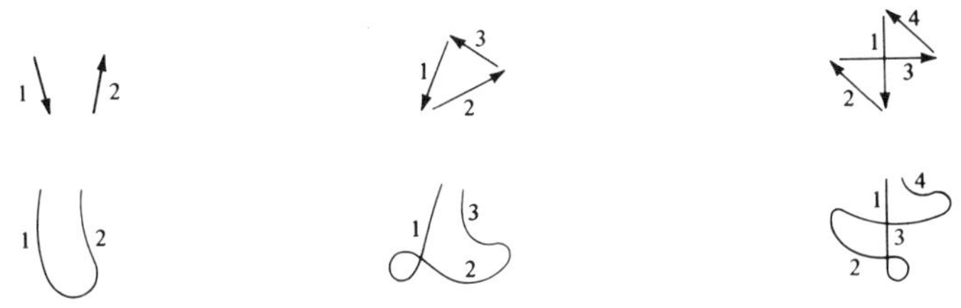

A summary of the most common meters and their components is given in the table beginning below and continuing on page 32. This information should be mastered before proceeding to the Exercises that follow.

Meter Type	*Signatures*	*Accentuation*	*Number of Beats*	*Beat*	*Division*	*Subdivision*
Simple duple	2/4	Sw	two	♩	♪	𝅘𝅥𝅯
	2/8	Sw	two	♪	𝅘𝅥𝅯	𝅘𝅥𝅰
	2/2	Sw	two	𝅗𝅥	♩	♪

(cont.)

Meter Type	*Signatures*	*Accentuation*	*Number of Beats*	*Beat*	*Division*	*Subdivision*
Simple triple	3/4	Sww	three	♩	♪	𝅘𝅥𝅯
	3/8	Sww	three	♪	𝅘𝅥𝅯	𝅘𝅥𝅰
	3/2	Sww	three	𝅗𝅥	♩	♪
Simple quadruple	4/4 (C)	SwSw	four	♩	♪	𝅘𝅥𝅯
	4/8	SwSw	four	♪	𝅘𝅥𝅯	𝅘𝅥𝅰
	4/2	SwSw	four	𝅗𝅥	♩	♪
Compound duple	6/4	Sw	two	𝅗𝅥.	♩	♪
	6/8	Sw	two	♩.	♪	𝅘𝅥𝅯
	6/16	Sw	two	♪.	𝅘𝅥𝅯	𝅘𝅥𝅰
Compound triple	9/4	Sww	three	𝅗𝅥.	♩	♪
	9/8	Sww	three	♩.	♪	𝅘𝅥𝅯
	9/16	Sww	three	♪.	𝅘𝅥𝅯	𝅘𝅥𝅰
Compound quadruple	12/4	SwSw	four	𝅗𝅥.	♩	♪
	12/8	SwSw	four	♩.	♪	𝅘𝅥𝅯
	12/16	SwSw	four	♪.	𝅘𝅥𝅯	𝅘𝅥𝅰

EXERCISES

1. Locate each of the items listed below in the musical example. Then write the letter of each item at the point of its occurrence in the music.

   a) the note equivalent of one beat
   b) the note equivalent of two beats
   c) the note equivalent of three beats
   d) the note equivalent of one half-beat
   e) the note equivalent of one quarter-beat
   f) the rest equivalent of one beat
   g) the meter signature
   h) a dotted note equal to a beat and a half
   i) a note falling on a strong beat   j) a note falling on a weak beat
   k) a flag   l) a beam   m) a note stem
   n) a note lasting three-quarters of one measure

2. a) Establish several measures of common time by tapping beats at a moderately fast pace; keep tapping the meter and intone the rhythm of the musical example in Exercise 1 as accurately as possible.
   b) Play d^1 on the piano and then sing the same example at the tempo established above.
   c) Locate and mark all half-steps that occur in the first two lines of the example, as shown in the first four measures (⌢).

3. Locate each of the items listed below in the musical example and write the letter of each item at the point of its occurrence in the music.

a) the note equivalent of one basic duration (assuming there are two principal beats per measure)

b) a note equal to one-third of the beat unit

c) a note equal to one-sixth of the beat unit

d) a measure revealing the normal beat division in 6/8 meter

e) a note falling on the weak beat of a measure

4. Establish several measures of 6/8 meter by tapping two main pulses per measure; maintain the tapping and intone the rhythm of the musical example in Exercise 3 as accurately as possible.

5. Circle all the notes of the Great Octave that occur in the example in Exercise 3. (Write on the music.)

(optional)

6. Transcribe the musical example in Exercise 3 to 6/4 meter by doubling the duration of all notes. Observe the principles of beaming, etc., cited earlier.

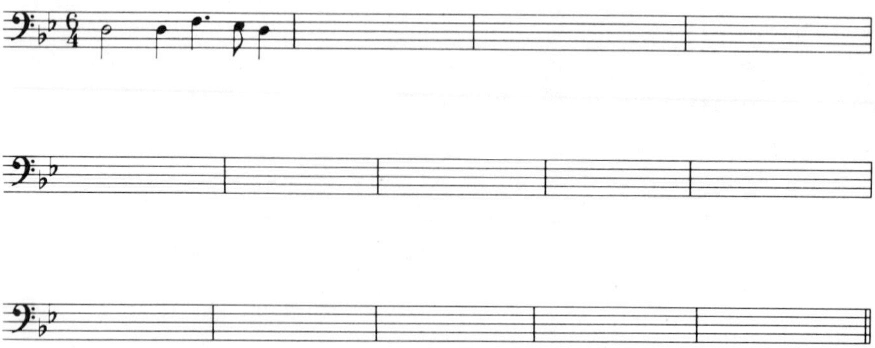

7. Write the note equivalent of the basic duration for each of the meters noted here:

3/8 ______, 6/4 ______, 3/4 ______, ¢ ______, 9/8 ______, 3/2 ______, 6/16 ______.

8. Write rest equivalents for each of the following durations:

(optional)

9. Complete each of the following measures with one note. Observe the given meter signature for each measure. See the sample solution.

Chapter 3

MELODY: MATERIALS AND ORGANIZATION

Melody involves the coordination of musical time and space, that is, rhythm and pitch. The pitch relationships of the successive tones of a melody constitute the melody's contour or tonal profile; the successive durations constitute the melodic rhythm and create an impression of continuity in time.

Melody appears to be the most memorable aspect of music. We recall and identify compositions through memory of their melodies and associations. We hum, whistle, or sing melodies from compositions consisting of many other competing and interacting elements. Comprehension of a piece of music usually begins with an understanding of melodic content, the most easily grasped part of a composition, and then proceeds to the other factors.

INTERVALS

Melodic contour, as we have said, is the profile of melodic rise and fall. On hearing a particular melody, we may be impressed by its contour and remember it because of its unique pattern. Another melody may have a less engaging design, but may still arouse our interest or have some appeal for us for some other reason. Compare the two melodies in Example 3-1. Note that while the first has a very pronounced rise and fall, the second has little variety in its contour, remaining for the most part within a very limited span.

To describe contour in a precise way, we use the nomenclature of musical *intervals.* Intervals are relative pitch distances; they indicate the precise span embracing two different notes in terms of their positions on the staff and the number of steps between them. However, the meaning of an interval is a recognizable *sound* relationship; an interval cannot be described solely in terms of the lines and spaces of the staff.

Example 3-1

a) Beethoven

b) Chopin

There are three types of melodic motion which can be described in terms of intervals. Movement by *step* (conjunct motion) involves movement between adjacent notes—that is, between a note on a line and the note on the space immediately above or below it, or between a note on a space and the note on the line immediately above or below it. The last two measures of Example 3-1(a) consist entirely of step motion. Example 3-2 illustrates an entire melody composed of step motion.

Example 3-2

Steps predominate in most melodies, particularly vocal melodies. Movement by *leap* (disjunct motion) affords variety to a melody and creates a sense of motion and activity not attainable by the use of steps alone. Example 3-1(b) contains both steps and leaps, although step motion predominates.

The third type of melodic motion is *repetition* of a note. Note repetition, as seen in Example 3-1(b), does not affect melodic contour; instead, its effect is primarily rhythmic.

The interval name for the step is the *second.* There are two commonly found kinds of second: the *minor* second, or half-step (for example, from *b*

Example 3-3

Example 3-4

Example 3-5

Brahms

to *c*, from *e* to *f*, from *a* to *b*♭, or from *f*♯ to *g*), and the *major* second, or whole step (for example, from *c* to *d*, from *e* to *f*♯, or from *a*♭ to *b*♭). The minor second (m2) appears several times in Example 3-3; note the effect it creates of a tight, binding connection. This effect, when produced by an ascending minor second, is often described as a leading tone progression. The major second (M2), or whole step, is a wider step than the minor second; in fact, it is twice as wide. The major second is probably the most frequently occurring interval in most melodies. Sing Example 3-4 and note the contrast between major and minor seconds.

Example 3-5 is typical of innumerable melodies from music literature in that it is fashioned largely from seconds. However, the complement of intervals found in this melody is not limited to seconds alone. Note that measures 4, 5, and 9 contain small leaps, namely thirds. Note the effectiveness of the thirds in creating variety and heightening interest without altering the essentially conjunct impression of the melody.

The interval of a *third* is the most frequent leap in many melodies. It involves movement from a note on a line to the note on the line immediately above or below it, or from a note on a space to the note on the space immediately above or below it. Like seconds, thirds may be major or minor. The minor third (m3), which is the smallest possible leap, spans a step and a half:

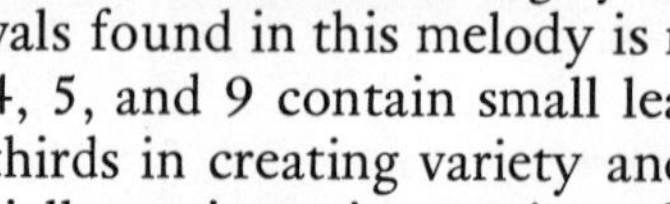

The major third (M3) consists of two whole steps:

Note the frequent use of thirds in Example 3-6.

Example 3-6

Beethoven

When we move from thirds to fourths, fifths, and octaves, we use a different set of terms; instead of being called major or minor, fourths and fifths (and also octaves and unisons) are called *perfect, augmented,* or *diminished.* The perfect fourth encompasses two and one-half steps:

The perfect fifth spans three and one-half steps:

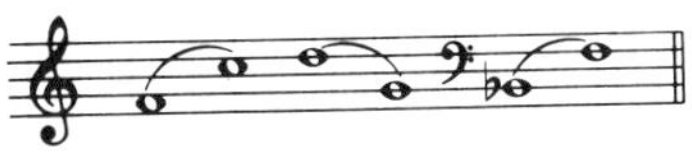

Both perfect fourths and perfect fifths are quite common melodic intervals, particularly at the beginning and end of melodic groups or phrases. Placed thus at the junctures of melodic design, as in Example 3-7, they help to delineate melodic structure and tonality.

Example 3-7

Beethoven

Although encompassing a wide melodic span, namely five whole and two half-steps, perfect octaves (P8) are easily grasped as higher or lower duplications of tones with identical note names. Note the octave leaps in Example 3-8, where they occur as elaborations of a simple step design, shown in the reduction below the excerpt.

Example 3-8

Mozart

An augmented interval is one semitone larger than the corresponding perfect interval, and a diminished interval is one semitone smaller. For most practical purposes, we need concern ourselves only with the augmented fourth and the diminished fifth. As it happens, these two intervals are identical in sound.* The sound they represent is called the *tritone.* A tritone, as the name suggests, consists of three whole steps:

+4 °5

It is useful to note that all the intervals in the treble clef that span four natural notes (i.e., notes that have not been altered by means of accidentals) are perfect fourths, with the exception of the interval between the first space and the third line, which is an augmented fourth or tritone:

Any perfect fourth enlarged by a semitone becomes a tritone. Similarly, a perfect fifth becomes a tritone if the upper note is lowered one semitone or if the lower note is raised one semitone:

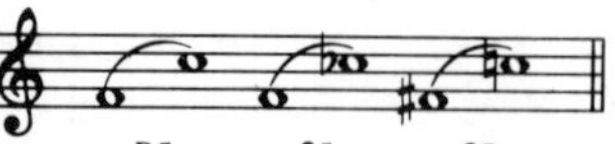

P5 °5 °5

*It is for notational convenience that they are given different names. For the same reason, the diminished fourth and the augmented fifth are available to the composer, but they are not frequently used. As you can see for yourself, the diminished fourth is identical in sound to a major third, and the augmented fifth is identical to a minor sixth.

All fifths in the treble clef consisting of natural notes are perfect fifths, except the interval from the third line to the fifth line, which is a tritone:

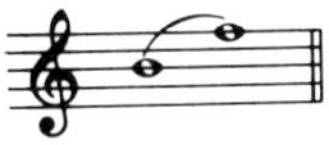

The tritone is characterized by an ambiguity of effect. Without previous associations with a tonic, or key center, the tritone can be difficult to sing. Note the effect of the tritones in Example 3-9.

Example 3-9

Brahms

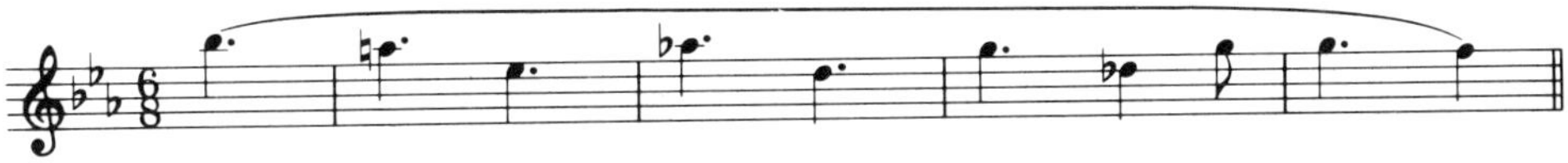

In discussing sixths and sevenths, we return to the nomenclature of major and minor intervals. If a third is inverted, that is, if the lower note of a third is raised an octave, as shown here:

the resulting interval is a sixth. When a minor third is inverted, it becomes a major sixth; an inverted major third becomes a minor sixth. The major sixth is a whole step wider than a perfect fifth, and the minor sixth exceeds the perfect fifth by a semitone:

Like other wide leaps, sixths occur less commonly than their smaller inversions, thirds.* Compare the thirds and sixths in Example 3-10.

The major and minor seventh, a half-step and a whole step less than a perfect octave, respectively, are wide leaps which produce a definite effect of

Example 3-10

French Folk Song

---

*Note that fifths are inversions of fourths, and sevenths are inversions of seconds.

angularity in the melodic contour. A leap of a seventh is usually followed by step motion in such a way that the leap is "resolved":

Note the use of such resolution in Example 3-11.

Example 3-11

J. S. Bach

Example 3-12 contains virtually all of the intervals that have been discussed. Identify each interval, then find the starting note (*c*) and sing the entire series of notes, intoning the note names.

Example 3-12

Intervals are analogous to the alphabet. Although it is essential to know the alphabet as a basis for reading and writing, we do not interpret speech by identifying each syllable in a sentence. Similarly, listening to music presupposes a working knowledge of intervals, because they constitute the basic ingredients of musical sentences and their subparts, phrases, motives, and figures. However, our "minds' ears" receive and process musical signals far more rapidly than we can isolate and identify each interval heard in a melody. Thus, when we listen to music, we rely on facility in the accurate recognition of intervals as a kind of subconscious process. Instead of recognizing each interval individually, we perceive a number of successive intervals as a musical pattern. Music, after all, is composed of patterned, not isolated, sounds.

The table on page 43 provides a summary of the intervals discussed, with the number of steps they contain and the number of lines and spaces they encompass on the staff. Examples are given in the treble clef, using g^1 as a starting point.

RANGE

The high and low peaks in the contour of a melody define its *range.* There are no rules which specify the allowable range of a melody; however, some limitations are imposed by the particular performing media. In general, vocal

Interval Nomenclature

Interval	*Specific Quality*	*Position on Staff*	*Size in Steps*	*Notation*
Unison or Prime	Note duplication	Same line or space	–	
Second	Major, minor	Adjacent line and space or adjacent space and line	1, ½	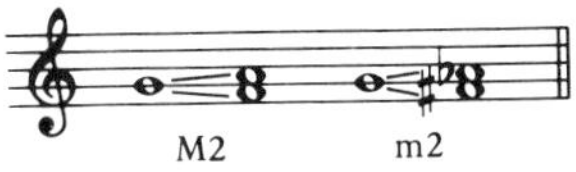
Third	Major, minor	Adjacent lines or adjacent spaces	2, 1½	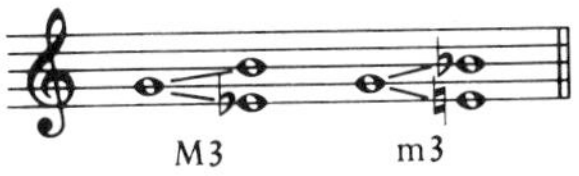
Fourth	Perfect, augmented	Two lines and a space apart or two spaces and a line apart	2½, 3	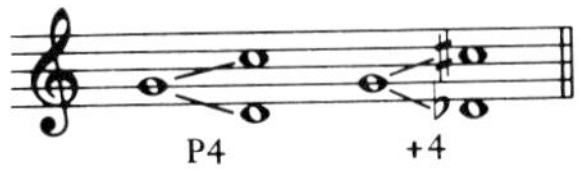
Fifth	Perfect, diminished	Three lines or three spaces apart	3½, 2½ ½	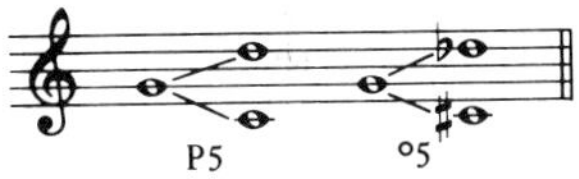
Sixth	Major, minor	Three lines and a space apart or three spaces and a line apart	4½, 3½ ½	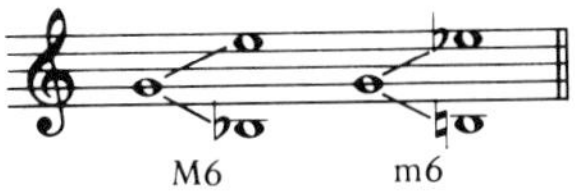
Seventh	Major, minor	Four lines or four spaces apart	5½, 4½ ½	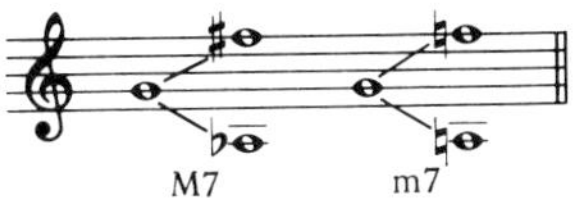
Octave	Perfect	Four lines and a space apart or four spaces and a line apart	5½ ½	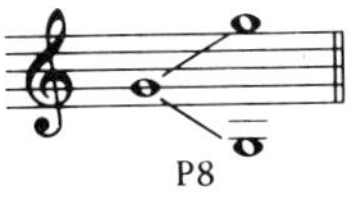

melodies, because of the physical limitations of the human voice, fall within a smaller range (usually no wider than an octave plus a fifth) than do those written for instrumental or keyboard performance. The range of most instruments is at least two octaves (a fifteenth).

Compare the ranges of the two melodies in Example 3-13. The first is a vocal melody; the second was written for orchestral instruments.

Example 3-13

a) *Dixie* (range: an octave plus a third)

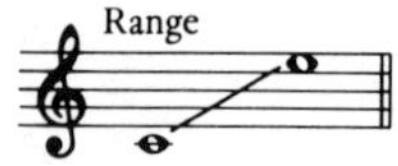

b) R. Strauss (range: two octaves plus a fifth)

Singers commonly describe a song in terms of its general "lie," that is, the mean or norm of its pitches—disregarding occasional notes occurring above or below the core of the song's melodic content. The word used to denote

Example 3-14

Mendelssohn

the general "lie" of a melody is *tessitura.* Compare the tessitura of the melody in Example 3-14 with its range.

MELODIC RHYTHM

Musical time is described in terms of the relation of the various note values (or durations) to the prevailing meter at a given tempo. To stretch a point, it might be said that meter and tempo provide a frame of reference for rhythmic activity just as key and range provide a framework for pitch organization. The successive durations of a melody, which divide or complement the beat or metered pulse, constitute the *melodic rhythm.* It is the interplay of melodic rhythm and meter that produces the wonderful illusion of forward motion in melody. Establish a moderate tempo (such as MM ♩ = 80) and perform Example 3-15. Note the melodic rhythm as contrasted with the rhythm of successive beats (metric rhythm), shown on the bottom line of the example.

Example 3-15

Brahms

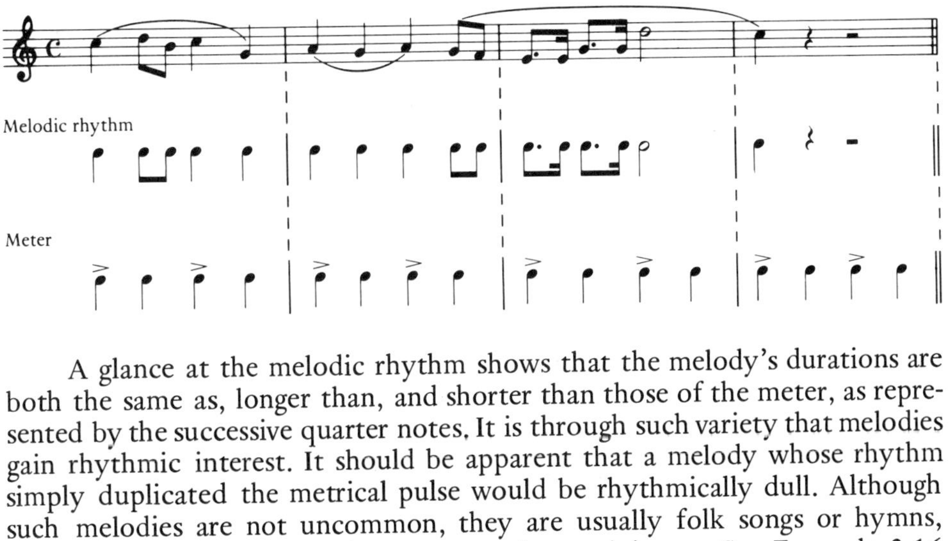

A glance at the melodic rhythm shows that the melody's durations are both the same as, longer than, and shorter than those of the meter, as represented by the successive quarter notes. It is through such variety that melodies gain rhythmic interest. It should be apparent that a melody whose rhythm simply duplicated the metrical pulse would be rhythmically dull. Although such melodies are not uncommon, they are usually folk songs or hymns, whose performance demands represent a bare minimum. See Example 3-16 for an example.

Example 3-16

Haydn

ACCENTUATION IN MELODY

Listen to the familiar melody in Example 3-17 and note its rhythm, shown beneath the music. Two factors in particular lead us to react to it as being in triple meter. The first is the *grouping* of durations (quarter notes) in threes. The second is the occurrence of longer notes on strong beats; that is, the notes that fall on the *first* beats of measures often produce accents by reason of their longer duration. Accents that occur on longer notes are called *agogic accents.* There are no agogic accents in Example 3-16, since all the durations are identical. Example 3-18 contains agogic accents, as indicated by the arrows above the notes.

Example 3-17

Example 3-18

Brahms

Musicians always consult the meter signature of a melody before beginning to perform it. They do so because the meter signature supplies the reader with information about grouping and accent placement in the example to be read, *not* because the meter predetermines the melody's rhythms. To demonstrate this, perform the following experiment.

Listen to a performance of Example 3-19 without any preconception of the meter. Then determine the meter (duple or triple) that is suggested by

Example 3-19

Beethoven (shown without barlines)

Example 3-20

Beethoven (renotated)

note grouping and by agogic accents and supply barlines accordingly. Then perform the melody to confirm your response. Assume that the melody is in a simple meter whose beat unit is the quarter note.

Having determined the triple meter implied by the melody's rhythm, perform the renotated version shown in Example 3-20, noting in particular the relation between agogic accents and the placement of strong and weak beats. The version of Example 3-20, notated in duple meter, reveals the placement of rhythmic accents that tend to disrupt the simple rhythmic motion of the successive beats. The notes marked (>) clearly produce agogic accents; however, they have been displaced in such a way that they fall on weak beats and continue to sound *through* the succeeding strong beats. The result of such displacement, commonly called *syncopation,* is a melodic rhythm that does not clearly affirm or comply with the given (notated) meter of the passage. The resulting "conflict" of accents may be used to heighten rhythmic interest and break up the tandem-like sequence of accents. For contrast, perform Example 3-21, which lacks syncopation. The rhythms of most melodies affirm

Example 3-21

Example 3-22

Muffat

the metric basis of the meter signature, but *in varying degrees,* and particularly at the beginning and the end of the melody. However, accent displacement is a vital aspect of many works. Perform Example 3-22 and note the points, marked ↑, at which syncopation occurs.

One can imagine numerous rhythmic patterns that would disrupt or displace the agreement of the metric accents with the accents of the melodic rhythm. For instance, *dynamic* accents (accent by means of louder articulation) applied to weak beats can also produce syncopation, as shown in Example 3-23 (*p* means "soft" and *f* means "loud"). That the accented notes of this passage are also distinguished by high or low placement tends to emphasize further the displacement of the metric accent.

Example 3-23

Example 3-24

J. S. Bach

A final example will serve, for the time being, to illustrate regular and displaced rhythmic accents. In Example 3-24 the opening two measures clearly affirm the beat (♩.) and its primary division (♪). Rhythmic interest is heightened in measures 3 and 4 by displacement of the note grouping—note articulation is shifted to the weak part of the beat:

The result of this syncopation is a kind of "lift"—a slight prod—that is timed to avoid the monotony of repetition that could result without such a device.

EXERCISES

1. Identify the sizes of all the intervals formed by successive pitches in the excerpts given below. Write beneath the music between the two notes of each melodic interval, as shown at the beginning of each excerpt.

English Folk Song

a)

Handel

b)

French Folk Song

c)

(optional)

d)

(optional)

Mozart

e)

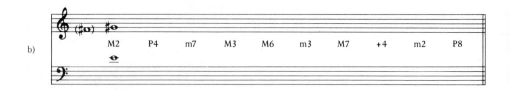

2. Write the notes that will form all of the intervals specified above and below each of the given pitches. Note the samples.

a)

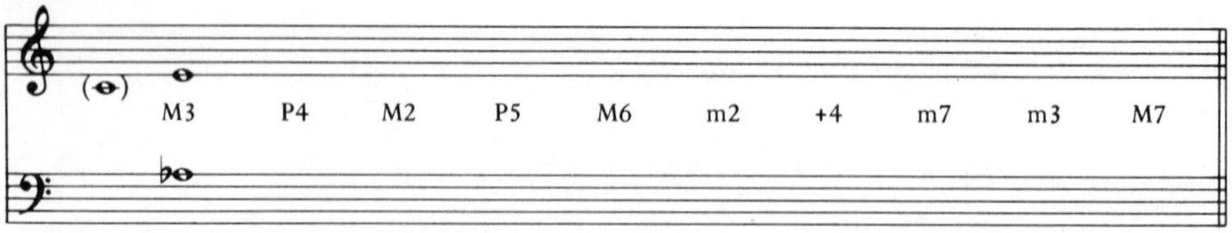

b)

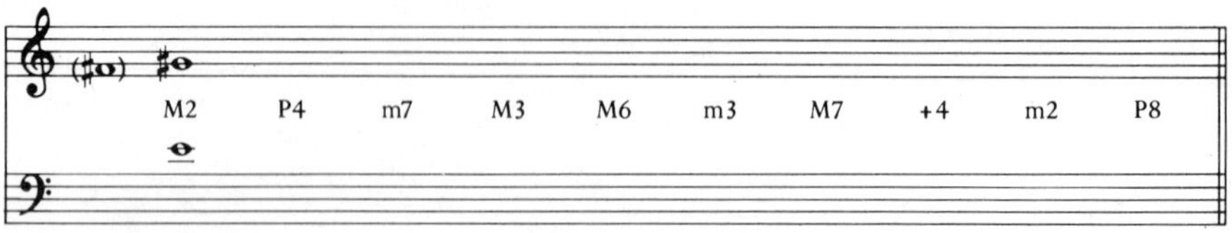

c) 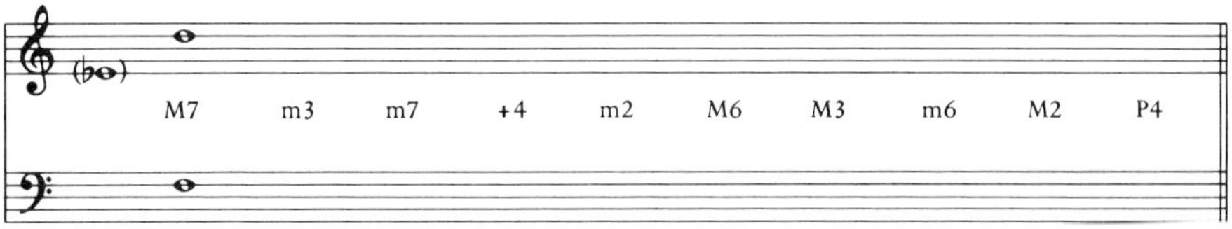

d) 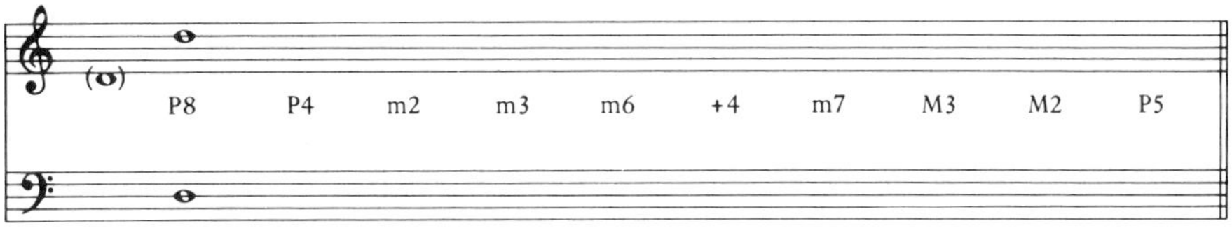

e) 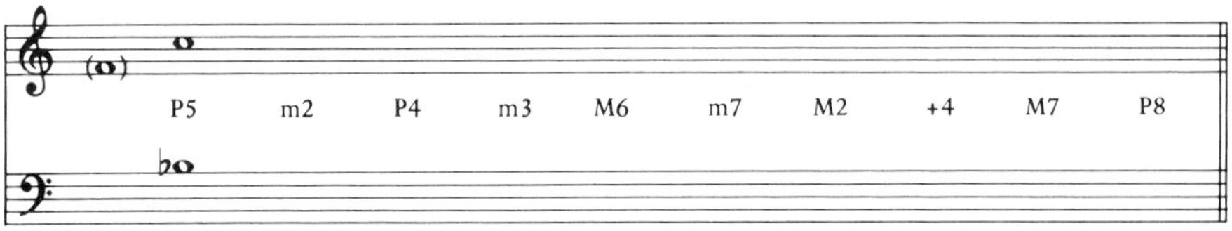

(optional)

3. Write the inversion of each of the following intervals. See the sample.

4. Read the rhythm of each of the melodies in Exercise 1. In each case establish the meter before beginning, and maintain the meter by tapping as you intone the rhythm. Strive to accomplish the following goals:
   1) Continue to *move ahead* regardless of any mistakes you make.
   2) Direct your attention to the accurate articulation of whatever durations fall on successive *accented beats* of the measure.
   3) Read one measure ahead. Avoid reading the measure or note that you are intoning by moving your hand over the music; doing so *forces* you to read ahead.
5. Establish a tempo, find the starting pitch, and sing each of the melodies in Exercise 1, applying the same three principles mentioned in Exercise 4.
6. Practice interval singing and recognition by playing the given pitch for each of the various parts of Exercise 2 and singing the intervals specified, above and below, in a comfortable register. Practice recognition of these and similar interval patterns by taking turns playing them with another person. Use the piano or any available instrument, or your own voice.

7. Sing or play the melody given below and answer the following questions about it. Answer in the spaces provided.

Brahms

a) Is the motion of the melody mostly conjunct or disjunct? ___________

b) Is the meter simple or compound? ___________

c) Draw the pitch profile of the melody.

Pitch Profile:

d) Describe the range of the melody. ___________

e) Which measure contains the most rhythmic activity? ___________

f) What type of accent coincides with the melody's high point? ___________

g) Does the melody contain syncopation? _____ If so, where? ___________

h) Transpose the opening phrase (measures 1 through 4) to the key of A major by writing each note a major second above its occurrence in the example.

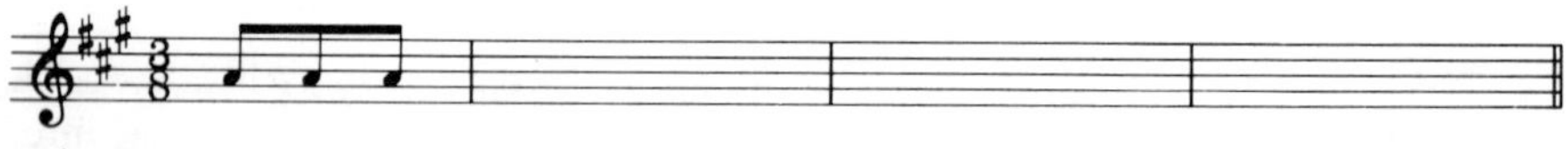

(optional)

8. Familiarize yourself with the following melody. Then locate each of the items listed on page 53 and write the measure number of its occurrence in the space provided.

Mozart

a) Placement of agogic accent on a strong beat. ____________

b) A measure containing only disjunct motion. ____________

c) The longest duration used. ____________

d) A note lasting three beats. ____________

e) The widest leap in the melody. ____________

f) A measure containing only step motion. ____________

g) A measure which reveals the same melodic rhythm as measure 8. ____________

(optional)

9. Perform the melody given below and locate syncopation in it. Where does a prominent tritone occur? Is the tritone resolved by step motion? Try to determine aspects of the melody's organization that result in unity.

Schubert

Chapter 4

TONALITY IN MELODY

Perhaps the most common trait of melodies written during the evolution of Western music prior to the twentieth century is that of *tonality.* Tonality, like many artistic phenomena, is more easily experienced, or felt, than verbalized. Compare the two melodies of Example 4-1, of which the first clearly implies a key, the second does not.

Example 4-1

a) *Yankee Doodle*

b) Schoenberg, *Sommermüd,* Op. 48

In Example 4-1(a) one note, *g,* acts as a central pitch or as a focal point of the melody's activity. Used at the beginning and the end of the melody, it is given a particular prominence that impresses it upon our minds. The frequent recurrence of *g* within the melody also serves to reinforce our aural recall of it. Because of the prominence of *g* in the melody, the other notes seem subservient to it and, in a way, dependent on it. Their role in the melody's structure seems to be governed by, and best heard in relation to, the tone *g*. As the focal pitch, or tonal center, of the melody, the note *g* is called the *tonic.* Any melody which reveals a focal pitch exemplifies, to one degree or another, the unique aspect of music called tonality. Although there are numerous causcs and cffccts of tonality, it is perhaps most easily grasped as an important facet of pitch organization and our psychological reaction to it. Indeed most melodies reveal some semblance of tonal-centeredness, examples such as Example 4-1(b) notwithstanding.

Upon hearing Example 4-1(b) one experiences little sense of tonality. This is due to the fact that no single note is indelibly impressed on our minds as a point of focus upon which all the other tones of the melody converge. On the contrary, such a maze of relationships occurs that virtually any of the notes may, at one time or another, act as a point of reference. Such melodies, characteristic of a great deal of recent composition, usually yield patterns of pitch organization other than those typified by tonal music. Such patterns are themselves neither good nor bad, simply different from the patterns of tonal music.

The tonic is not always stated as the first note of a melody, although it is usually heard as the concluding note. In Example 4-2 the tonic, *d,* is first heard at the end of measure 2. Its role in the melody's organization involves prominence as a high and a low point, and thus as a framework encompassing the body of the melody, as well as a closing (or cadential) pitch, one which in a sense acts as the tonal *goal* of the melody.

Example 4-2

Dvořák

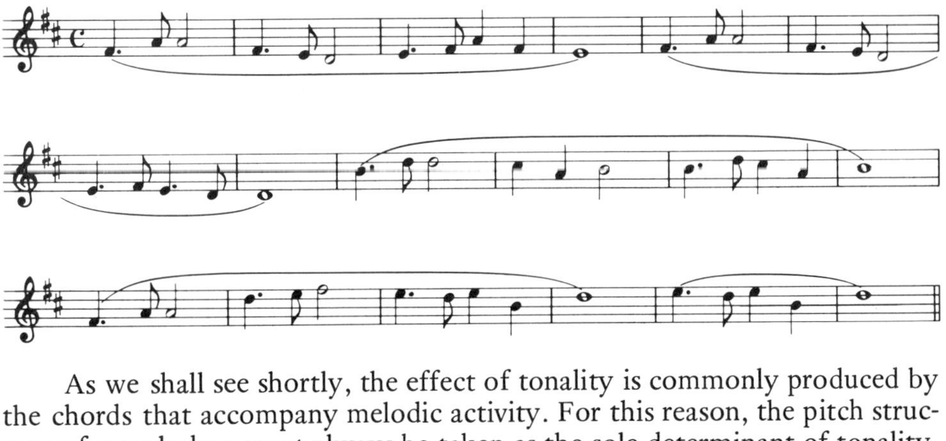

As we shall see shortly, the effect of tonality is commonly produced by the chords that accompany melodic activity. For this reason, the pitch structure of a melody cannot always be taken as the sole determinant of tonality. The feeling of the tonic conveyed by a melodic line will often be clarified and underscored by accompanying chords, but in some cases the harmonic accompaniment will suggest a reassessment of the tonality implied by the melody alone.

We may define tonality generally as the organization of pitch activity around a tonal center, the tonic. The degree to which we recall and aurally relate to a tonic hinges on the simplicity and directness with which it is projected by the pitch organization. Although pitch focus may be said to operate in varying degrees in practically all music, tonality, in the most commonly acknowledged sense of the term, is analogous to *key.* And when musicians speak of tonality, they are usually referring to the specific basis for creating tonal relationships denoted by the word key.

KEY

The term key describes a set of notes orbited, so to speak, around a tonic, or key center. The various pitches that constitute a key relate to each other as the various members of a family of notes. Furthermore, each note of a key is dependent on the tonic, which is the principal member of the tonal family and which defines and gives tonal meaning to the other notes. Listen to the melody in Example 4-3 and discover its tonic. Note the dependency of the other members of the melody on the tonic as a kind of rallying point.

The pitch materials of this melody constitute the key of D major. In fact, the pitches of this melody consist of seven different note names, including *d* and all the other note names between this *d* and the *d* an octave higher. An important aspect of this series of seven different notes is the set of whole-step and half-step relations within it. If we arrange the notes in ascending order, the result will be a *scale,* as described briefly in Chapter 1:

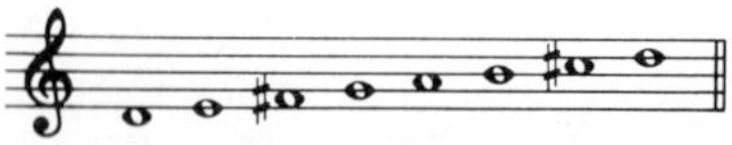

A scale is the simplest vehicle for picturing the pitches of a given key. As a matter of fact, the terms key and scale are commonly regarded as virtually synonymous.

Note that a given melody does not have to contain all of the pitches available in its key. Example 4-2, which is in the same key as Example 4-3, does not contain *g.* Nor is the content of a melody limited strictly to the basic set of available pitches, as we shall see later. Most melodies, however, are composed principally of the notes belonging to their scales.

Example 4-3

J. S. Bach

The particular arrangement of whole steps and half-steps revealed by the scale we have been considering constitutes the identifying characteristic of all *major* scales. A major scale consists of four whole steps and two half-steps, arranged in the following ascending order: whole, whole, half (two and one-half steps so far), followed by whole, whole, whole, half (three and one-half steps). It is convenient to think of the major scale as consisting of two parts, the break occurring between the fourth and fifth notes, because doing so demonstrates an important characteristic of this scale. The lower and upper halves of the scale,

 and 

have identical patterns of intervals. Such four-note spans are called *tetrachords.* The two tetrachords of the major scale are joined by the interval of a major second.

The major scale pattern, like any scale pattern comprising a total of five whole steps and two half-steps, is called a *diatonic* scale. Each member, or degree, of a diatonic scale has a name denoting its relative position in the scale pattern. These names are given in Example 4-4, in which the scale is based on *c.*

Example 4-4 The major scale based on c

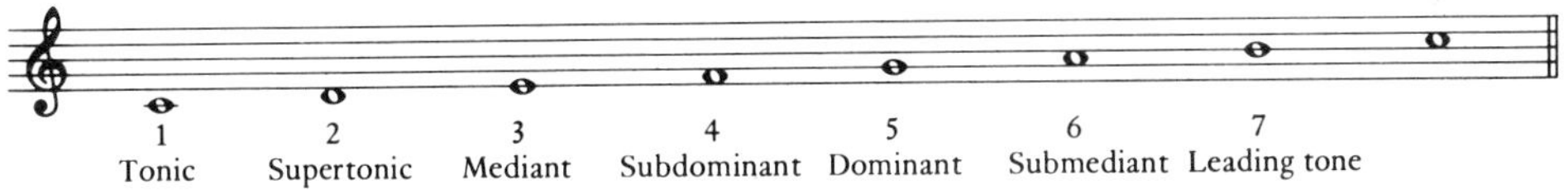

Although scales are always shown as step arrangements beginning on the tonic note, it is important to be aware of the distances between various non-adjacent scale members—for example, between tonic and mediant, between subdominant and leading tone, and between supertonic and dominant. It is only through an awareness of these intervals that one can fully appreciate the relationship between key patterns and their use in actual melodies. To illustrate this, study the interval content of Example 4-5.

The melody of Example 4-5 opens with the skip of a major third, which is identical with the interval between the tonic and the mediant of a major

Example 4-5

scale. Note also that the span of a perfect fifth in measure 2 is the interval between the tonic and the dominant, and that the half-steps in measures 3 and 5 represent the interval between the leading tone and the tonic (this is the leading tone progression mentioned earlier). One of the most telling features of the major scale (and some forms of the minor scale too) is the interval of a tritone between the fourth and seventh degrees of the scale:

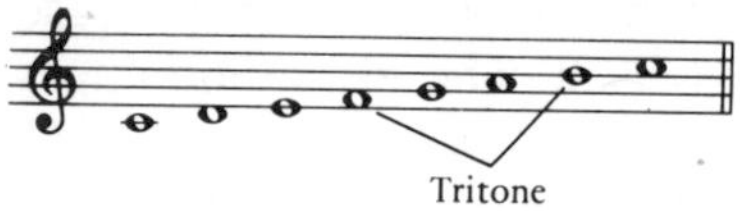

The tritone is often heard near the conclusion of a melody, producing a sense of instability or tension that is resolved with the arrival of the tonic, as in Example 4-6. For another example of this telling use of the tritone, see the excerpt reproduced in Exercise 9 of Chapter 3.

Example 4-6

Haydn

KEY SIGNATURES

In introducing the major scale, we have used C major as an example. The scale of C major consists of the white keys of the piano. Since it involves no sharp or flat alterations, it is often called the natural scale. However, as we know, tonal music is not limited to scales based on *c;* any note, including its sharp and flat variants, can act as a tonic. When a major scale is based on a note other than *c,* it is necessary to alter (lower or raise by a half-step, using a sharp or a flat sign) one or more of the notes in order to preserve the pattern of whole and half-steps peculiar to the major scale. Example 4-7 shows major scales based on *c, a,* and *e♭* for the purpose of comparison. Note that the A major scale involves the use of accidentals before the mediant, *c* (to produce a major third above *a*), before *f* (to produce a major sixth above *a*), and before *g* (to create a half-step interval between the leading tone and the tonic). Similarly, the E♭ major scale uses three lowered notes, *b♭, e♭,* and *a♭.*

Example 4-7 Major scales on c, a, and e♭

The sharps or flats of a key signature are usually written on the lines or spaces within or adjacent to the staff, ledger lines being avoided in signature notation. Any number of sharps or flats from one to seven may appear in key signatures. As a rule, sharps and flats are not mixed, although some recent composers such as Bartók have modified and enlarged upon traditional signature practices.

Various sorts of key signatures have been in use over the past 800 years, but the earlier types of signatures have presented numerous difficulties for musicians until recently. In the system which has been in general use over the past 200 years, the *order* of affixing the accidentals is related to a theoretical arrangement of keys based on the interval of a perfect fifth.

For keys whose signatures consist of sharps, this arrangement is called the *cycle of ascending perfect fifths.* Beginning with *c,* one progresses through a series of keys whose tonics are a perfect fifth apart:

Example 4-8 The cycle of ascending fifths

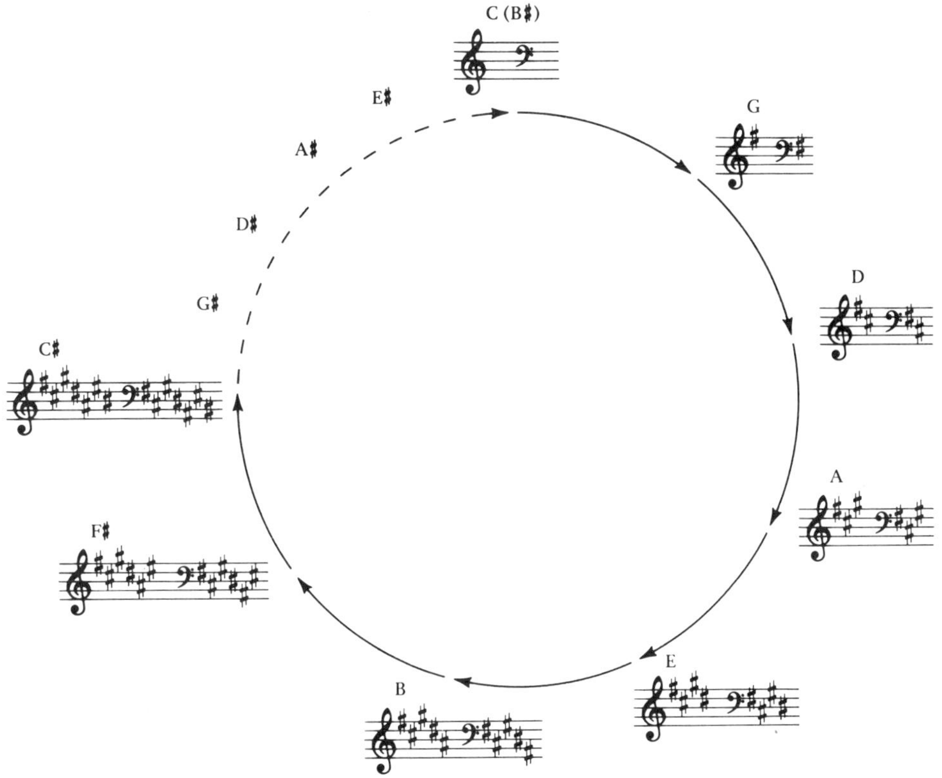

For the sake of notational convenience, we have inverted every other interval, making it a descending perfect fourth. The cycle is complete when we reach *c* again. However, we don't actually return to *c*, but rather to its enharmonic equivalent, *b*♯. Any two notes that are identical in pitch but, as the result of sharp or flat alterations, are notated differently are referred to as *enharmonic.*

If you write out the major scales based on each of these notes in succession, you will find that each progression by a perfect fifth requires the addition of a sharp to the key signature. The major scale of *g* requires one sharp, of *d* two sharps, and so on.

The cycle of fifths for the commonly used sharp keys is given in Example 4-8, with the respective key signatures written in both treble and bass clefs. Note that the order of the sharps is *f-c-g-d-a-e-b,* and that the last sharp of each signature corresponds to the leading tone of the major key.

For flat keys there is a *cycle of descending fifths,* shown in Example 4-9. The order of the flats is *b-e-a-d-g-c-f,* and the last flat always corresponds to the subdominant note of the major key.

It is relevant to note that, when the use of a particular key would necessitate an impractical number of sharps or flats, the sound equivalent (that is,

Example 4-9 The cycle of descending fifths

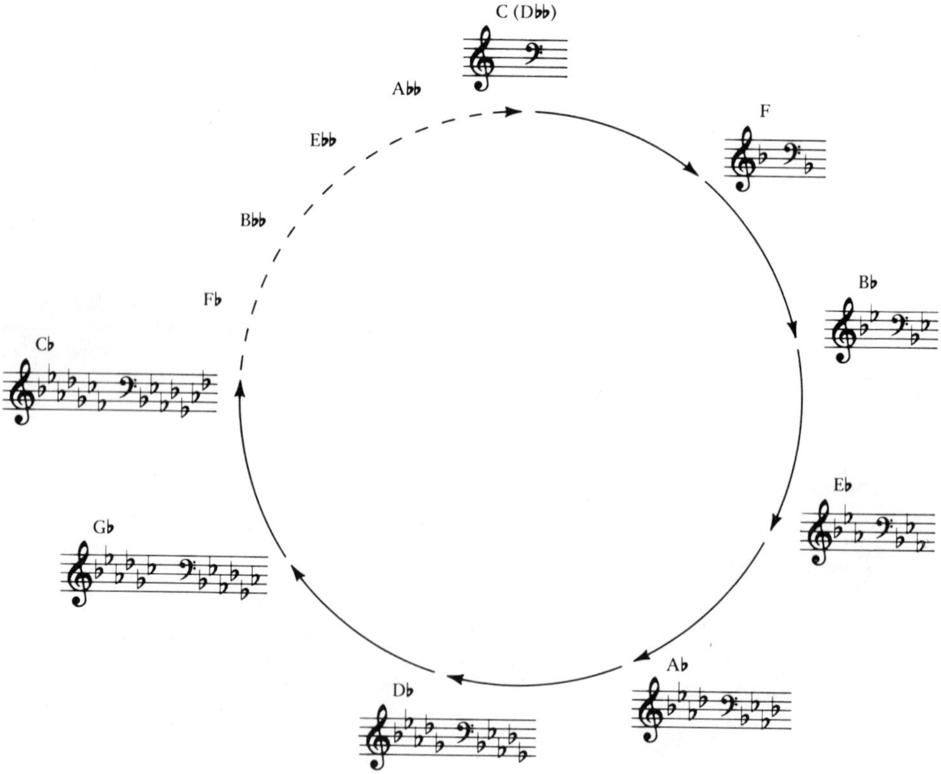

the enharmonic equivalent) of such a key can be employed. For example, B♭ major can be used in place of A♯ major, E major in place of F♭ major. In some cases the performance capabilities and the mechanical construction of certain instruments, winds in particular, dictate to some extent the notation of a part. In general, however, the choice of a particular key is based more on artistic factors than on notational convenience. This is the only reasonable explanation that can be given for the fact that composers frequently elect to write in the key of C♯ major (seven sharps) rather than D♭ (five flats).

By combining, so to speak, the two cycles of perfect fifths, one can obtain a clearer grasp of how the use of enharmonic equivalents permits the duplication of keys. Enharmonicism is part and parcel of Western musical notation and a by-product of the equal temperament system of tuning. In Example 4-10, the keys in parentheses represent theoretical possibilities that are impractical because of the large number of sharps or flats they would require.

Example 4-10 The composite cycle of fifths

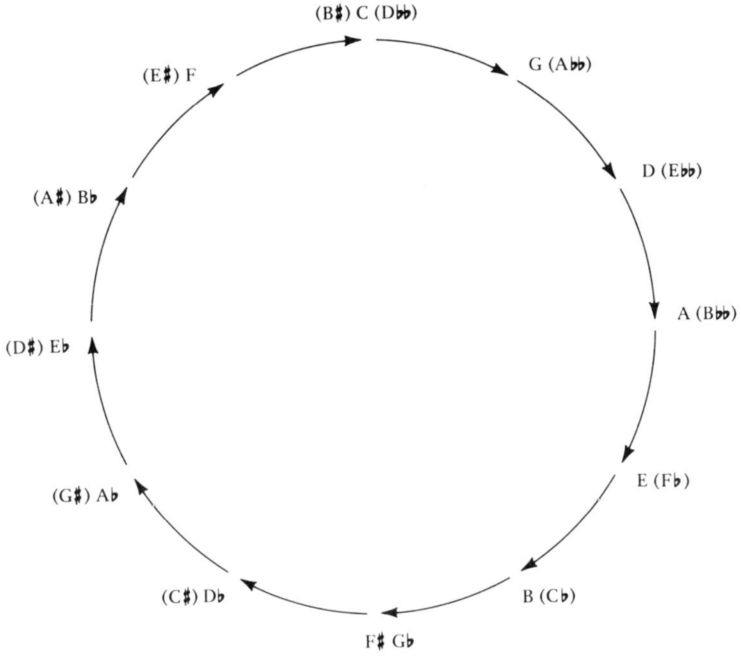

In this chapter, key and scale have been treated as roughly analogous. Although to do so is quite practical and convenient, it is, in a sense, an oversimplification. Key is more than a theoretical grouping of the main pitch materials of a composition; more important, it is a unique determinant, a kind of *set,* denoting the materials and relations which constitute the pitch organization. Key is a *felt* and *heard* aspect of musical pattern through which all the various tonal events of a composition may be perceived. Key provides a sense of direction, an inbound-outbound relation of tones to a tonic, which is produced by both melody and harmony and which both influences and is influenced by many other aspects of music. In later chapters we shall note some of the ways in which key, or tonality, affects our musical experiences in ways not suggested by a discussion of scale alone.

EXERCISES

1. Sing or play each of the following melodies. Then decide whether or not the various melodies reveal tonality, or key. For those melodies that do reveal a key, indicate the tonic and the scale basis.

a)

Analysis: ______________________

b)

Analysis: ______________________

Bartók (Quartet No. 6)

c)

Analysis: ______________________

d)

Analysis: ______________________

2. Show the tonal bases of the following major melodies as scales. Part (a) is done for you as a sample.

German Folk Song

a)

Scale Basis (use the appropriate clef):

b)

Scale Basis:

Mendelssohn

c) 

Scale Basis:

Haydn

d) 

Scale Basis:

3. Write the key signatures for the following scales, each of which is major and each of which is identified by a particular given scale degree. See the sample.

Sample:

Mediant is *d*

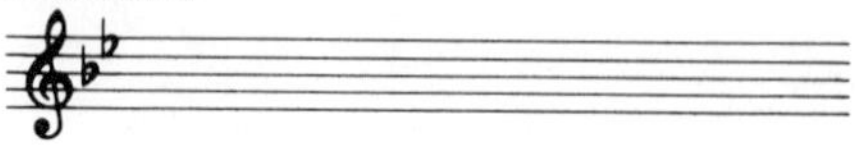

Tonic is *a*

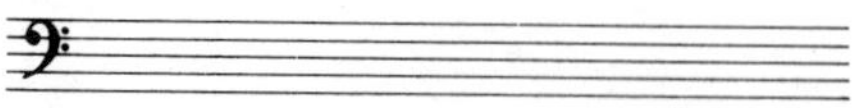

Dominant is *e♭*

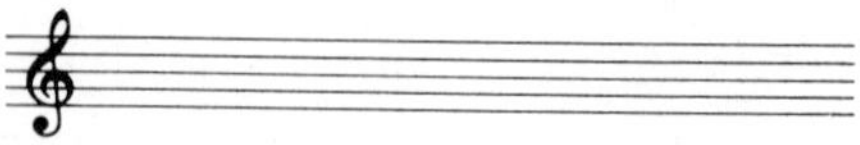

Leading tone is *f*

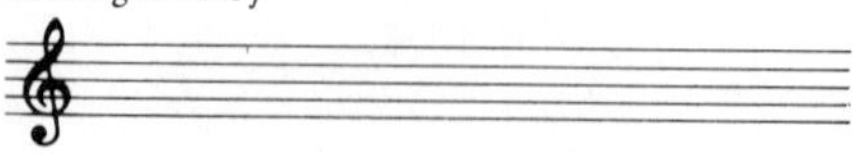

Subdominant is *f♯*

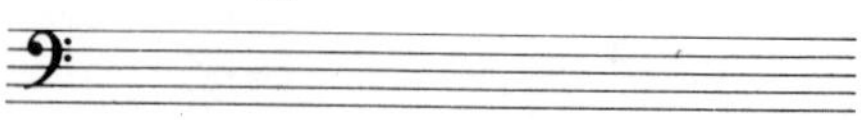

Submediant is *e*

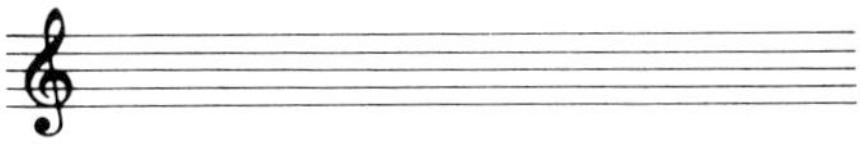

Supertonic is *f*

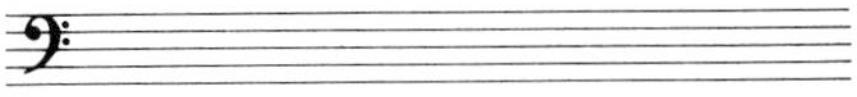

Tonic is *a*♭

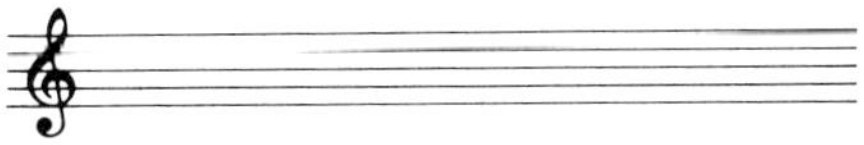

Dominant is *d*

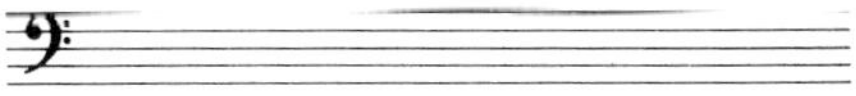

Subdominant is *e*♭

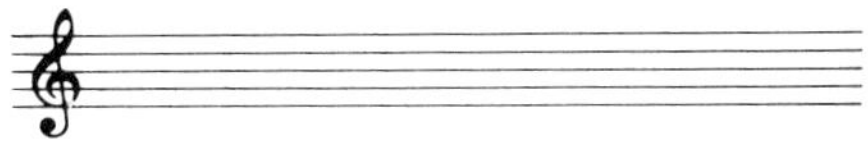

Leading tone is *b*

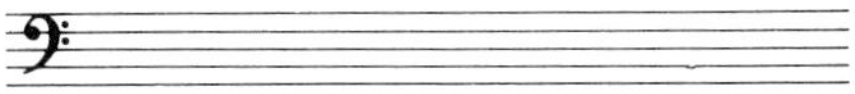

(optional)

4. In the melodies of Exercise 2 find an example of each of the following items, and indicate the example letter and measure number (where applicable) of its occurrence.

   a) Octave range. ____________

   b) An ending revealing syncopation. ____________

   c) A predominantly disjunct phrase. ____________

   d) A predominantly conjunct phrase. ____________

   e) A melody whose tonic occurs only twice. ____________

   f) A melody whose tonic occurs as the high and low peaks of the entire line. ______

   g) A measure in (b) where the tonic does not occur. ____________

Chapter 5

COMPLEX AND MIXED METERS; MINOR AND MODAL SCALES

Simple and compound meters have in common the regular, periodic recurrence of accented and unaccented beats. When alternate beat groupings by two and three (or four and three) occur within the measure, producing irregular patterns, the result is *complex meter.* Any meter whose signature indicates five, seven, eleven, thirteen, or fifteen beats per measure is called complex. In effect, however, such meters are more easily grasped as constituted of two or more main pulses of uneven length, as Example 5-1 suggests.

The meter signature of Example 5-1 indicates five eighth notes (or their equivalent) per measure; in this instance the eighth notes are grouped in units of three followed by two, as shown beneath the first measure. However, a broader pulse of two units of uneven length (♩. ♩) is also established, as shown beneath the music. This pattern represents a two-beat measure with unequal beats; it is an asymmetrical pattern.

Example 5-1

Example 5-2

Some melodies reveal the continuous use of one such beat pattern; others are not consistent in their grouping. If the pattern used in Example 5-1 is revised as shown in Example 5-2, a different accentuation results. Grouping in a complex meter such as 5/8 (quintuple meter) is usually reflected in the note beaming. Patterns consisting of 2 + 3 or 3 + 2, consistently or interchangeably used, represent the norm in quintuple meter. A further revision of the same melody's rhythm occurs in Example 5-3. Here the rhythmic grouping involves alternation between ♩. ♩ and ♩ ♩..

Example 5-3

Septuple meter commonly reveals pulse groupings of 3 + 4 or 4 + 3. The former grouping occurs throughout Example 5-4. Note that the main pulse organization of this example can be shown as ♩. ♩ ♩, three beats of uneven length. By *thinking* the prevailing beat *division* of eighths and conducting the broad pulse grouping noted above, an accurate rendition of the passage's rhythm is easily achieved.

In this chapter (and in the Exercises) examples involving complex meters are limited to quintuple and septuple patterns. An understanding of the principles pertinent to the realization of these patterns can readily be applied to other, less common meters such as 8/8 (3 + 3 + 2, 2 + 3 + 3, or 3 + 2 + 3), 11/8, 11/4, 13/8, and 15/8, which represent extensions of the principle of

Example 5-4

Falla

uneven beats. Of greatest importance in grasping such patterns is to remember that a constant, equal length for the duration representing the signature's lower figure, such as the eighth in 5/8 or the quarter note in 7/4, be maintained. This is the major problem in accurate performance of complex meters; see Example 5-5, which is to be performed with particular attention to the rendering of equal eighth notes. Note that the measures are consistently grouped , thereby producing a conductor's beat of three main pulses: 

.

Example 5-5

Mexican Folk Song

CHANGING OR MIXED METERS

Meter change is an important means of achieving rhythmic variety and delineation of form. Changing meters, or *mixed meters,* as they are frequently called, are more abundant in music written before 1600 or after the beginning of the current century than in music of the seventeenth, eighteenth, and nineteenth centuries. However, even in nineteenth-century compositions, examples of meter change within a composition, section, or phrase are by no means rare. Sometimes a consistently employed scheme of metrical change is used for an entire passage or composition, as in Example 5-6. Far more often, however, mixed meters signal the use of asymmetrical rhythms, characterized by the absence of evenly spaced accentuation, as in Example 5-7.

Example 5-6

Mussorgsky

Example 5-7

Stravinsky

Changes of meter may involve (1) a change in the number of beats per measure, (2) a change in the duration of the beat, (3) a change in the prevailing beat division, i.e., from duple to triple or from triple to duple, or (4) combinations of these. Composers often facilitate the performer's task of interpreting changes in meter by designating a *common duration,* that is, a note value which has the same duration in both the meters used, as a link between the two meters. An example of such a designation is ♪ = ♪, used to indicate a common duration where the meter changes from 2/4 to 6/8. Read the passages in Example 5-8, which illustrate the four types of meter change noted above.

Example 5-8

a) Meter change from 3/4 to 4/4. The quarter note serves as a common duration.

b) Meter change from 2/4 (simple time) to 6/8 (compound time). In this case the composer, as is customary, has indicated that the eighth note is to be treated as a common value.

c) Meter change from 3/4 to 9/8. In this instance the quarter note of 3/4 is to establish the length of the dotted quarter in 9/8, as shown at the point of meter change.

d) Meter and tempo change. Note that no common duration is retained.

MINOR SCALES

The contrast between major and minor is best understood by aural comparison of the two melodies of Example 5-9. The particular effect of the minor version is due to its intervals. Note that the major third from 1 to 3 (from the tonic to the mediant), that is, from *d* to *f*♯, becomes a minor third in the second version. Also note that the descending pattern of measures 5 and 6 has the intervals m2, M2, and M2 in Example 5-9(a), but M2, M2, and m2 in Example 5-9(b). Shown as scales, the pitch materials of the two melodies clearly reflect the bases for their contrast (see Example 5-10).

Example 5-9 (Haydn)

a) In major (the original)

b) Adapted to minor

Example 5-10 Scale reductions of Example 5-9(a) and (b)

a) Major Scale

b) Minor Scale (natural minor form)

Example 5-11

Gluck

Scale Basis (B minor)

Like the major scale, the minor scale shown here has five whole steps and two half-steps. It is in their arrangements, or successions, of whole steps and half-steps that the two scales differ. The minor scale shown above, commonly called the *natural* (that is, unaltered) minor scale, contains half-steps between 2 and 3 (the supertonic and the mediant) and between 5 and 6 (the dominant and the submediant). The minor third from the tonic to the mediant, more than any other factor, determines the *minor* quality of the scale and, as a result, of melodies for which it serves as a basis. Sing the melody of Example 5-11 and extract its scale.

Unlike the melody of Example 5-9(b), this melody makes use of two variants of the seventh scale degree, *a*♯ and *a* natural. The explanation for this is implicit in the melody's contour. Note that *a*♯ occurs as a leading tone to *b*, in conjunction with ascending step motion which emphasizes the tonic. On the other hand, *a* natural is used in a descending step pattern from 8 to 7 to 6, with the major second emphasizing the falling contour. Such variability of the seventh scale degree is a feature of many melodies in minor keys. This flexibility of intervals is embodied in the three theoretical minor scale patterns: *natural minor, harmonic minor,* and *melodic minor.* In showing them (Example 5-12), it is essential to point out that such scale forms do not dictate or predetermine the details of minor melodies, but merely reflect frequently observed treatments of them in general practice. Logically, ascending patterns more often contain raised sixth and seventh steps, thus heightening the sense of motion toward the tonic. Conversely, descending patterns commonly employ the lowered sixth and seventh degrees of the natural minor scale. It seems appropriate to view "minor" as a generic term embracing three scale patterns which have in common the telling minor third from tonic to mediant.

As noted above, the harmonic minor scale contains an altered (raised, in this case) seventh step. This alteration of the natural minor pattern is *not* shown in the key signature itself and, as a result, must *always* be written as an accidental (a sharp or natural, depending on the context). Like the major scale, the harmonic minor contains the 4-7 tritone, which is *not* present in the natural minor pattern. The harmonic minor scale also contains a gap in the form of an augmented second (+2) between 6 and 7.

The name "harmonic" minor derives from the relation of this scale to traditional harmonic practice and to its influence on harmonically oriented melody. Example 5-13 lies entirely within the sphere of the harmonic minor. Note the altered seventh degree and the characteristic augmented second.

Example 5-12 Minor scale patterns on d

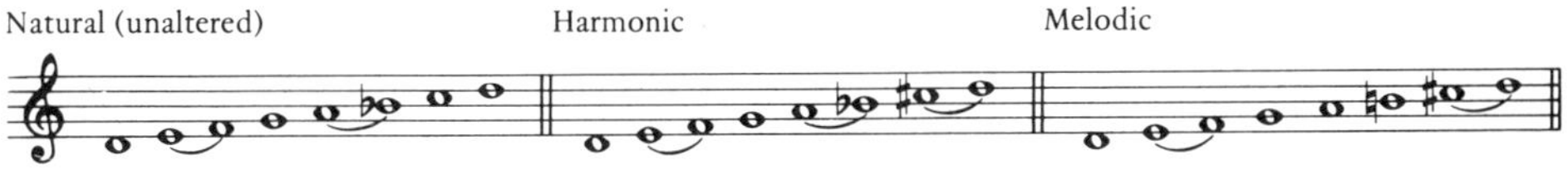

Example 5-13

Mozart

The melodic minor pattern is best understood as an ascending scale which differs from the major only in the interval of a minor third from 1 to 3. The altered (that is, altered in comparison with the natural minor) sixth and seventh notes reflect the tendency of many melodies to emphasize ascent by means of raised notes. It has been pointed out many times that, by raising the sixth degree, the augmented second associated with the harmonic minor pattern is avoided, and a smoother melodic progression results. Such explanations, although theoretically expedient, fail to acknowledge the numerous melodies in music literature which exhibit just such a relation. Example 5-14 illustrates a typical use of the melodic minor scale, used in this example in both ascending and descending patterns.

Example 5-14

French Folk Song

Perhaps the most distinctive aspect of the melodic minor pattern is found in the succession of four whole steps from the mediant through the subdominant, the dominant, and the submediant to the leading tone, a succession which is sometimes found in melodies of predominantly step motion. Note also that, like the major and harmonic minor forms, the melodic minor scale contains a tritone between 4 and 7. In notation, the melodic minor pattern always requires accidentals to modify the sixth and seventh degrees.

Example 5-15

Example 5-15 demonstrates the variability of note patterns typical of many minor-mode compositions. In this example, as indicated below the music, one can hear patterns derived from all three minor scale forms. Indeed, the feeling of minor elicited by such a melody is a product of several factors embodied in a variable, rather than singular, scale basis. It seems wiser to determine such factors from specific contexts than from theoretical abstractions.

MINOR KEY SIGNATURES

The signatures used for denoting minor keys are the same as those used for major keys; only their application differs. As we noted earlier, the signatures for minor keys are based on the natural minor scales; accidentals are used within the body of the music to indicate alterations of the sixth and seventh degrees. Major and (natural) minor scales employing identical notes, but centered on tonics a minor third apart (for example, D major and B minor, C major and A minor), are called *relative* scales, or relative keys; F major serves as the relative major key to D minor, and conversely D minor is relative to F major.

Relative keys have identical signatures; therefore, F major and D minor have identical signatures of one flat. Similarly, F♯ major and D♯ minor both employ a signature of six sharps. Study the following chart of relative key signatures.

Relative Key Signatures

Major Key	*Relative Minor Key*	*Signature*	
C	A	None	
G	E	*f*♯	One sharp
D	B	*f*♯, *c*♯	Two sharps
A	F♯	*f*♯, *c*♯, *g*♯	Three sharps
E	C♯	*f*♯, *c*♯, *g*♯, *d*♯	Four sharps
B	G♯	*f*♯, *c*♯, *g*♯, *d*♯, *a*♯	Five sharps
F♯	D♯	*f*♯, *c*♯, *g*♯, *d*♯, *a*♯, *e*♯	Six sharps
C♯	A♯*	*f*♯, *c*♯, *g*♯, *d*♯, *a*♯, *e*♯, *b*♯	Seven sharps
F	D	*b*♭	One flat
B♭	G	*b*♭, *e*♭	Two flats
E♭	C	*b*♭, *e*♭, *a*♭	Three flats
A♭	F	*b*♭, *e*♭, *a*♭, *d*♭	Four flats
D♭	B♭	*b*♭, *e*♭, *a*♭, *d*♭, *g*♭	Five flats
G♭	E♭	*b*♭, *e*♭, *a*♭, *d*♭, *g*♭, *c*♭	Six flats
C♭	A♭†	*b*♭, *e*♭, *a*♭, *d*♭, *g*♭, *c*♭, *f*♭	Seven flats

*Usually written as B♭ minor, the enharmonic equivalent of A♯, since to do so involves a signature of only five flats, as opposed to seven sharps.

†Also usually treated enharmonically.

MODES

Mode is a historical name for scale, as is suggested by such expressions as "major mode" and "melodic minor mode." However, the word mode is also used to refer to a collection of scales which antedate the more recently established major and minor key systems. This group of patterns, redundantly called "modal scales," consists of a family of scales whose origin stems mainly from the codification of ecclesiastical music of the Middle Ages. Although these patterns were used primarily in medieval vocal church music, their influence has been felt in other periods and other media, particularly during the Renaissance. Furthermore, many folk melodies from all periods reveal a tonal basis more akin to the church modes than to the major-minor system. Both the melodies shown in Example 5-16 are fashioned from modes. Perform them and abstract their scale bases.

Example 5-16 Dorian mode

a) *L'homme armé* (Anonymous)

Scale Basis

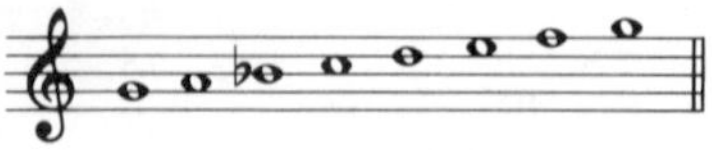

b) Gregorian Chant

Scale Basis

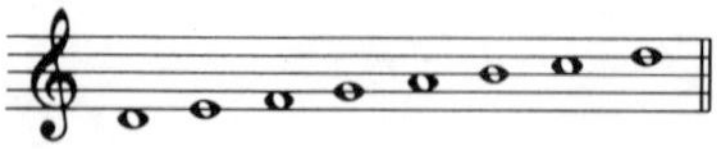

The scale bases of both melodies are identical, although their tonics, *g* and *d* respectively, are different. Note the absence of a leading tone half-step relation in both melodies. Note also that the minor third from tonic to mediant establishes an essentially minor character in both melodies. Also, as in both the major scale and the melodic minor, the sixth scale degree of the mode employed here is a major second above the fifth; in other words, this mode has a raised sixth degree. The name for this mode is *Dorian,* and it is one of a group of modes whose effect is primarily minor. The names used to denote the various ecclesiastical modes are of Greek origin, and stem from pre-Christian times.

There are three other important modal scales: the Phrygian, Lydian, and Mixolydian. Examples of all three, together with their scale bases, are given in Examples 5-17, 5-18, and 5-19. Sing each melody and its scale basis, noting carefully the three different arrangements of whole steps and half-steps, which give a total of five whole steps and two half-steps in each case.

The *Phrygian* mode (Example 5-17) contains a minor third between 1 and 3, employs a whole step between 7 and 8, and, like no other church mode, reveals a half-step from the tonic to the supertonic (from 1 to 2). It is this last characteristic which, perhaps more than any other, characterizes melodic construction in the Phrygian mode.

Example 5-17 Phrygian mode

Walther

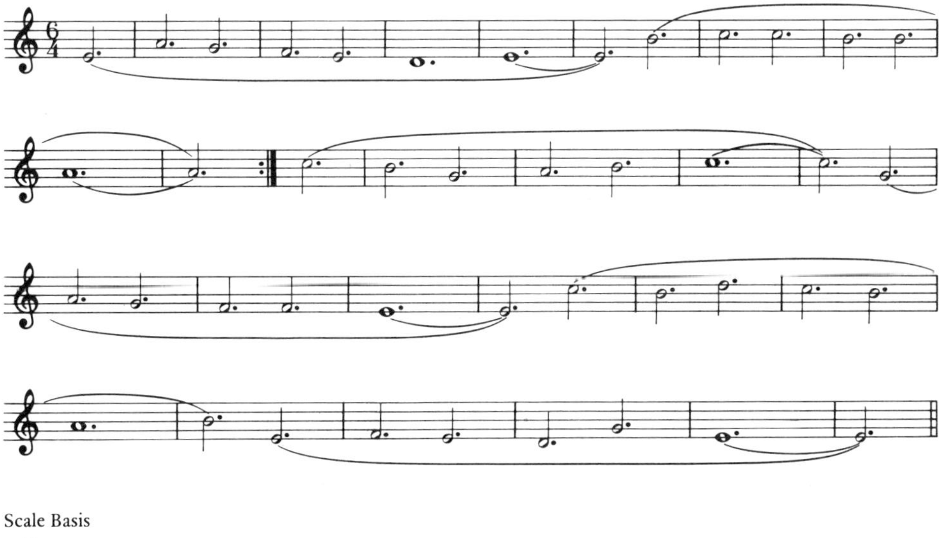

Scale Basis

The scale basis of the melody of Example 5-18 is most easily recognized by its obvious similarity to the familiar major scale. The *Lydian* mode is unique, however, because of the presence of a tritone between the tonic and the subdominant. There is also a half-step between 4 and 5.

Example 5-18 Lydian mode

Hungarian Folk Song

Scale Basis (transposed) (untransposed)

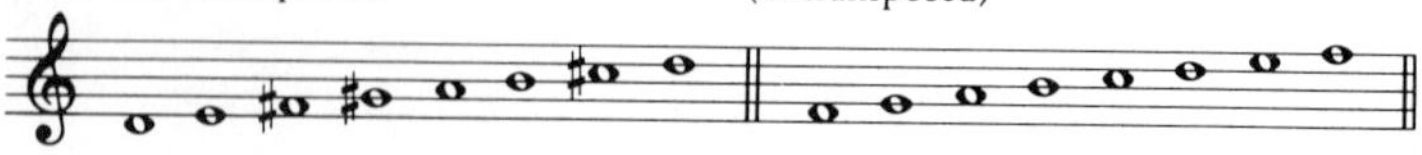

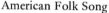

The *Mixolydian* mode (Example 5-19), like the Lydian, has an essentially major quality because of the major third between 1 and 3. Unlike the Lydian mode, however, it contains a subtonic note; that is, instead of having a leading tone a half-step below the tonic, this scale has a seventh degree

Example 5-19 Mixolydian mode

American Folk Song

Scale Basis (transposed) (untransposed)

which is separated from the tonic by a whole step. As a result, Mixolydian melodies do not reveal the familiar leading tone progression of the major scale.

Like other scales, modal patterns can be centered on any of the twelve tones of the chromatic scale. Thus any note or altered note may appear as the tonic of a modal melody. However, modal melodies are often made up of unaltered notes, that is, notes which correspond to the white keys of the piano keyboard. Example 5-17 consists of unaltered notes; but the melodies of Examples 5-18 and 5-19 both use transposed forms of their respective modes. The untransposed, or "pure," form of each mode is given beside the form used in the melody. The signatures for transposed modes, those involving pitch alteration by means of accidentals, are arrived at in the same manner as for major and minor keys. Review the melodies in Examples 5-16, 5-17, 5-18, and 5-19 and determine the signature of each.

Theoretically there exists a modal scale on each of the seven notes of the diatonic system: *d, e, f, g, a, b,* and *c.* Since the pattern for the scale centered on *a,* the *Aeolian* mode, is identical to the natural minor pattern, no special attention is given to it in this discussion. Similarly, the mode centered on *c,* the *Ionian,* is identical with the major scale. The mode on *b,* the *Locrian* (Example 5-20), is rarely found in music literature, and needs little attention other than an acknowledgment of its theoretical availability. Contemporary composers, among them Debussy, Hindemith, and Bartók, have occasionally used it.

Example 5-20 Locrian mode

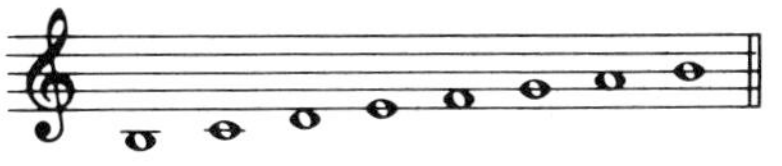

Compare the untransposed forms of the Dorian, Phrygian, Lydian, and Mixolydian modes. Familiarize yourself with them by playing, singing, and notating each type from several different starting notes.

PENTATONIC SCALES

Pentatonic scales consist of five-note patterns. They are gapped scales; that is, they employ both steps and leaps between adjacent tones. Their historical beginnings and present-day use are associated to a great extent with the exotic.

One of the characteristics of the pentatonic scale is the absence of strong tonic definition. The natural pentatonic scale consists of the notes *c, d, f, g,* and *a;* but any of these notes can act as the tonic. Consequently, a series of five pentatonic scales can be constructed from this set of tones:

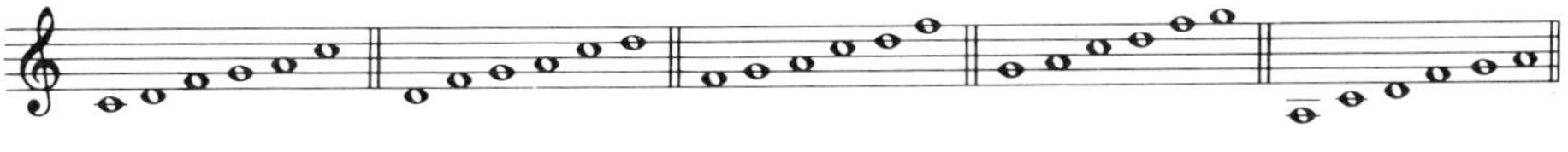

An obvious feature of these scales is the absence of any half-steps. This aspect of pentatonicism is probably the main reason why pentatonic melodies, such as the one in Example 5-21, do not project a strong sense of tonic definition.

Example 5-21 Pentatonic scale

Ravel

Scale Basis

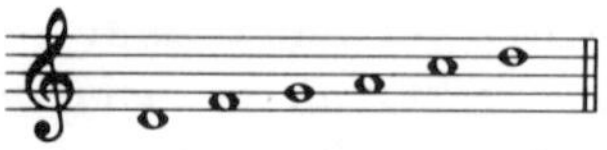

Pentatonic scales, like other scales, can be transposed.

CHROMATIC SCALES

The chromatic scale encompasses all twelve pitches within an octave span. Played on the piano, a chromatic scale activates all white and black keys of an octave. As it appears in musical compositions, the chromatic scale can have either of two distinct functions: (1) it may constitute the *elaboration* and embellishment of essentially diatonic writing, that is, writing based mainly on the tones of one of the major, minor, or modal scales; or (2) it may be the *basis* for music which treats all twelve available notes more or less equally, without deference to any clearly defined key or tonic. Both functions can be seen in Example 5-22. Example 5-22(a) is clearly based on a diatonic scale, while Example 5-22(b) reveals no strong feeling for a key and treats each tone as an entity.

The subject of scales raises a question analogous to the question of the chicken versus the egg. Scale is often regarded as a kind of musical palette from which the composer selects tones for a melody. In some recent music, such as the excerpt shown in Example 5-22(b), the scale is indeed the direct source of the tonal materials of the composition. However, it seems unlikely that past generations of composers have been guided to such an extent by theoretical considerations. It would appear more logical to regard scale as a product, rather than a determinant, of melody. In doing so we may observe that a working knowledge of scale theory has undoubtedly provided musicians with a useful discipline for composition and a workable reference for its interpretation and realization.

Example 5-22

a) Mozart

Scale Basis (black notes represent members of the chromatic scale that lie outside the key of C minor)

b) Schoenberg

Scale Basis

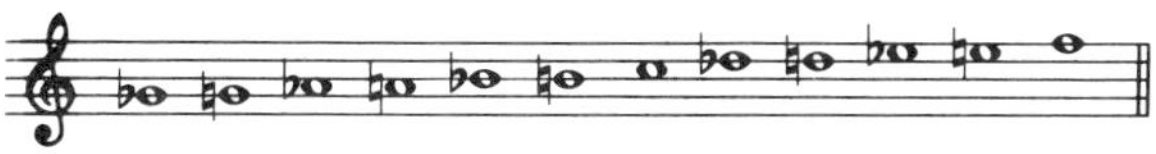

EXERCISES

1. Build the scales indicated in the given clefs. Use the given key signatures as a basis for determining each scale's tonic. Familiarize yourself with each pattern by singing it.

Minor, harmonic (ascending)

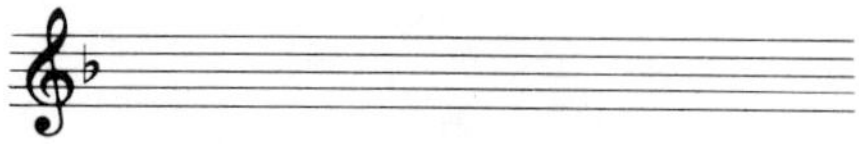

Phrygian (ascending)

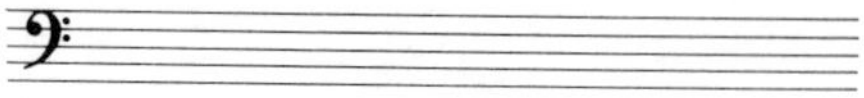

Minor, natural (descending)

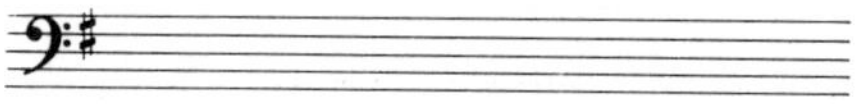

Minor, melodic (ascending)

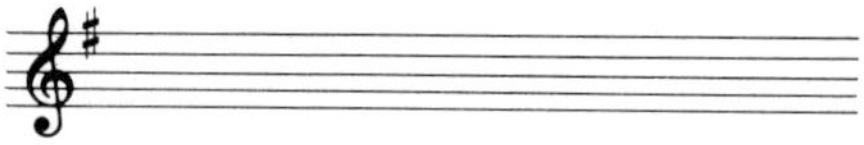

Minor, harmonic (descending)

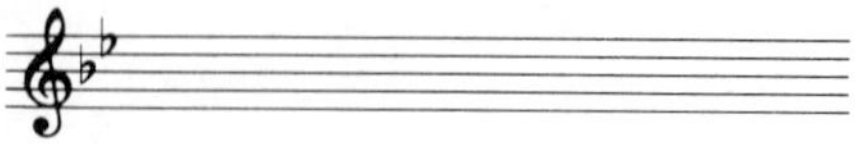

Major (descending)

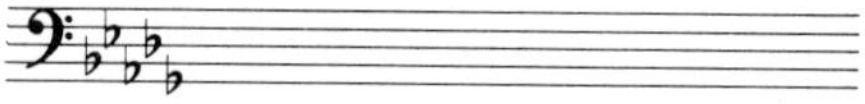

Major (ascending)

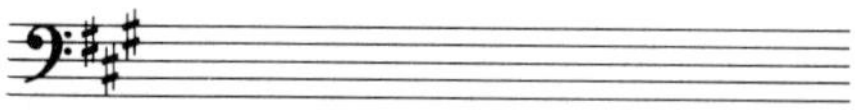

Lydian (ascending)

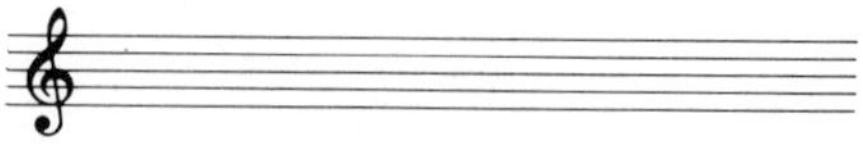

Minor, melodic (ascending)

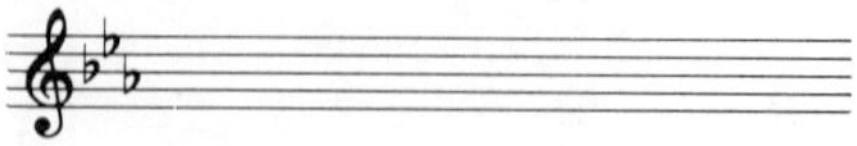

Mixolydian (descending)

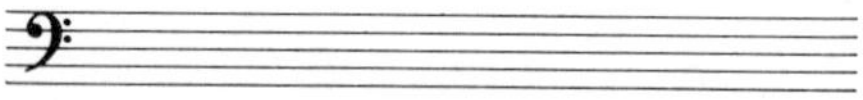

Dorian (descending)

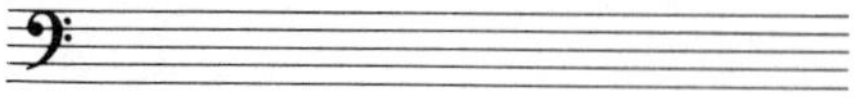

Minor, melodic (ascending)

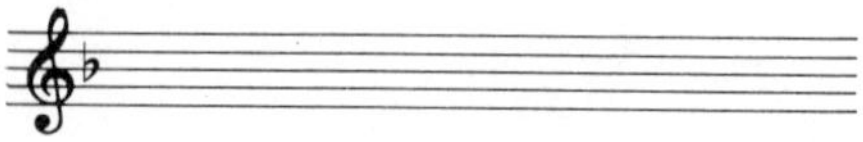

Minor, natural (ascending)

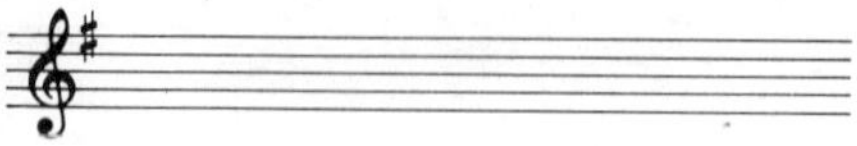

Dorian (ascending)

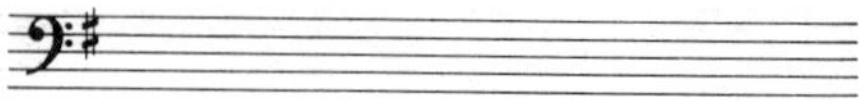

2. Sing or play each of the excerpts that follow. Then identify the following items in each melody: (1) tonic, (2) type of scale basis, (3) type of meter, i.e., simple, compound, complex, or mixed (changing), and (4) the basic duration (note value) of the melody. See the sample exercise.

Sample:

J. S. Bach

Answer: tonic, *d;* scale basis, major; meter, simple (triple); basic duration, ♪.

a) 

Bartók

b) 

Schubert

c) 

Breton Folk Song

d) 

Franz

e) 

3. a) Devise four measures in 5/8 meter using only quarter and eighth notes in the arrangement of 3 + 2.

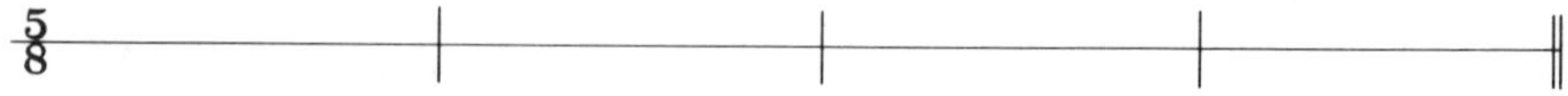

Perform these four measures at a moderately quick tempo.

b) Rewrite the same four measures in 5/4 meter.

c) Use the 5/8 passage of (a) as the rhythmic basis for a short melody in D natural minor. Use only steps in the melody.

4. Write a brief definition of each of the following terms: *scale, complex meter, Dorian, pentatonic, chromatic, melodic minor, asymmetrical rhythm, harmonic minor.*

(optional)

5. Make up short melodic phrases (two to four measures each) illustrating the items in Exercise 4.

Scale

Complex meter

Dorian

Pentatonic

Chromatic

Melodic minor

Asymmetrical rhythm

Harmonic minor

6. Revise the pitches of the melody below so as to conform to each of the scale bases indicated. Retain the original tonic. Introduce an appropriate change of key signature.

J. S. Bach

Minor, harmonic

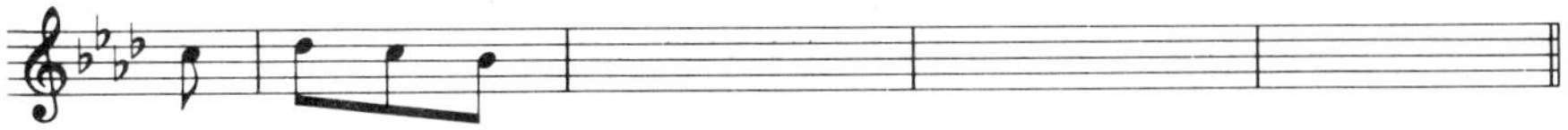

Dorian

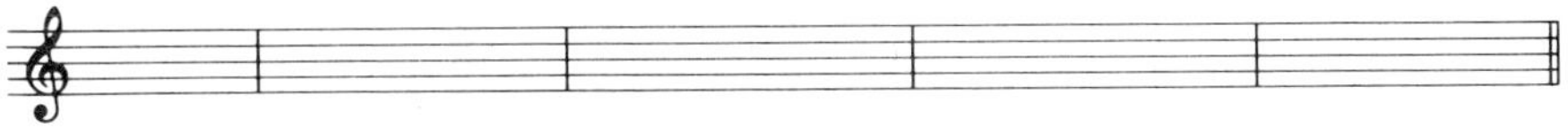

Minor, natural

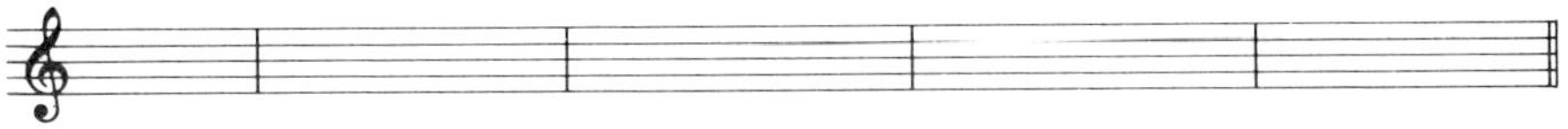

Mixolydian

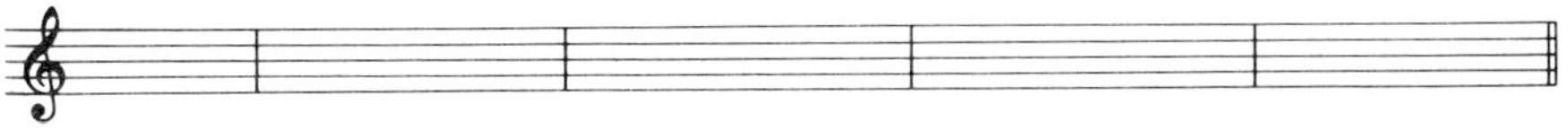

Chapter 6

HARMONIC MATERIALS

HARMONIC INTERVALS

In a broad sense, *harmony* means combined tones, notes sounded together. In a restricted sense, harmony is often taken to mean "pleasant sounding" combinations of tones. In this chapter we shall refer to harmony in the broad sense of the word.

Example 6-1, a simple example of two-part writing, provides a useful point of departure for a consideration of harmony, since harmony is produced whenever two or more parts sound together. The harmonic content of the passage consists of various *harmonic intervals,* that is, pairs of notes sounded simultaneously. The nomenclature of harmonic intervals is the same

Example 6-1

J. S. Bach, *Anna Magdalena Notebook*

as that of melodic intervals. However, when discussing harmony, musicians commonly disregard the precise span of a harmonic interval when it exceeds an octave.* In other words, they mentally change the register of one of the notes so that the interval is contained within the span of an octave. Thus the opening interval of Example 6-1, between *b*♭ and d^1, is called simply a major third in common parlance, although its precise distance is a major tenth. Similarly, the first interval of measure 2 is called a minor sixth. This system of naming harmonic intervals will be used throughout this book except where more precise identification is needed.

The harmonic staples of most traditional music are usually called *consonances.* These consist of perfect octaves, perfect fifths, perfect fourths, and major and minor thirds and sixths. Note that Example 6-1 contains a decided majority of consonances. Those combinations which sound unstable, or seem to be in a state of unrest, are traditionally called *dissonances.* They consist in the main of seconds, sevenths, and tritones.

The terms consonant and dissonant have lost much of their meaning to today's musicians, and many avoid such hard and fast classifications of sonority, suggesting that descriptions of *relative* degrees of consonance (stability) and dissonance (instability) are more meaningful. Listen carefully to the progression from relative consonance to sharp dissonance produced by the intervals in Example 6-2. The question of where dissonance is first heard seems moot.

Example 6-2

Reconsidering Example 6-1, one notes that, in combining the two melodies, the composer has used a variety of harmonic intervals. Seconds, sevenths, and one tritone add variety to a basic palette of thirds and sixths. Although it can be useful and instructive to figure out the various intervals that constitute the harmonic materials of a composition, to do so provides only diminishing rewards, since harmonic materials do not occur in isolation from other important components of music. This fact is particularly pertinent to any study of dissonances, since dissonance in most cases is a product of melodic and rhythmic activity, that is, motion. This aspect of dissonance will become more evident when we pursue questions of texture and rhythmic elaboration. For the moment, we shall view harmonic intervals as the building blocks of chords, just as melodic intervals form the building blocks of melody.

---

*Intervals which exceed an octave are called compound intervals. For example, a ninth is an octave plus a second, and a tenth is an octave plus a third. Intervals larger than a thirteenth are seldom described in compound terms, for reasons of practicality.

CHORDS

Three or more notes sounded (or perceived) as a unit form a chord. There are numerous types of chords, and each of those shown in Example 6-3 represents a group of similarly constructed sonorities. Play them on the piano and note their various intervallic combinations.

Example 6-3 Types of chords

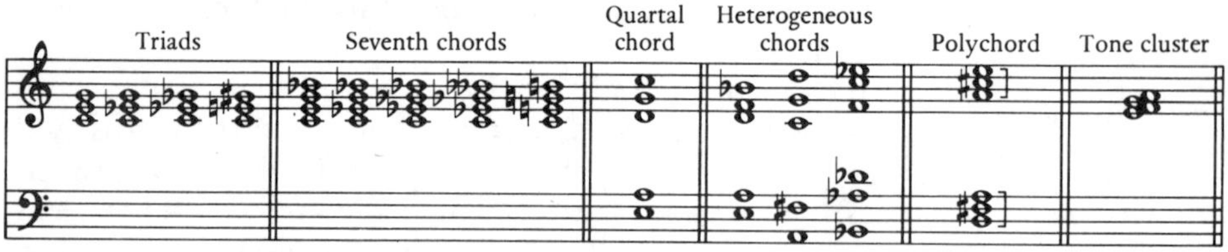

The smattering of chords shown above gives only a suggestion of the variety of chord types obtainable through random experiments at the keyboard. Such experiments may prove misleading, however, because the vocabulary of chords used throughout the development of most Western music before the current century is remarkably simple and unencumbered. It can be summarized as consisting of consonant and mildly dissonant combinations comprising a group of chords called *tertian,* or "third-based." Tertian harmony is most simply represented by a collection of three-note chords called *triads*—major triads, minor triads, augmented (+) triads, and diminished (o) triads:

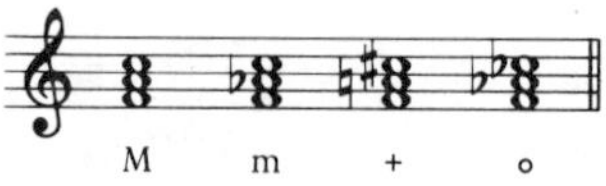

For the sake of clarity of definition, it must be pointed out that any chord whose structural basis is the interval of a third is called a tertian chord. The following are all tertian chords:

However, each of these chords is more complex than a triad. A triad is a tertian chord consisting of three notes. Whereas all triads exemplify tertian chord construction, the class of tertian chords is by no means limited to triads. The most common type of extended tertian chord used in Western music before the twentieth century is the seventh chord. Note with care the intervallic makeup of the following seventh chords:

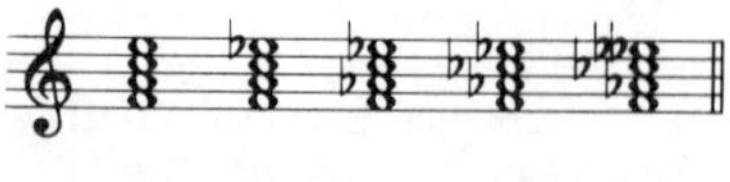

It should be obvious why they are called "seventh" chords.

A clear understanding of the tonal basis of traditional music requires a solid grasp of tertian harmony, particularly triads and seventh chords. Such an understanding can in turn serve as a beginning for subsequent work with music having more diverse and complex harmonic materials.

THE OVERTONE SERIES

Musical tuning, instrument construction, acoustical science, and indeed musical audition are affected to varying extents by the natural makeup of musical tone, as represented in the *overtone series* (sometimes called the *harmonic series).* The overtone series is a pattern, or complex, of relative vibrations which produce the phenomenon of a single musical tone. For example, when we listen to *C* performed on the cello's lowest string, we hear not only the tone *C,* but also a number of pitches called *overtones.* The simultaneous sounding of the fundamental tone *C* and the less prominent overtones produces a composite tone whose richness depends on the relative prominence of the various overtones.

Overtones are produced by partial vibrations, that is, vibrations of parts of the whole sounding body (string, air column, or membrane). In other words, whatever transmits musical sound vibrates not only as a whole, but also in halves, thirds, fourths, fifths, and so on ad infinitum. The most significant overtones, those which most affect the quality of a given tone, are those produced by the larger divisions of the string, membrane, or air column, that is, divisions by halves, thirds, fourths, and fifths. The pitch equivalents of these and of smaller divisions, together with the pitch of the vibrating whole, are shown as an overtone series based on *C* in Example 6-4. A similar overtone series can be constructed for any note in the entire pitch gamut by following the pattern of intervals shown here.

Note that the term "overtone" refers to all tones in the series *other than* the fundamental note. The term "partial," which is frequently used as a synonym for "overtone," can be applied to *any* note in the overtone series. In Example 6-4 the partials are numbered. The fundamental tone, *C,* is referred to as the "first partial," the first overtone, *c,* is called the "second partial," and so on.

Example 6-4 Overtone series on C

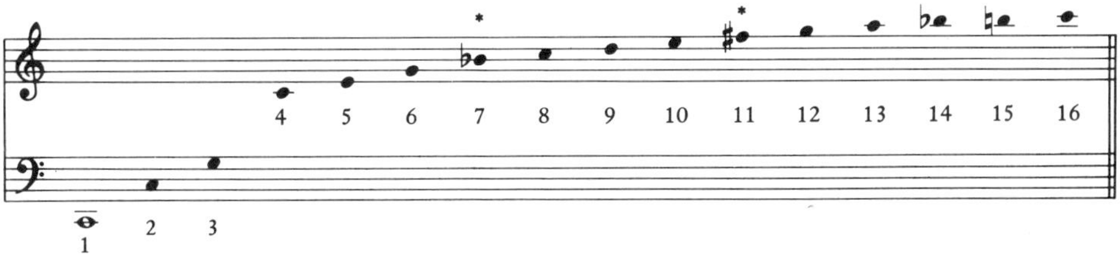

* Out of tune (flatter than indicated) by our current tuning standards.

It is generally acknowledged that the major triad, the basic unit of traditional harmony, is closely related to the natural properties of sound as reflected in the overtone series. Note that the fourth, fifth, and sixth tones of an overtone series form a major triad. For this reason the major triad is a "natural" part of the composition of any musical pitch. Thus harmonic practice, an explicitly artistic phenomenon, has its roots in the physical phenomenon of tone structure. Many musicians and scientists have speculated considerably about the "influence" of the harmonic series on Western music in general, and traditional harmonic practice in particular. Our purpose is served, for the present, by an awareness of the "derivation" of the major triad from the overtone series, which itself affects the composition of musical tone and, to varying degrees, our perception of it.

TRIADS

As we have seen, a triad consists of a combination of three notes arranged in a series of thirds; the particular thirds (major, minor, augmented, or diminished) used in any given triad determine its unique *quality.* When a triad is arranged as a series of stacked thirds (other possible arrangements will be discussed shortly), it is said to be in *fundamental position,* or *root position,* and the lowest note is referred to as the *root.* The note immediately above the root—precisely, a major or minor third above—is called the *third,* and the uppermost tone is called the *fifth:*

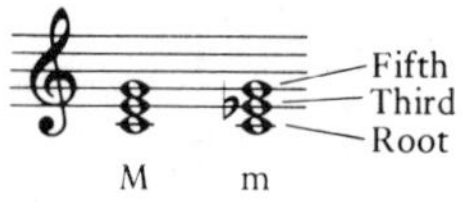

The major and minor triads are named for the interval between the root and the third; in the major triad this is a major third, and in the minor triad it is a minor third. In both cases the interval between the root and the fifth is a perfect fifth. Note that the major triad contains the interval of a minor third from the third to the fifth of the chord, whereas this interval is a major third in the minor triad. Thus the intervals of the major and minor triads mirror each other.

The major and minor triads are essentially stable in effect, in contrast to two other types of triads, the augmented (+) and the diminished (o). Compare their intervallic makeup with that of the major and minor triads shown above:

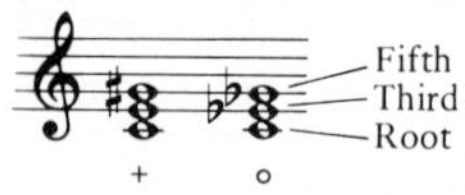

Note that the augmented and diminished triads are named for the interval between the root and the fifth. Both the augmented and the diminished triads sound unstable in most *tonal* contexts, that is, contexts revealing tonal-centeredness. The former occurs rarely in traditional music, while the diminished triad, which consists of two superposed minor thirds spanning the interval of a diminished fifth, occurs more often.

Play the series of three-note sonorities in Example 6-5, some of which are triads, and identify each triad as major, minor, augmented, or diminished. Compare by ear the various effects of triadic and nontriadic sonorities.

Example 6-5 Triadic and nontriadic sonorities

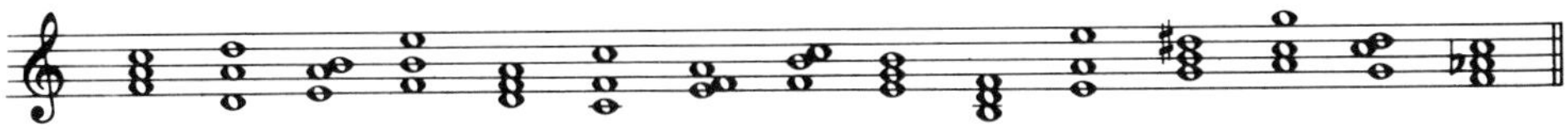

Any triad can be deployed in numerous ways, depending on the context in which it is to be heard. Each of the sonorities given in Example 6-6 is a C major triad in root position (that is, with the root as the lowest sounding tone). Note the variety of effects achievable with such simple material by dispersing the notes over an octave or more. Also note that in some of the arrangements one or more members of a chord have been *doubled,* that is, duplicated in a different octave register. The designations of the chord's root, third, and fifth, as determined when the chord is in its simplest arrangement as two superposed thirds, remains unchanged, regardless of the dispersal of chord tones or their doubling; *e* is always the third of the chord in Example 6-6, no matter where it occurs, and *g* is always the fifth.

Example 6-6 Various arrangements of a root-position major triad on C

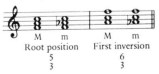

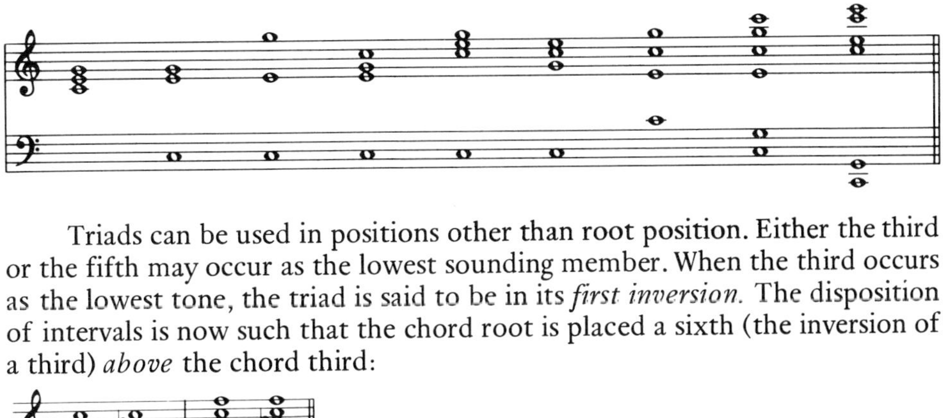

Triads can be used in positions other than root position. Either the third or the fifth may occur as the lowest sounding member. When the third occurs as the lowest tone, the triad is said to be in its *first inversion.* The disposition of intervals is now such that the chord root is placed a sixth (the inversion of a third) *above* the chord third:

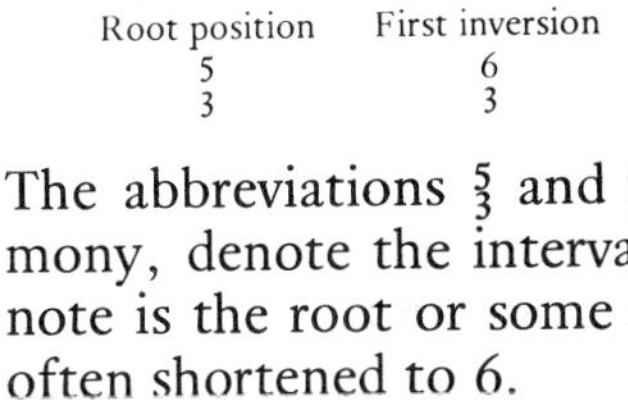

The abbreviations $^{5}_{3}$ and $^{6}_{3}$, which are frequently used in discussions of harmony, denote the intervals that occur above the lowest note (whether that note is the root or some other member of the chord); the abbreviation $^{6}_{3}$ is often shortened to 6.

A somewhat less frequently encountered inversion, the *second inversion,* is produced by arranging a triad with the chord fifth as the lowest note:

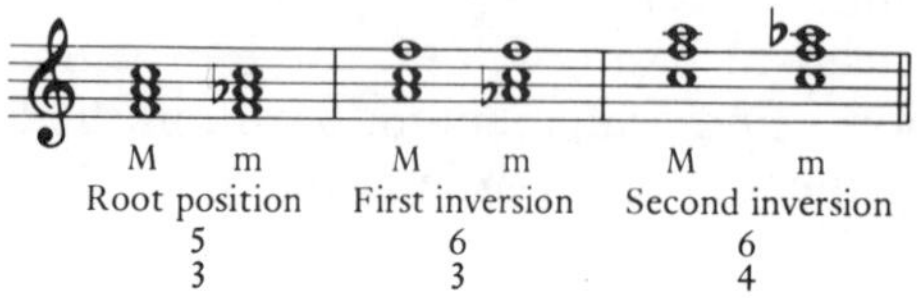

Second-inversion triads contain the intervals of a sixth and a fourth above the bass.

The concept of triad inversion is one of the most significant features of traditional Western musical theory. The concept stems from theories put forth by the eighteenth-century theorist and composer, Jean-Philippe Rameau, and is generally accepted by musicians.

Play the chords in Example 6-7 and note the variety of effects obtainable with various deployments of root-position and inverted triads.

Example 6-7

HARMONIC FUNCTIONS OF TRIADS

In an earlier discussion of key it was noted that each scale degree or key member has a clearly defined relation to the tonic, and that each note of a given key has an assigned name (tonic, supertonic, mediant, subdominant, dominant, submediant, and leading tone or subtonic) denoting its scalar relation to the tonic. If each individual key member is taken as the root of a triad whose members all belong to the same key, a system of chords results that constitutes, in effect, an amplification and reinforcement of the tonal relation to the tonic of each chord root. The dominant note becomes the root of a dominant triad, the tonic acts as the root of a tonic triad, and so on for every scale degree. In Example 6-8 the seven notes of the F major scale appear as the roots of triads. Note that the various scale degrees also occur as thirds and fifths of other triads as well. For example, the tonic appears as the root of the tonic triad, but also as the fifth of the subdominant triad and the third of the submediant triad. Also note the various qualities (major, minor, augmented,* and diminished) of the triads.

Example 6-8 Diatonic triads based on the major scale of F

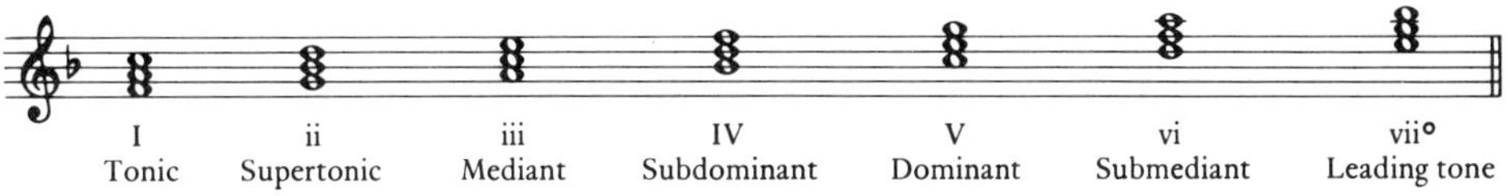

A series of triads similar to that of Example 6-8 can be constructed for any major scale. Each such series of chords constitutes the basis of harmonic activity in its particular key. The tonic, dominant, and subdominant triads are commonly called *primary triads,* while the remaining four—supertonic, mediant, submediant, and leading tone—are called *secondary.* These designations reflect the typical usage of the various triads. The primary triads occur quite frequently in traditional music, and often at important points in the melodic design. The secondary triads tend to be used less often and in less conspicuous locations.

Listen to Example 6-9 and note the chords used; also note the way in which the tonic triad produces a convincing beginning and end for the passage, thereby contributing to the sense of key stability and direction implied in the progression of chords. To demonstrate this effect of the tonic triad, replay the progression in Example 6-9, substituting the triad appearing in brackets as a closing chord. When this is done, the expectation of an F major triad that is developed by the beginning and continuation of the passage is frustrated. This simple experiment suggests that the family relationship of chords

Example 6-9 Diatonic progression in F

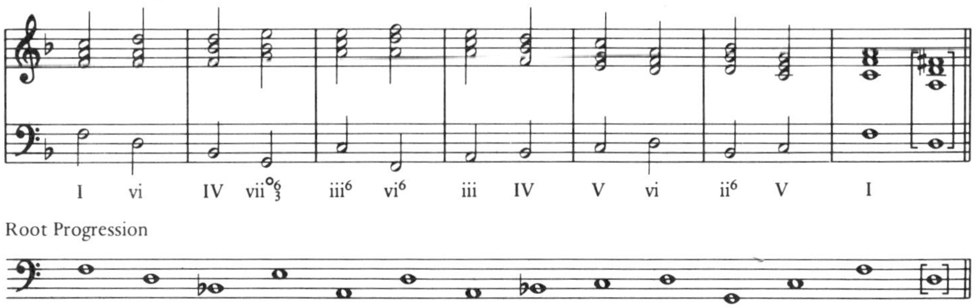

---

*Augmented triads do not occur as unaltered members of major keys.

that constitute a major or minor key is predicated on the concept of tonality, that is, the audible presence of a central tone (or chord) on which all others are dependent, so to speak, for key identity and tonal meaning.

Note in Example 6-9 that upper-case roman numerals denote major triads, while lower-case roman numerals are used to represent minor triads. Numerals representing diminished triads are shown as lower-case numerals followed by a small circle (o), as in the diminished triad vii$^{\circ}$. Augmented triads, which do not appear in Example 6-9, are denoted by an upper-case numeral followed by +. For example, if the *g* in the fifth chord from the end of Example 6-9 were preceded by a sharp sign, the chord would be denoted by V^{+}. If a triad is inverted, the numerical symbol for the inversion is placed after the symbol denoting the chord's name and quality: ii^{6}, vii$^{\circ 6}_{4}$, etc. These symbols supply only a minimum of data about the passages to which they are applied—they say nothing about the distribution of the notes of the triad, or about melody or rhythm. However, they are a simple and convenient means for communicating about sonority and chord content.

Another means of indicating the harmonic content of a passage is provided by the *fundamental bass,* or so-called *root progression.* This is simply a representation of the succession of chord roots that occur in a passage. Where a chord occurs in root position the fundamental bass note (root) is simply the lowest sounding pitch. Inverted chords, however, are represented by their actual roots, rather than the lowest sounding tones. Note the fundamental bass line for Example 6-9, which is shown below the music.

MINOR-KEY TRIADS

The harmonic minor scale is usually adopted as the basis for constructing minor-key triads. It should be noted, however, that the variability in the sixth and seventh scale degrees, which was discussed earlier in terms of melody, applies also to minor-key chord usage. Note the triads shown in Example 6-10(a) in the key of F minor; study their use in Example 6-10(b).

Example 6-10

a)

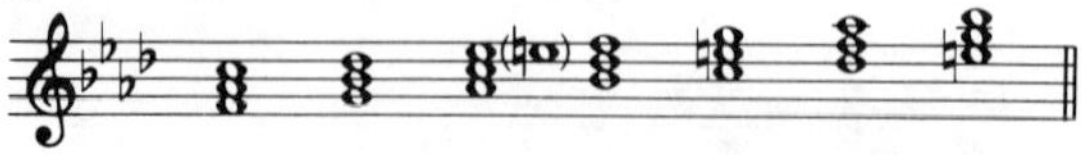

b)

THE DOMINANT FUNCTION

As we become attuned to the traditional harmonic patterns of concert music, opera, film music, folk music, and jazz, it becomes increasingly apparent that certain kinds of harmonic relations occur in countless works of the past, regardless of the particular stylistic garb in which they are clothed or the medium of a particular composition. A symphonic movement of Mozart has more in common, so far as harmony is concerned, with a current specialty of the Dave Brubeck Quartet or a recent favorite by the Beatles than is often recognized. By far the majority of the music we hear is based on traditional harmonic concepts, and is organized within a tonal framework. One of the most obvious exemplifications of traditional tonality is the patterning of chords so as to produce a sense of motion toward the tonic. This sense of direction is usually accomplished by means of the dominant triad or its relative, the leading tone triad. Both chords have the leading tone itself in common. The dominant-tonic progression produces a root relation of a descending perfect fifth (or its inversion, an ascending perfect fourth). Note the examples of dominant-tonic (that is, V-I) progressions, as deployed in C major and C minor, in Example 6-11.

Example 6-11

a)

b)

The V-I progression is usually treated rhythmically in such a way that the tonic triad arrives on a strong beat, with the preceding dominant occurring on the previous weak beat. In this way the dominant triad leads both rhythmically and harmonically toward the tonic. Note the V-I progression at the close of Example 6-12.

Note that the dominant triad, whether it occurs in a major or a minor key, is most often a major triad. Thus the V-I progression always has the qual-

Example 6-12

Mozart, *Concerto No. 1 in B♭ for Bassoon,* 3rd movement

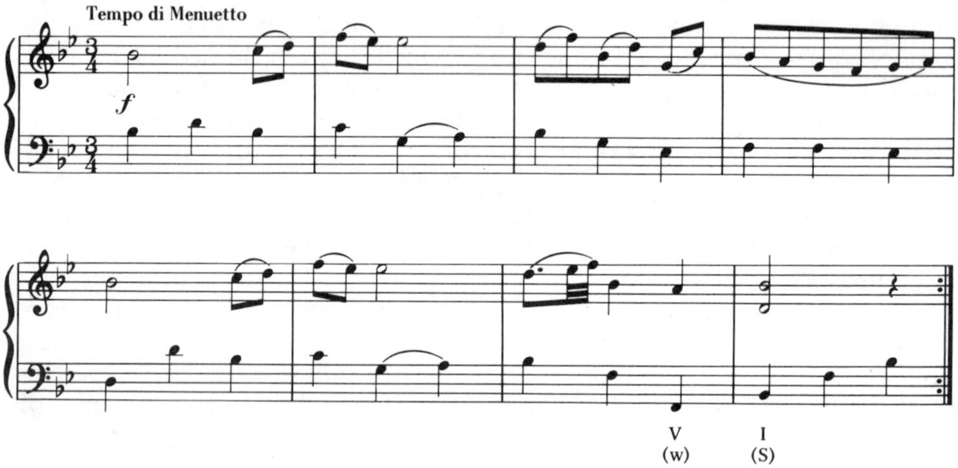

ity of a major triad revolving to a major or a minor triad. It also contains the leading tone progression and the root progression of a fifth down (or fourth up). The effectiveness of the pattern is further attributable to the binding effect of the common tone (the dominant degree) that exists between the two chords. This common tone is often sounded in the same part, or horizontal strand, as the progression is resolved, as in Example 6-13.

Placing either the tonic or the dominant triad in the first inversion affords some variety in chord tone dispersal and allows for step motion in the bass part, thereby giving some melodic interest to the bass line and at the same time bringing about a smoother connection of chords than is possible when the bass moves by leap:

(The *c* in the bass line is called a "passing tone." Passing tones will be discussed later in this chapter.) First inversions of chords produce a "lighter" effect than do chords in root position. Thus, when either of the two chords in the V-I progression is inverted, the tonal impact of the progression is lessened. Such inversions are useful at points other than the beginning and end of a passage, where one does not desire an overly strong emphasis on the passage's tonality.

Example 6-13

J. S. Bach, *Ach Gott, vom Himmel sieh' darein* (Chorale) (V-I with common tones)

The tonic triad is often used in its second inversion on a strong beat immediately preceding the dominant chord:

In this situation the second inversion of the tonic triad is often described as an "embellishment" of the dominant chord. Note the use of triad inversions in Example 6-14.

Example 6-14

Beethoven, *Piano Concerto No. 1 in C major,* Op. 15, 2nd movement

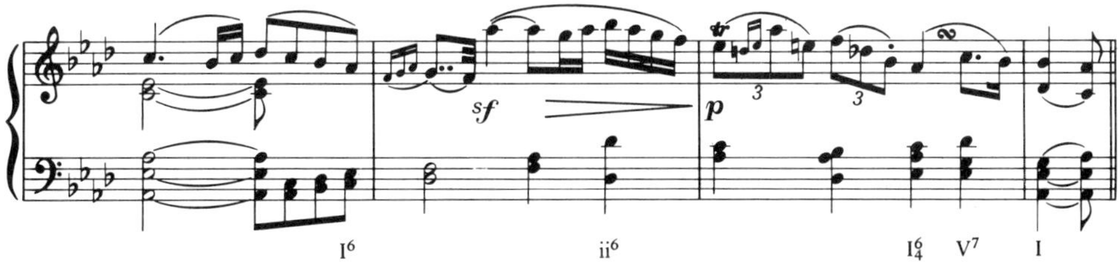

The dominant function is often enhanced by the addition of a fourth note, a chord *seventh*, to the basic triad, producing a *dominant seventh* chord:

This additional chord member, which forms a tritone with the chord third, has become part and parcel of the V-I progression in traditional music. It adds considerable impulse to the sense of motion toward the tonic. Compare the two progressions given in Example 6-15 and note the role of the tritone and its resolution in increasing the thrust toward the tonic.

Example 6-15

a) b)

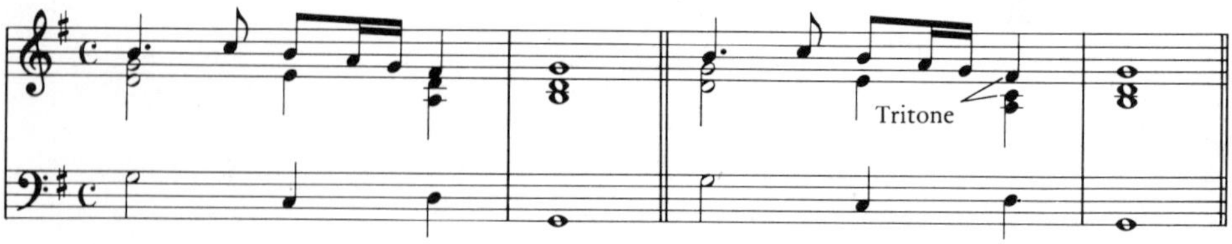

Like simple triads, the V^7 (four-note) chord may also be inverted so as to capitalize on the varieties of position, voice leading, and spacing implicit in any chord of several notes. Also observe that the various inversions of V^7 given in Example 6-16(a) allow for an enormous number of dominant approaches to the tonic. The V^7-I progression is probably the most frequently heard harmonic progression in traditional Western music of the past 200 years. Although it has been discarded by most composers of current concert music, it continues to thrive, in various guises, in most tonally oriented folk music, jazz, and pop music, and in school songs and beginners' music for solo instruments and ensembles. Note the use of V^7 and its inversions in Example 6-16(b), (c), and (d).

OTHER HARMONIC FUNCTIONS

There has been a great deal of discussion concerning the details of harmonic progression involving chords other than tonic and dominant (and V^7). Such discussion quite properly lies outside of the realm of this book. However, a few general observations can be made.

Tonality, as determined by chord progression, is usually produced by the interaction of tonic and dominant chords. Other chords derive their tonal meaning and identity from their relation to a tonic, rather than being considered as isolated, independent chords. In other words, the chords of a given

Example 6-16

a) Inversions of the Dominant Seventh Chord

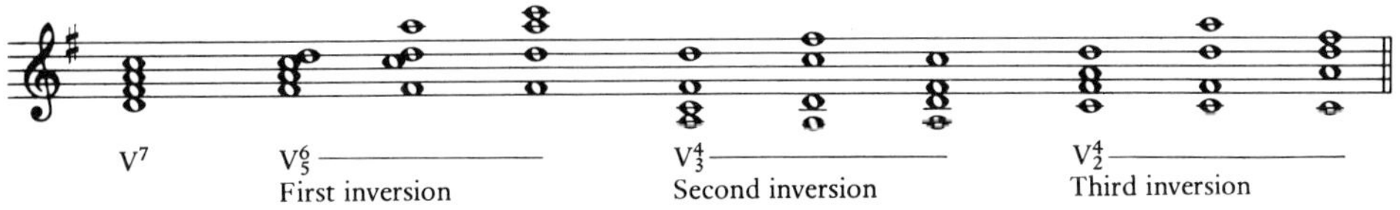

b) J. S. Bach, *Partita in D minor for Solo Violin*

c) Mozart, *Fantasia in C minor for Piano,* K. 475

d) Mendelssohn, *Sonata in C minor for Piano,* 1st movement

composition, operating in a given key, become significant in terms of harmonic function as members of *patterns* leading to or from a tonic triad, rather than as single chords as such. "Normal" patterns of harmonic progression, as evidenced by enormous numbers of works of the past, can be summed up as follows:

Tonic →	*Digression* →	*Approach to tonic* →	*Return to tonic*
I	IV	V or V^7	I
	II	VII^6	
	VI		
	III		

Example 6-17 reveals this "normal" harmonic progression.

The harmonic movement of this piece consists of a series of digressions from and returns to the tonic. The first digression—to vi and ii—occurs almost immediately after the opening tonic chord. This digression is followed by a return to the tonic via the dominant triad. Another "return to tonic" occurs immediately, with no intervening digression. A brief digression to ii is followed by another return to the tonic, this time "embellished" by the second inversion of the tonic chord.

A thorough study of the anatomy of chord relations would have to take into account the numerous "exceptions" to "normal" harmonic patterns. Such exceptions, many of which have been incorporated into traditional harmonic practice, constitute some of the most memorable events in the history of Western music.

The following points may help to clarify the preceding digest:

1. The tonic may occur at any point in the cycle; it may be interpolated after a digressive chord (that is, between a digressive chord and the dominant) or between two digressive chords. It is not essential that a digressive chord occur in the cycle; thus, in its simplest form, the cycle consists of the progression I-V-I.

2. An expected tonic triad is sometimes evaded in favor of VI. When this occurs cadentially, after V or V^7, the pattern is called a *deceptive progression*, or *deceptive cadence.*

3. Phrases or sections are commonly extended by evading a return to the tonic after the dominant. Doing so can effectively postpone the psychological effect of return while offering the composer a vehicle for tonal exploration and further digression.

4. Any chord can succeed any chord. The composer's choice of chord succession depends on the degree of key stability and fulfillment of harmonic expectation that he desires.

Example 6-17

Mozart, *Sonata in B♭ for Piano,* K. 333, Finale

HARMONIC CADENCE

The term *cadence* has been used but not fully explained. A cadence is a point of juncture in the design of a composition; it signals the end of a phrase, of a section, or of the entire composition. It is typically marked by a slackening of rhythmic pace and melodic motion, but harmonic progression is often an even more important element in cadence. Tonal music allows only three "psychological" possibilities for cadence:

1. The affirmation of the tonic. This produces a *terminal cadence.*

2. The implication that more music is to follow. This is accomplished by closure on a nontonic degree (or chord) such as V, VI, VII, II, III, or IV, producing a *progressive* or *half cadence.*

3. The projection of a new, temporary focal point. This is done by using a terminal pattern such as V-I or V⁷-I based on a tonic other than the initial tonic. The result is a *transient terminal cadence.* (The technique of moving from one tonic to another, called modulation, will be discussed in Chapter 7.)

Example 6-18 Cadences

a) Terminal (Schubert, *Sonata in D for Violin and Piano*)

b) Progressive (Brahms, *Intermezzo,* Op. 118, No. 2)

c) Transient Terminal (Chopin, *Prelude in C minor*)

Compare the cadences shown in Example 6-18. Besides the harmonic progressions, note also the rhythmic and melodic characteristics of each pattern. As observed above, cadence is a product of several interacting factors. A chord progression is not in itself cadential. It becomes cadential only if it is accompanied by rhythmic or melodic differentiation producing a sense of arrival or relaxation of activity.

DECORATIVE TONES

In most melodies certain notes seem to be of greater importance to melodic design and structure than others. These notes usually include those occurring at the beginning and end of motives, phrases, and sections, and at high and low peaks of the melodic profile. Rhythmically accented notes and those which most clearly delineate tonality also stand out as important to melodic design. Such notes, called *basic pitches,* constitute the structural scaffold of a melody. Note the basic pitches in Example 6-19.

Example 6-19

Christmas Carol (traditional)

Several observations can be made about the structure of this melody that may serve as a basis for similarly appraising other melodies as well:

1. Basic notes commonly occur on accented beats or accented parts of the beat, and often form agogic accent.
2. Each phrase begins and ends with a basic pitch.
3. Those notes that are not basic are usually unaccented or of short duration; they tend to embellish the basic notes.

The significance of nonbasic (commonly called "decorative") pitches is mainly *rhythmic,* since these notes help to project a sense of movement, or the illusion of motion in music, without seriously altering the essential "sweep" or "gesture" of linear design.

The most frequently occurring type of decorative note is the *passing tone,* a note (or group of notes) that joins *by step* two basic melodic tones. Passing tones occur (marked PT) in measures 1, 3, 6, 7, 13, and 14 of Example 6-19. Note that passing tones are usually unaccented notes of relatively short duration, seldom exceeding the length of the basic duration.

Example 6-20 Harmonization of the melody given in Example 6-19

Another important type of step decoration of a basic pitch is the *neighbor tone.* The neighbor tone (NT) creates a brief departure from and return to a single basic pitch; the decorative note may be either above or below the basic note. Measures 2, 4, and 7 of Example 6-19 contain upper neighbors. Like passing tones, neighbors are most often unaccented. Both accented and unaccented types may be found, however, as in this passage:

The basic pitches of a melody are usually treated as members of the accompanying chords, whereas decorative tones are regarded as being outside the harmonic content of a passage. Look at Example 6-20, which is a harmonization of the Christmas carol quoted in Example 6-19. The upper part in Example 6-20 projects the melodic line and is supported by an accompaniment of mainly harmonic and rhythmic (i.e., nonmelodic) interest in the three lower voices. If the passage is reduced to its harmonic basis, one can more easily appraise the various forms of elaboration that create rhythmic interest in the main voice. Such a reduction, together with the labels denoting harmonic functions, is provided in Example 6-21. Listen to a performance of the harmonic basis and then compare this to the music in Example 6-20.

Example 6-21 Harmonic reduction of Example 6-20

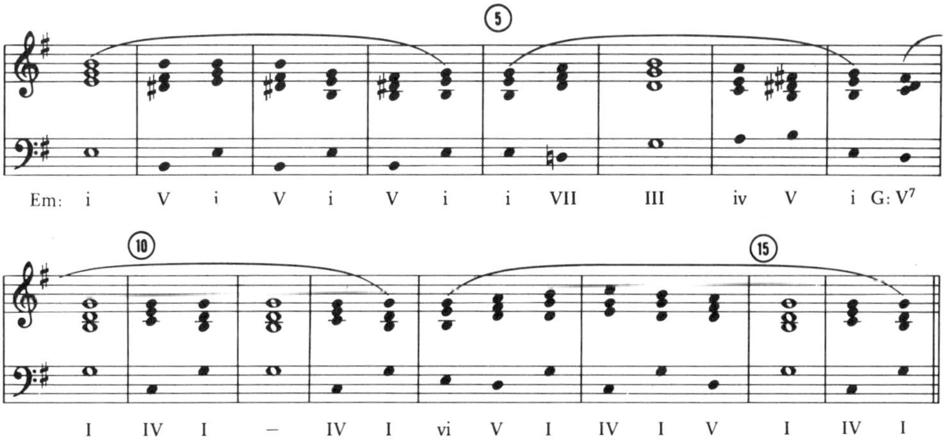

Several conclusions can be drawn from such a comparison:

1. Most accented pitches of the melody are chord members.
2. Neighbor and passing tones are commonly used as nonchord tones in the passage; these frequently produce unstable intervals with one or more of the simultaneously heard voices.

3. Note repetition is a simple means of creating movement.
4. Adding a seventh (as a harmonic dissonance) to a simple triad by passing motion in one voice produces a heightening of harmonic motion and interest. This is done in measures 2, 3, and 4.
5. The sense of motion is enhanced by moving the bass to a different chord member while repeating one chord, as in measure 6.
6. Changes in chord distribution (spacing) can also create the illusion of motion without a chord change. This occurs in measures 1, 7, and 10.

These conclusions may serve as a starting point for appraising the chordal and nonchordal materials of other compositions. One should keep in mind, though, that the relation between melody and chords is a supple one and that the composer selects progressions to complement a melody from virtually endless possibilities. More complex melodies naturally suggest greater complexity of harmonic setting than there is in the example we have been discussing.

Example 6-22

Beethoven, *Sonata in C minor for Piano,* Op. 10, No. 1, 2nd movement

Example 6-23

Pachelbel, *Chorale Prelude*

A considerably more varied, colorful, and complex relation between melody and harmony is developed in the passage in Example 6-22. The intensity and mood of the passage are a product of many interacting factors such as tempo, melodic contour, chords, texture, and dynamics. Perhaps most of the effectiveness of this example comes from the harmonic treatment of the main voice. Note that, in contrast to the carol discussed earlier, this melody's accented notes are twice treated as *nonchord* tones, that is, as step embellishments of chord members; see the second beats of measures 1 and 3. The note c^2 in measure 1 is accented; furthermore, it is reached by a leap and resolved by a descending step to the *b*♭ sixteenth note that forms the fifth of V^6_5. This type of decorative pattern is called a *leaning tone,* or *appoggiatura.* It appears again in measure 3. Although less common than passing and neighbor tones, the leaning tone, a nonchord tone reached by leap and resolved by step, is an important and interesting means for enhancing the relationship between melody and chords.

When the anticipated arrival of a basic pitch is delayed, or displaced from a strong beat to a subsequent weak beat (or beat part), a figure called the *suspension* results. Suspensions occur in Example 6-23; each suspension is marked with an arrow. The suspension is a figure made up of three separate elements; these are usually described as *preparation, suspension* (or dissonance), and *resolution.* The three steps are marked P, S, and R in the following:

P S R

The preparation consists of the introduction as a basic pitch, or chord tone, of the note that is to be suspended. The same note is delayed, usually as a sustained (or tied) note, in its movement *by step* to the note of resolution. This delay takes place while the other voice or voices move to produce a *change of chord,* one of the members of the new chord being displaced by the suspended note. The suspended note is usually resolved on an unaccented beat; when this is done, syncopation results from the rhythmic pattern of the suspended voice. Such is the case in Example 6-24(a), which reveals several uses of suspensions. The same passage is shown in Example 6-24(b) without any suspensions. Compare the two versions, noting how the suspensions have made Example 6-24(a) considerably the more interesting of the two.

Example 6-24

a)

b)

The suspension figure is unquestionably the most significant means for heightening rhythmic interest and part individuality. A noteworthy feature of the suspension is the fact that it usually creates dissonance.

It is apparent that there are numerous ways of introducing step decorations of important notes. The key word here is *step,* because most decorative notes form steps with notes that they embellish either at the point at which they are introduced, at the point of resolution, or at both locations. The term *resolution,* in the most common sense, denotes a step interval formed by a decorative note (often a dissonance) and its successor. An exception to this definition occurs with the *escape tone* (see the circled notes in Example 6-25), which is reached by step but "resolved" by a leap.

The *anticipation* is an unaccented note, usually of brief duration, reached by *step or leap,* that precedes a more important accented articulation of the same pitch. Anticipations are often found as elaborations of cadences, as in Example 6-26.

Example 6-25

Mozart, *Sonata in D major for Piano,* K. 576

Example 6-26

Chopin, *Piano Concerto in F minor,* 1st movement

PEDAL POINT

Pedal points, or pedal tones, are sustained or resounded pitches, most often the tonic or the dominant, which continue to sound in one part while various types of harmonic and rhythmic activity take place in the other voices. Pedal tones are most frequently found in the bass voice, underscoring motion in the upper parts. They commonly create dissonances with one or more members of the succession of notes or chords that are projected above (or below) them. They are a most arresting means of creating harmonic tension while at the same time prolonging a stable member of a key. It is this interaction of stability and motion that produces the unique effect associated with a pedal. See Example 6-27.

Example 6-27

Schumann, *Papillons,* Op. 2, No. 12

An analysis of the decorative figures characteristically used in a composition is far more valuable than a note-by-note description of melodic and harmonic relations. Many passages, if not entire sections or compositions, will be found to reveal certain characteristic decorative patterns, which have an important effect on the melodic and rhythmic style of the piece. Some pieces reveal a predominance of passing or neighbor tones, while others rely more consistently on suspensions or leaning tones. Other works may evolve a pattern of varied types of decorative figures. Obviously, decorative figures are meaningful only as they occur in specific contexts, rather than as isolated events. Their value, as we have said, is essentially rhythmic. They allow motivic activity without which melody would seem comprised of streams of more or less equally structural notes, with little differentiation by duration, placement, consonance and dissonance, or level of importance.

EXERCISES

1. Play all 22 of the chords given below, each of which contains three pitches. Place a check above each *triad,* and indicate its quality—major (M), minor (m), augmented (+), or diminished (o).

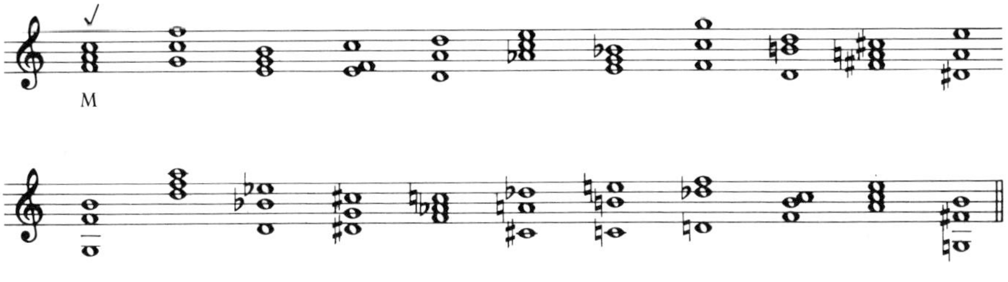

(optional)

2. Write the first 16 members of the overtone series whose fundamental is *E♭*.

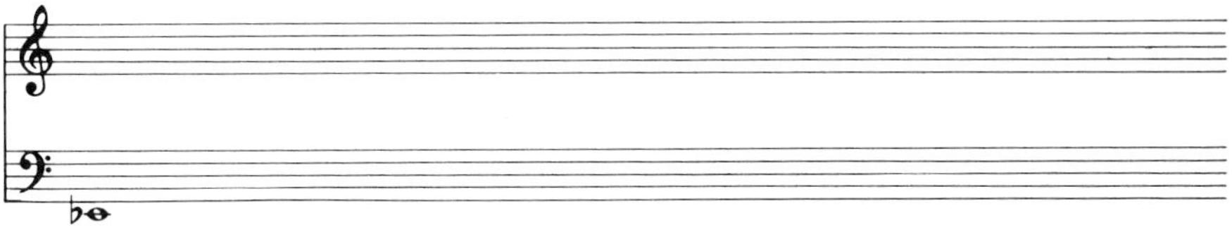

3. Invent 10 different arrangements of a root-position E♭ major triad, using as few as three or as many as six pitches, as desired. Deploy them in different registral arrangements, as illustrated in the text in Example 6-6. Play the chords on the piano and note the aural effect of each arrangement.

(optional)

4. Construct each of the chords indicated below in the key requested ("m" indicates a minor key). Note the sample.

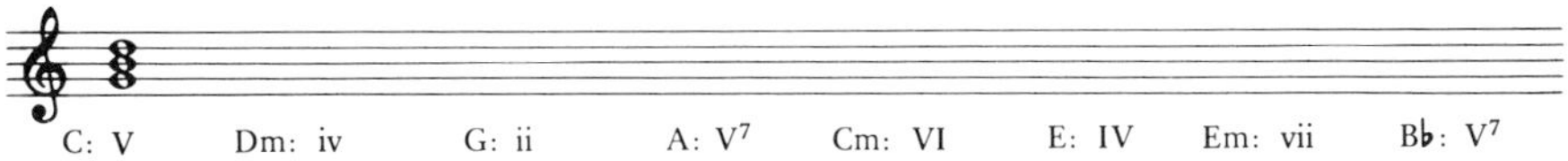

C: V Dm: iv G: ii A: V^7 Cm: VI E: IV Em: vii B♭: V^7

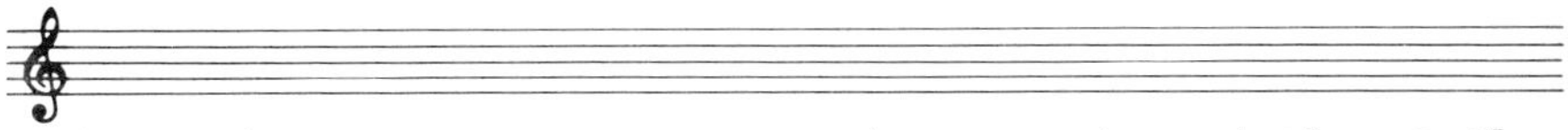

D♭: I E♭m: V Gm: ii Am: III A♭: IV Bm: i G♭: V^7 D: V^7

5. Play or sing the following example, which is taken from a collection of piano pieces written to illustrate some of the materials of twentieth-century composition. Label all dissonances that occur (as has been done in the first phrase). Then write a brief paragraph in which you take stock of the rhythmic location and melodic resolution of dissonant intervals in general in the piece.

Bartók (Mikrokosmos, Vol. 2)

6. Continue the analysis of all on-the-beat harmonic intervals found in the following passage. Treat all compound intervals as simple intervals.

J. S. Bach (Invention in D major)

7. Use the two preceding musical examples as a basis for practicing interval singing; play one member of each interval analyzed and sing the other in a comfortable register. Check your performance with the piano or have another person listen to you and note errors that you make. Maintain a consistent pace of performance (about MM = 80 per interval).

8. Study the following composition by Haydn.

Haydn (The Creation)

(cont.)

a) Analyze the functions of all harmonic changes between measure 1 and measure 16. Use appropriate roman numerals.

b) Locate and indicate on the music examples of terminal, progressive, and transient terminal cadences. Indicate the harmonic functions at these cadence points.

c) Name the predominant type or types of nonchordal activity in the vocal line. Refer by measure to examples of such activity.

d) Locate any occurrences of pedal points in the accompaniment.

e) Locate examples of the various inversions of the dominant seventh chord and write the appropriate numerical abbreviations beneath the music.

9. Familiarize yourself with the following musical example.

J. S. Bach (Chorale, "Gottes Sohn ist kommen")

a) The cadences in this piece are signaled by fermata symbols. Indicate whether each cadence is progressive, terminal, or transient terminal.

b) Indicate the functions of all chords that occur in measures 5 to 7 and 12 to 13. Use appropriate roman numerals.

c) Write the root progression for measures 1 through 4.

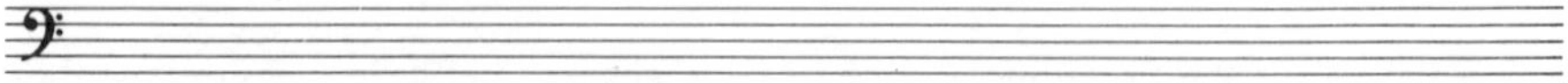

(optional)

10. Arrange the following chords to produce a typical root progression as described in the text, keeping in mind the cycle of tonic, digression, approach to tonic, and return to tonic.

11. Study the recitative shown below. Sing the vocal line and play the accompanying chords on the piano. Place a check above each dominant seventh chord in the accompaniment. Then place a numeral 6 below the bass note of each first-inversion triad used in the recitative.

Haydn (The Creation)

Chapter 7

MODULATION AND MUTATION

There are numerous ways in which composers create tonal variety in music. Most compositions, even those consisting of the most concise and simple materials, reveal some degree of tonal variety produced by the introduction of pitches lying outside the realm of the composition's principal key, i.e., the key in which it begins and closes. The means for effecting tonal variety are almost as limitless as the resources of composers' imaginations. In this chapter we shall merely ripple the surface of the subject of tonal variety, a subject which is almost as critical to most musical organization as is tonality itself.

TONALITY CHANGE: MODULATION

Tonality change involves a change of tonic; the initial tonal center is erased and a new focal point is established. Tonality change, in other words, is a change of key. Example 7-1 contains a clear and unadorned change of key from C major, the principal key of the composition, to the key of its dominant, G major.

The tonality change in this example is direct and clear. A terminal cadence on the tonic of C major occurs at measure 8, and is followed by the beginning of a new section in G major. In many cases the line of demarcation between two keys is not so clearly defined, and the listener or reader may not be aware of the precise point at which a new key is introduced. Listen to Example 7-2 and try to discover through listening, without visual reference to the music, the measure in which a new key is made evident.

Musicians commonly describe passages such as the one in Example 7-2 as effecting *modulations.* As is suggested by the passage, a modulation is a change of key that is more subtly or gradually introduced than in Example 7-1. In a sense, the composer conceals the point of key change by employing

Example 7-1

Schumann, *Album for the Young,* "Humming Song"

chords or tonal materials whose key identity is ambiguous; then he confirms and clarifies the new key quite commonly by a V-I progression or cadence. The ensuing music further clarifies and emphasizes the new key. Thus the process of modulation consists of three steps: (1) preparation by the use of tonal materials which could belong to either the old or the new key; (2) confirmation of the new key, usually by means of a V-I progression; (3) further emphasis on the new key in the following music.

Returning to Example 7-2, one can discover each of the steps just cited. The chord at measure 8 is ambiguous, since it can be understood either as iv of D minor or as ii of F major. In measure 9, F major is implied by the absence of the leading tone of D minor (*c*♯), which is replaced by *c* natural, the dominant of F. The V-I progression in measures 9 and 10 confirms the key of F; the following six measures, in which *c*♯ is still conspicuously absent, clarify the sense of F major tonality; and the terminal cadence in F at measures 16 and 17 gives further emphasis to the key of F.

Example 7-2

J. S. Bach, *Invention in D minor*

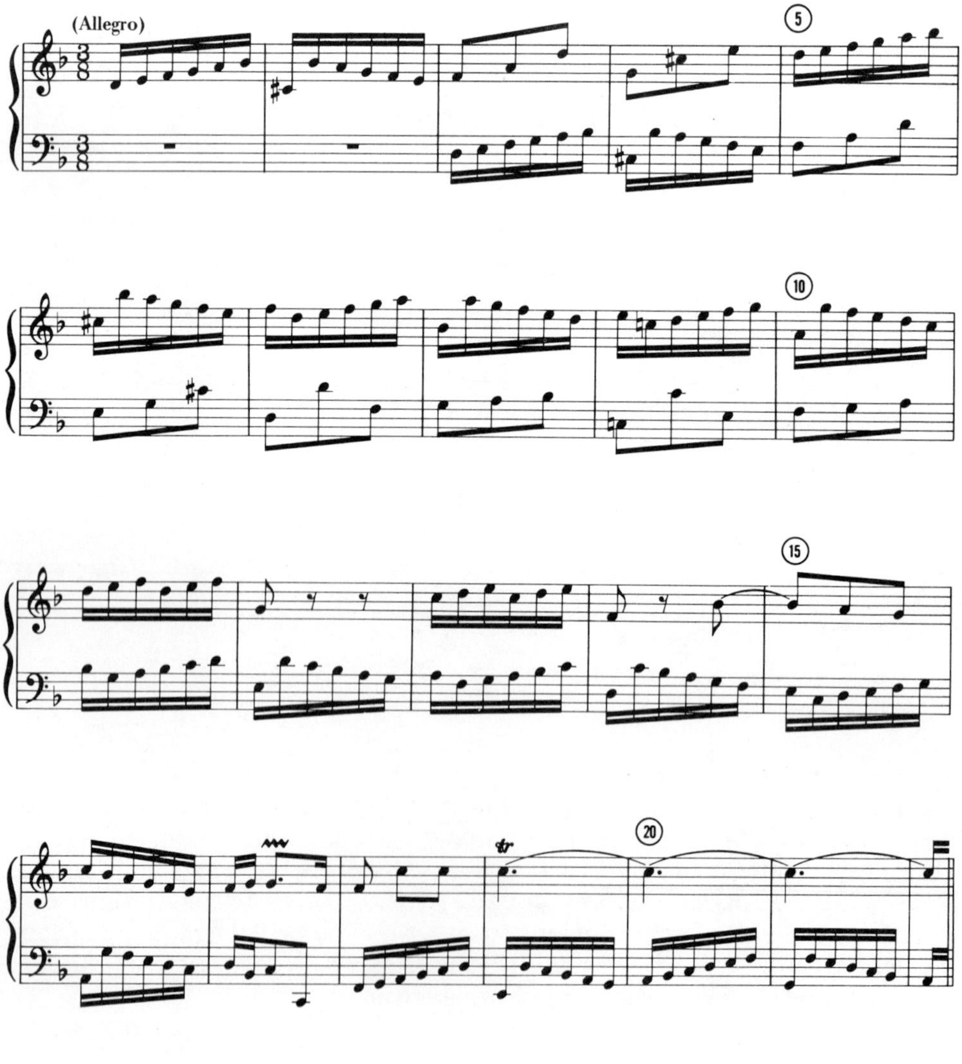

Thinking back over the entire passage, one can surmise that the change of key to F major was initiated about measures 8 and 9. However, such a conclusion could hardly have been made on first hearing. Indeed one of the essential properties of modulation is a passage that is *pivotal,* that is, tonally relatable to either of two keys, the original key or the one serving as the goal of the modulation. The chords occurring at such key junctures are usually called *pivot chords,* or common chords. The common chord in the example cited here is the G minor triad outlined in measure 8, and identifiable as iv in D minor or ii in F major. The harmonic reduction of this passage, shown in Example 7-3, can serve as a basis for better understanding the process of modulation. Each of the three steps cited above is marked.

Example 7-3 Harmonic reduction of Example 7-2

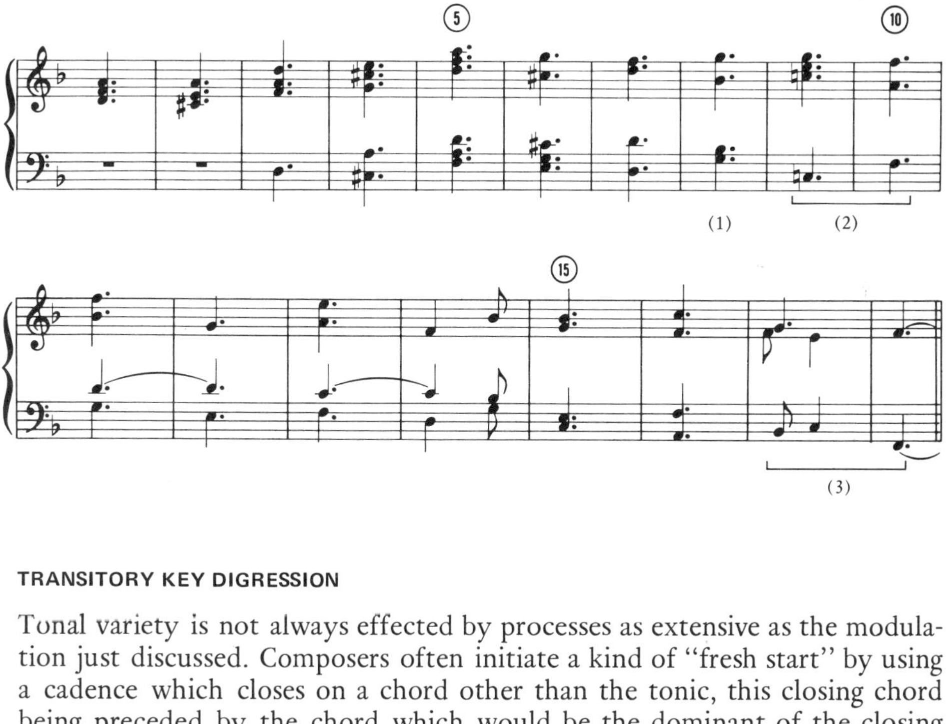

TRANSITORY KEY DIGRESSION

Tonal variety is not always effected by processes as extensive as the modulation just discussed. Composers often initiate a kind of "fresh start" by using a cadence which closes on a chord other than the tonic, this closing chord being preceded by the chord which would be the dominant of the closing chord were the closing chord considered as the tonic.

Study the cadence in measure 2 of Example 7-4. The key of the selection is A major. The closing chord of the cadence is the major triad on *e,* V in the key of A major. The chord preceding this triad is the major triad on *b,* which is the dominant triad of the key of E major. What we have in this cadence is a momentary digression from A major to E major. Note, however, that the *d*♯, which is a tone distinctive to E major, becomes *d* natural again

Example 7-4

J. S. Bach, *Jesu Leiden, Pein und Tod* (Chorale)

in the first chord of measure 3. Since the passage returns to the key of A major before E major is firmly established, the term "modulation" is scarcely appropriate. Such patterns are commonly referred to as dominant embellishments. They give a momentary surge to tonal interest by weakening the main key and implying a new one; the passage that follows, however, reaffirms the original key. Dominant embellishments may occur either at cadences, as in measure 2 of Example 7-4, or within phrases, as in measure 11.

Whether cadences like the one in measure 2 of Example 7-4 should be called terminal or progressive is a moot question. From the point of view of the new key, this cadence is terminal. However, it could just as easily be regarded as a progressive cadence in the key of A major, with the chord preceding the dominant modified to suggest the new tonality. By way of compromise, one may call such cadences *transient terminal* cadences. The chord which acts as the dominant embellishment of the "new" key is called a *secondary dominant.*

Dominant sevenths can be used in the same way as dominant triads to produce tonal digressions. Dominant sevenths used in this way are, of course, called *secondary dominant sevenths.* Several of these occur in Example 7-5 (indicated by check marks). Note that, even though no modulation occurs, considerable tonal variety is achieved in this passage within a short musical span.

Example 7-5

Mozart, *Sonata in B♭ for Piano,* K. 333, 1st movement

Secondary, or embellishing, dominants are perhaps most clearly signaled in notation by the appearance of *raised* accidentals denoting the temporary new leading tones (for example, the *d*♯ in measure 2 of Example 7-4). Of greater consequence, however, is the clearly audible root relation of a perfect fifth between the secondary dominant and its chord of resolution:

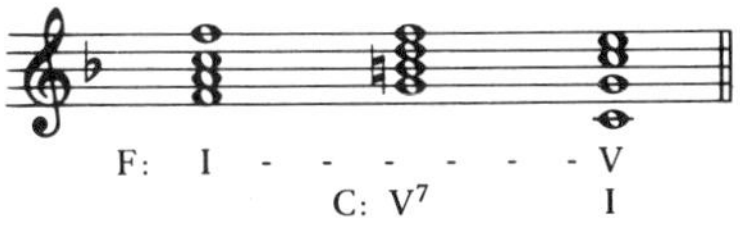

The use of secondary dominants is one of the most flexible ways of achieving tonal variety. There are, in fact, many examples of sections or phrases which are subject to numerous tonal interpretations. It is as important to acknowledge this potential for tonal ambiguity as it is to be aware of the *limitations* posed by key organization. In fact, composers often capitalize on the psychological implications of tonal ambiguity in the formal design of a composition. A passage like that in Example 7-6 illustrates the susceptibility of tonal patterning to various aural interpretations.

Each of the first four measures of Example 7-6 pays homage to a different key: measure 1 to C minor, measure 2 to A♭ major, measure 3 to F minor, and measure 4, the cadential measure, to G major. Were each tonal digression considered as a full-scale key change, the piece could be upheld as an outstanding example of measure-by-measure "modulation." A more "musical" (i.e., more realistic and less theoretical) explanation of the passage would describe the elaboration of four measures in C minor through extensive secondary dominant embellishments. Of greater significance to the composition's organization and its realization in performance is the fact that the four opening measures effect *unity* by repeating the same rhythm (♩ ♩ ♪. ♬ ♩) and

Example 7-6

Chopin, *Prelude in C minor,* Op. 28

contrast by emphasizing a different degree of the C minor scale as a temporary focal point—the tonic *(c)* in measure 1, the submediant *(a♭)* in measure 2, the subdominant *(f)* in measure 3, and the dominant *(g)* in measure 4. Considered in this light, the four measures constitute an elaboration of the chord progression I-VI-IV-V in the key of C minor. With the return to I in measure 5, the "normal" harmonic progression—tonic, digression, return to tonic—is complete.

In analyzing a passage such as the first four measures of Example 7-6, one must remember that the overall structure is more important than the individual details. What is important to note in Example 7-6 is that four degrees of the scale of C minor, the principal key of the passage, have been embellished through the use of tonal digressions employing secondary dominant sevenths. Though the details of the tonal digressions may be somewhat complicated, the broad harmonic outline of the phrase conforms to the simple pattern of "normal" harmonic progressions.

It is through procedures such as those used by Chopin in this example that tonality becomes a more significant form-determining factor than the mere notions of scale and chord imply. These procedures enable a composer to incorporate all twelve tones of the chromatic scale into melodic and harmonic patterns that are articulated in diatonic *units;* each of the first four measures of Example 7-6 is such a unit.

CHROMATICISM

Chromaticism is the result of using pitches which lie outside the prevailing key of a composition. Note alterations—sharps, flats, and naturals—signal chromatic tones in notation. A prolonged use of chromatic tones often indicates a modulation. Secondary dominants also involve chromatic notes. Equally important, however, is the use of chromatic tones as purely decorative notes to enrich an essentially diatonic passage. Decorative chromaticism thus constitutes yet another type of tonal variety.

Listen to Example 7-7 and note the use of decorative chromatic tones. This passage is clearly based on an E♭ major tonality, emphasized by both the melodic and harmonic materials. But notes foreign to the diatonic key of E♭ contribute measurably to melodic design and expression. Each of the checked pitches (measures 2, 3, 6, and 7) is a half-step embellishment—a chromatic passing or neighbor tone—of the diatonic note to which it moves. The rich hue of chromaticism, which contributes immensely to the effect of this passage, is due entirely to these decorative pitches. Most traditional music reveals some use of decorative chromatic notes.

Compare the chromaticism of Example 7-7 with that of Example 7-8, which reveals *no* diatonic underpinning in any major or minor key. In this passage, representative of many works from the current century, key, as a source of tonal materials and basis for tonal organization, is abandoned, and each of the available twelve tones is treated independently in the pitch structure; no homage is given to a tonic or to any pitch hierarchy. Such organization is commonly called *atonal.*

Example 7-7

Mozart, *Piano Concerto in E♭*, K. 482, 1st movement

Example 7-8

Schoenberg, *Pierrot Lunaire,* "Gebet an Pierrot"

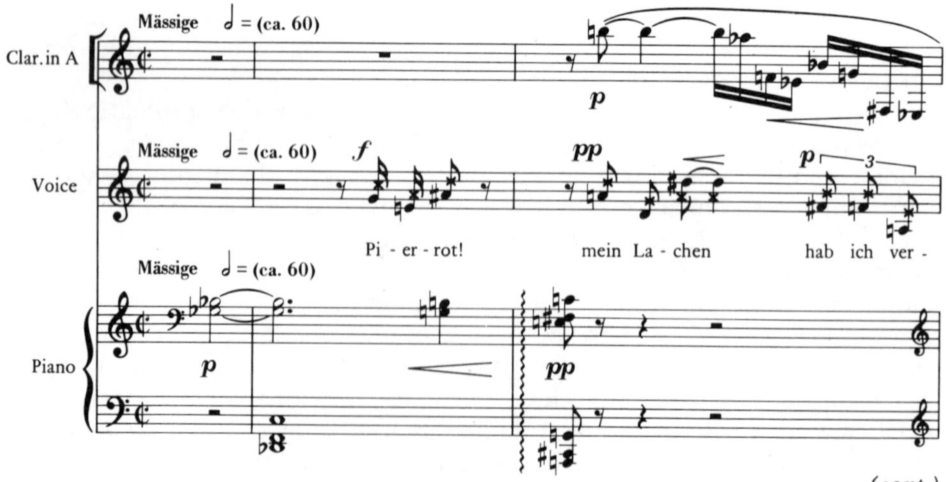

(cont.)

Example 7-8 (continued)

MUTATION

Modulation is a change of key; another way of creating tonal variety and contrast is to change the mode, that is, the scale basis, of a composition while retaining the initial tonic. This process, change of mode, is often called *mutation.* In the melody of Example 7-9 the note *a* persists as the tonic throughout, while the scale basis changes from major to minor.

Example 7-9

Brahms

Example 7-10

Brahms, *Intermezzo,* Op. 118, No. 2

(cont.)

Example 7-10 (continued)

The effectiveness of mutation in shaping musical form, that is, in helping to delineate sections of a composition, can easily be seen in Example 7-10, which involves a change of mode from F♯ minor to F♯ major and then back to F♯ minor.

The processes briefly described in this chapter constitute only a few of the means at a composer's disposal for creating variety and heightening interest in the pitch materials of a piece of music. Although we have considered them separately, these processes are by no means mutually exclusive. For example, a progression of secondary dominants could easily serve as the basis for creating tonal ambiguity before a change of key. Or mutation could be introduced to prepare the listener for a change of key, as in Example 7-11, in which a mutated chord on *c* prepares the new key of A♭ by introducing the note *e*♭ (the dominant of A♭).

Example 7-11

Some works involve so much interchange of mode, so-called "mixing of modes," that an assessment of their major or minor quality is neither possible nor realistic. Such modal mixtures are particularly common in works of the late nineteenth century, when the traditions of the major-minor tonal system were being abandoned to a great extent. Example 7-12 is difficult to appraise as either major or minor; it is, in fact, both.

Example 7-12

Wagner, *Tristan und Isolde*

EXERCISES

1. Circle the measure in each of the following melodies in which a change of key is *initiated.* Locate the cadence at which the change of key is confirmed and indicate the new key beneath the music, as shown in the sample. Draw a square around the measure in which a return to the principal key (the beginning and ending key) occurs. Sing each melody before analyzing it.

Sample:

French Folk Song

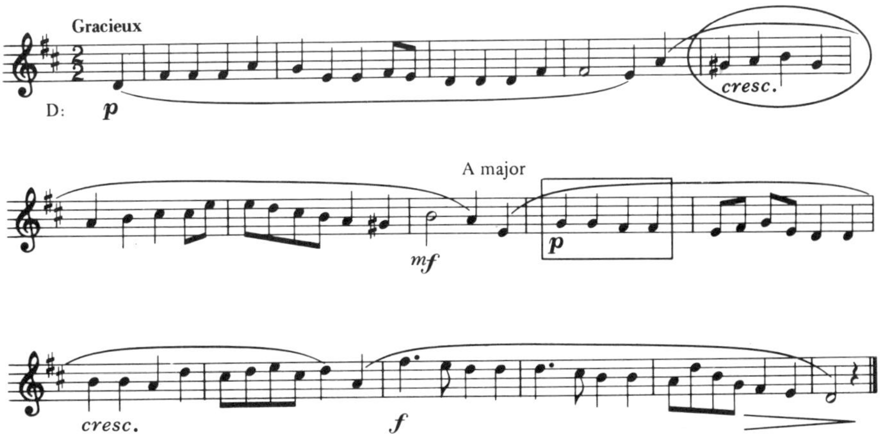

Corelli

a)

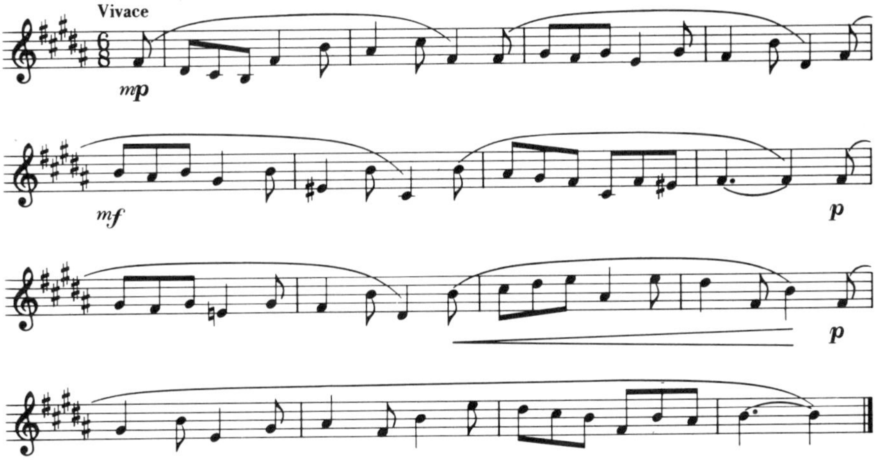

Schubert

b)

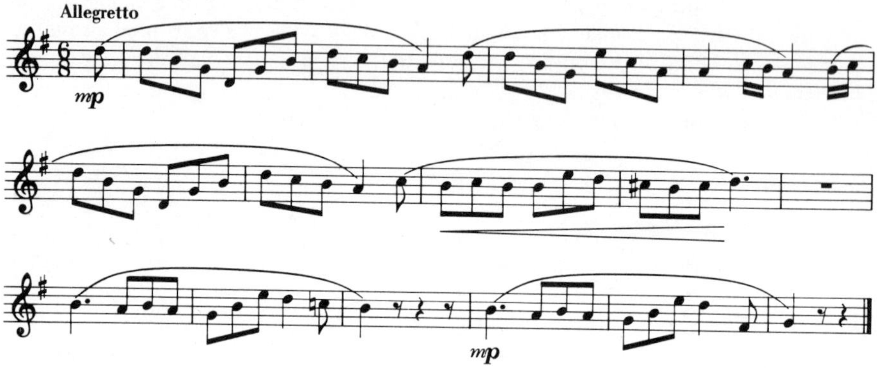

Swedish Folk Song

c)

Italian Folk Song

d)

Haydn

e) 

Rossini

f) 

(optional)

2. a) Perform or listen to a recording of the song by Schubert on page 132. Mark the phrase structure (the first phrase has already been marked). Identify the modulation that occurs by circling the measure in which it is initiated, identifying the key at the confirming cadence, and placing a square around the measure in which a return to the principal key occurs.

   b) Identify the chord changes in the piece with appropriate roman numerals, as has been done in the first four measures, and place a small check mark above all non-chord tones in the vocal line.

   c) Identify briefly those factors (at least three) that create *unity* in the composition; be as specific as possible. What factors produce *contrast?*

   d) Indicate briefly what you consider to be the most important musical attributes or characteristics of the piece insofar as its realization in performance is concerned. For example, in what way is the pianist responsible for projecting the mood of the song? How is the mood of the song reflected by its accompaniment?

Schubert ("Heidenröslein")

3. a) Play or sing (with help) the following composition. Identify all checked chords as secondary dominants in A minor and indicate their functions with roman numerals. For a sample, see measure 5.

   b) Locate and identify any accented (on-the-beat) nonchord tones (e.g., suspensions or passing tones) that occur in the upper voice.

   c) Place an "M" under any cadence chords involving mutated pitches.

J. S. Bach (Chorale, "Ach wie nichtig, ach wie flüchtig")

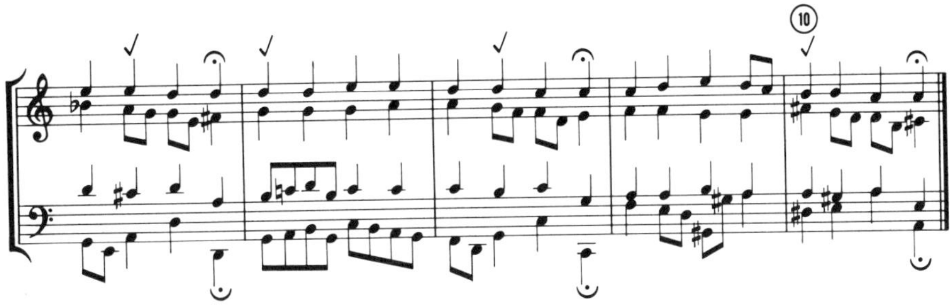

(optional)

4. Make an adaptation of the Bach Chorale in Exercise 3 for two voices—soprano and bass—or two wind or stringed instruments. Introduce continuous eighth-note activity in the lower part, returning to longer notes at cadences. Retain the same basic harmonic structure as that of the model. See the sample beginning.

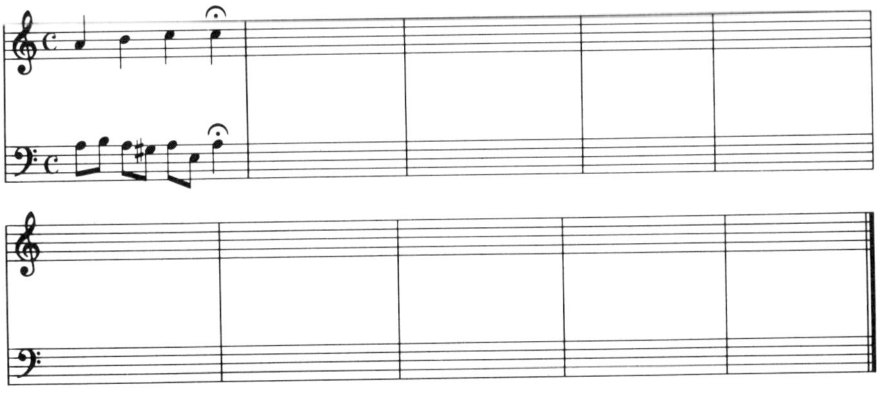

5. a) Listen to a reading of or play the example below on the piano at a moderately quick tempo. Indicate the harmonic changes that are implied by the two parts (this has been done for you in the first two measures). There are two or three changes per measure. It is not necessary to indicate implied triad inversions.

J. S. Bach (English Suite No. 3)

(optional)

b) Revise the piece for three strings—first violin, second violin, and cello—by adding a middle voice for the second violin part. This part should not detract from the prominence of the outer voices, nor should its addition cause any important revisions of the harmonic structure.

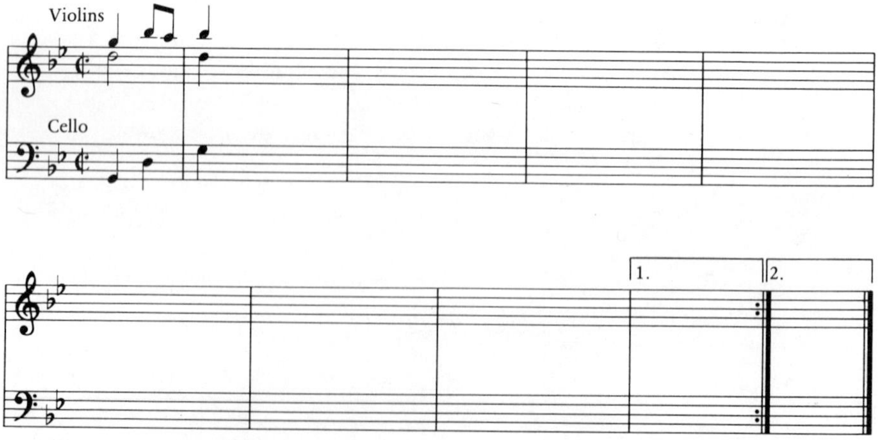

c) In what ways does this example manifest the cycle of tonic, digression, and return to tonic? Cite at least three ways, using measure references.

6. a) Play the excerpt below. Then identify three ways in which tonal *variety* is produced in the piece's pitch structure. Be as specific as possible.

   b) Describe briefly the most characteristic forms of nonchord activity found in this excerpt.

Chopin (Mazurka, Op. 7, No. 2)

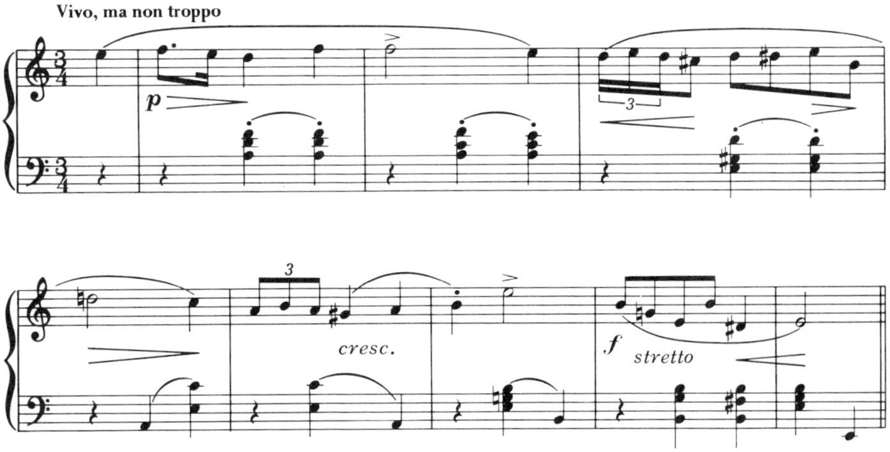

(optional)

   c) Invent eight additional measures of music based on the melodic materials found in the example. Retain the same harmonic rhythm and keyboard style. Plan your addition to begin in E minor and return to the principal key (A minor) in the closing phrase. Choose an appropriate pivot chord to initiate the return to A minor.

Chapter 8

MUSICAL TEXTURE

A description of the *texture* of a composition or section of a composition takes into account the number of parts or "strands" (voices or instruments), and the way in which they are deployed, or "woven." Most compositions contain between two and five parts. In many works, however, the specific number of separate parts is of less consequence than the way in which the parts are grouped into units or strata. Part deployment, that is, the manner of treating the various parts or textural units of a composition, is an important facet of the problem-solving and manipulation of materials that is composition itself.

MONOPHONY

The simplest, most transparent texture is that of unaccompanied melody. As the term suggests, *monophony* means "one voice." Some melodies, by outlining triads or other chords, imply a specific harmonic basis, as does Example 8-1. By way of contrast, Example 8-2 reveals *no* clear chordal basis. Both examples, however, are monophonic. Other melodies are fashioned in such a

Example 8-1 Alabama

Example 8-2

Matheus de Perusio

way as to imply more than one melodic line. Note how the pitch activity in Example 8-3(a) is distributed on two distinct levels. This bi-level distribution of pitches suggests the two-part harmony shown in Example 8-3(b).

Example 8-3

Corelli, *Sonata in E minor for Violin*

a)

b)

HOMOPHONY

Homophonic textures employ two or more voices; yet they remain relatively simple, because melodic activity and interest are concentrated in one voice, usually the upper, while the remaining parts provide tonal and rhythmic support. The nonmelodic parts are in effect an accompaniment. The simplest form of homophony is that of Example 8-4, which consists of a solo voice supported by a succession of unobtrusive, sustained chords realized by a keyboard instrument.

Example 8-4

Monteverdi, *Orfeo,* Act I

Composers often enliven homophonic textures by breaking up the accompanying chords into various kinds of figures or patterns. Such patterns, many of which are geared to the special capabilities of the keyboard instruments used to accompany soloists, abound in music literature. Some of the most common patterns are shown in Example 8-5. Note that such patterns are usually the result of *rhythmic* elaboration of a chord progression. By repeating chords or notes, by arpeggiating chords, or by outlining chords by unfolding them in a semimelodic manner, the composer can invest accompanying chords with a sense of forward motion and activity.

Homophonic textures usually reveal a complementary relation between the main voice and the accompaniment. The accompaniment supplies rhythmic continuity and harmony while detracting very little from the concentration of interest in the main voice. The accompaniment usually assumes a leading role only when the main voice is temporarily inactive. Occasional passages of melodic interest in such accompaniments do not alter their essentially homophonic character. It should be apparent from Example 8-5 that, despite the fundamental simplicity of homophony, the possibilities for enlivening homophonic textures are enormous.

As has been said repeatedly in this book, the various materials of musical composition are seldom heard in isolation. Example 8-6 shows a homophonic texture which demonstrates an unusually close relationship between melody and harmony, that is, between the main voice and the accompanying

Example 8-5 Various homophonic passages

a) Repeated chord accompaniment (Beethoven)

b) Simple broken chord figure—Alberti bass (Mozart)

c) Expanded chordal outlining—arpeggiation (Brahms)

d) Articulated pedal point (Mozart)

(cont.)

Example 8-5 (continued)

e) Broken octaves (Mozart)

f) Waltz-style accompaniment involving rapid shifts of register in the left hand (Chopin)

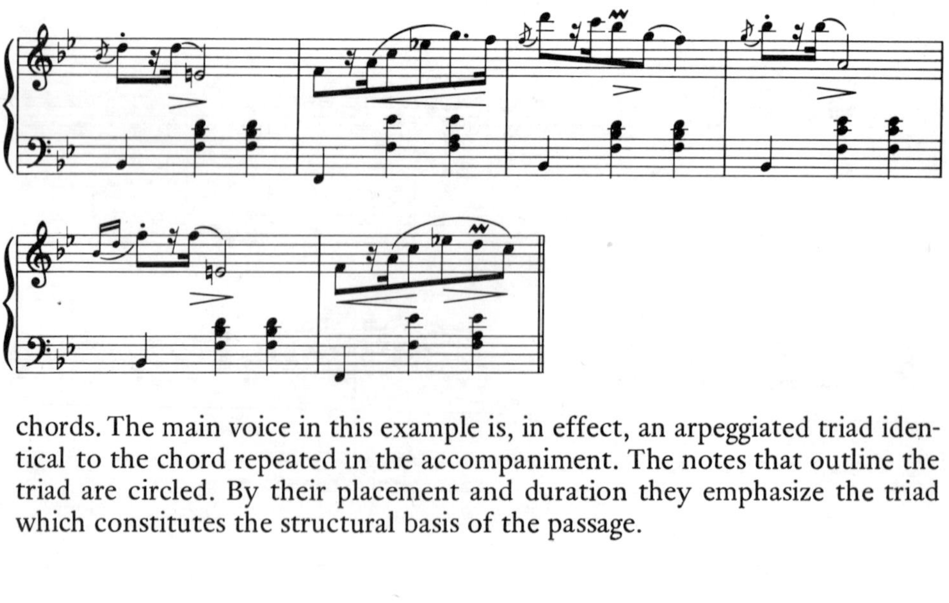

chords. The main voice in this example is, in effect, an arpeggiated triad identical to the chord repeated in the accompaniment. The notes that outline the triad are circled. By their placement and duration they emphasize the triad which constitutes the structural basis of the passage.

Example 8-6

Mozart, *Sonata in F major for Piano,* K. 574, 1st movement

Melody and harmony are as one in Example 8-6, each reflecting the other. That notes other than those corresponding to the prevailing triad (F major) occur interpolated between successive triad members in the melody further accentuates the interdependency of the melodic line and the chords. This is true because the melodic pitches that correspond to chord tones define the tonal structure, while the interpolated nonchord notes constitute elaboration and embellishment of them. The significance of such embellishment, as has been indicated earlier, is essentially rhythmic. When the relation between melody and chords is obscured, they tend to be heard more as separate, independent parts of a texture which derives unity from factors other than tonality.

COUNTERPOINT

Contrapuntal textures result from the combination of two or more melodies. The essence of counterpoint is *individuality* of the various parts. Individuality can be achieved through either contour or rhythm, frequently both. Two melodies sounding in tandem, that is, having identical contours and rhythms, will produce an effect that is homophonic and homorhythmic, as in Example 8-7. In such passages contrapuntal interest is practically nonexistent.

Another important aspect of contrapuntal writing is the *relative activity* of the parts. In contrapuntal music the parts are of more or less equal interest

Example 8-7

Mozart

Example 8-8

Beethoven, *Sonata for Piano,* Op. 2, No. 1, Minuet

and contribute equally to the development of the musical ideas on which the composition is based. In Example 8-8, the two parts are distinctive in both their contours and rhythms; yet this passage fails to qualify as contrapuntal, because the lower part has a considerably less melodic role than the upper part. A lower part such as this, primarily a product of chord outlining, would most likely be perceived as accompaniment rather than as a partner in counterpoint produced by two simultaneously projected melodies.

Listen to Example 8-9, which is a *contrapuntal* passage. Note that, at any given moment, the two voices are differentiated by both contour and rhythm. Also, the two voices are equally active and equally interesting. As one listens to the example, one's attention is drawn from part to part as the two voices compete for attention. Observe, however, that the lower part in measures 3 and 4 is virtually identical to the upper part in measures 1 and 2. The lower part, in effect, imitates the upper part.

The technique of *imitation*—the successive stating and restating, exactly or in a modified form, of a melodic segment by two or more parts—is one of the fundamental techniques of counterpoint. Imitation is the basis for various

Example 8-9

J. S. Bach, *Fugue in E♭ for Organ*

Example 8-10 Various passages illustrating imitation

a) J. S. Bach, *The Well Tempered Clavier,* Book II, Prelude in A minor

b) Mozart, *Sonata in A minor for Violin and Piano,* K. 402, Finale

c) Schoenberg, *Fourth String Quartet,* 1st movement

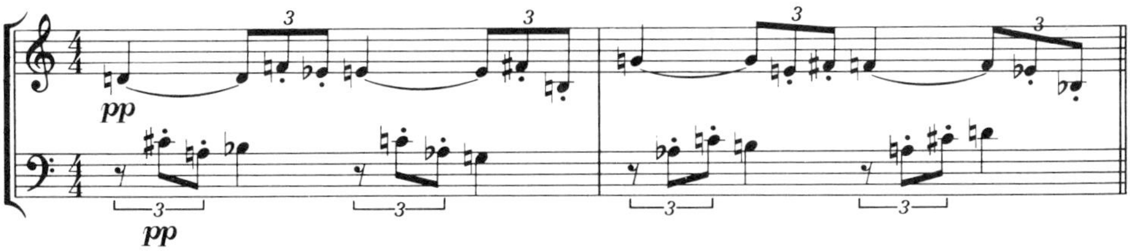

contrapuntal devices and forms such as canon, invention, fugue, chorale prelude, and others to be discussed later. Note that imitation, as defined by musicians, occurs *between* voices; the mere restatement of material by one voice does *not* constitute imitation. Listen to Example 8-10(a), (b), and (c) and note the various occurrences of imitation.

Counterpoint by definition implies the sharing of melodic interest by more than one voice. In *imitative* passages, such as those in Example 8-10, melodic activity is shared by two or more voices using *similar* melodic materials. *Nonimitative* (or "free") counterpoint results from combining *different* melodies. Imitation is by far the more common type of counterpoint. Whether imitative or nonimitative, there is probably no procedure that is more closely associated with the craft of composition than is that of creating effective counterpoint.

Example 8-11

a)

b)

VOICE LEADING

Melody and harmony serve to define and clarify each other, melody acting as a basis for the effective *connection* of successive chords, harmony creating tonal boundaries for melodic lines. In Example 8-11(a) a series of chords is unfolded without attention being given to the linear consideration of chord connection. The result is a succession of apparently arbitrarily selected chords which succeed each other in helter-skelter order. Example 8-11(b) shows the same chord series with the chords connected by the creation of lines, melodies of a sort, linking the four parts of each successive chord. In this version the chord series takes on a sense of logical forward motion that is not present in the former version.

The process of chord connection is called *voice leading*. Rarely does effective music fail to demonstrate some principles of melodic organization of the chord succession. Step motion is the simplest and most effective technique for creating smooth, cohesive chord connections. Note the predominance of step motion within the various voices of Example 8-12.

Example 8-12

J. S. Bach, *Es ist gewisslich an der Zeit* (Chorale)

Voice leading involves various types of motion relationships, that is, between-voice directional relations that can exist between simultaneously active parts. Such directional patterns constitute one of the basic elements of polyphonic music that reveals part independence. The following patterns are possible:

1. Contrary motion (the voices move in opposite directions):

2. Similar motion (the voices move in the same direction):

3. Parallel motion (the voices move in the same direction and maintain the same intervallic distance):

4. Oblique motion (one voice remains stationary while another moves by step or leap):

All of these types of motion may involve either steps or leaps; the former occur more often.

Effective voice leading may be found to be an organizing principle in many compositions which on the surface do not reveal voice-leading procedures as obvious as those cited above. This is probably most frequently the case with keyboard music. Example 8-13, written for a keyboard instrument, is based on an elaboration of a simple chord progression by means of arpeggiation. The musical effectiveness of the passage can be attributed, to a great extent, to the step connection of successive chord members. The composition's texture can be viewed, as shown in the reduction below the music, as a progression of logically joined five-note chords, one or more notes of which are usually doubled chord tones.

Example 8-13

J. S. Bach, *The Well Tempered Clavier,* Book I, Prelude in C major

Each of the types of motion enumerated above can be found in the voice leading subtly employed by Bach in Example 8-13. Although the listener will probably not be aware of the compositional basis for the logic and smoothness of harmonic motion in the passage, it is the composer's command of voice leading that helps to produce such a result.

CHORD SPACING AND DOUBLING

Harmonic *continuity* is in part a product of effective chord joining. On the other hand, harmonic *color,* the result of simultaneously sounded harmonic intervals, is greatly influenced by two other, related factors: the registral (high-low) distribution of chord tones and the reinforcement through octave duplication of one or more of the chord tones. Note the contrasting effects of various arrangements of the C major triad in Example 8-14.

Example 8-14 Various distributions of the C major triad

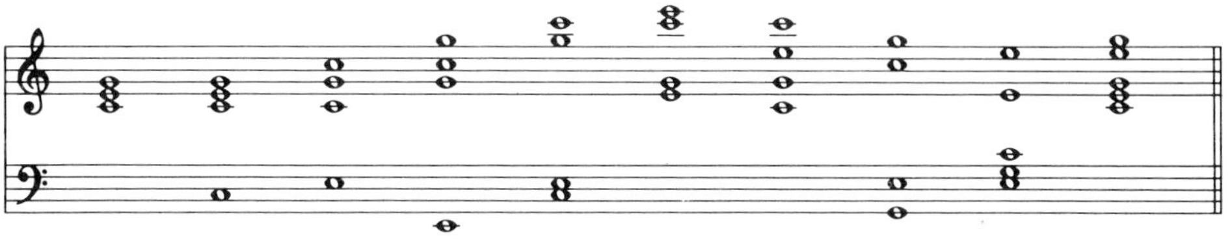

The topic of chord spacing is a complex one, for which musicians have not really agreed upon adequate descriptive terms. One might compare the endless number of possible chord spacings to the infinite number of hues obtainable from an artist's palette. In speaking of the spacing of vocal parts, musicians commonly describe arrangements in which the span separating the sopranos and tenors is an octave or less as *close position.* Each of the arrangements of the C major triad in Example 8-15 is scored for four voices—soprano, alto, tenor, and bass—in close position. The arrangements of the triad in Example 8-16 are characterized by a span of more than an octave between the tenor and the soprano. Each of these arrangements exemplifies *open-position* scoring. The variety of chord deployments available in each of these two main categories, close position and open position, is impressive.

Most of the chords in Example 8-17 contain more tones than the three that constitute a simple triad; the presence of these additional tones adds to the complexity of sonority. Note the great variety of sonority in this small sampling, and consider how the use of such media as an orchestra or a band would multiply the number of available sonorities. Note also that the effect of a chord may be altered by a change in the dynamic level, from *piano* (soft) to *forte* (loud) or vice versa; the use of various dynamic levels in a composition further increases the possible variety of sonority.

Example 8-15 Close-position arrangements of the C major triad for S. A. T. B.

Example 8-16 Open-position arrangements of the C major triad for S. A. T. B.

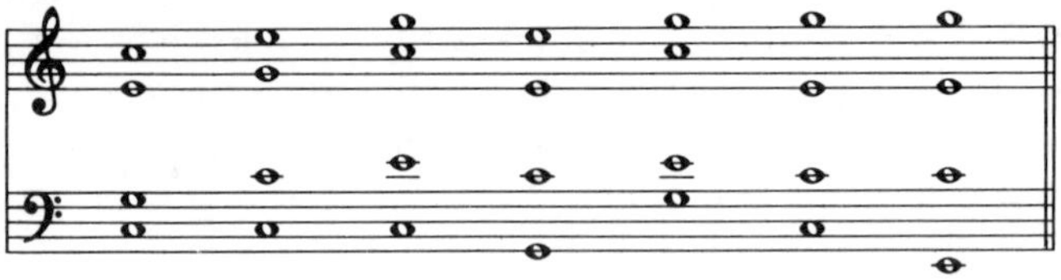

Example 8-17 Various types of sonority

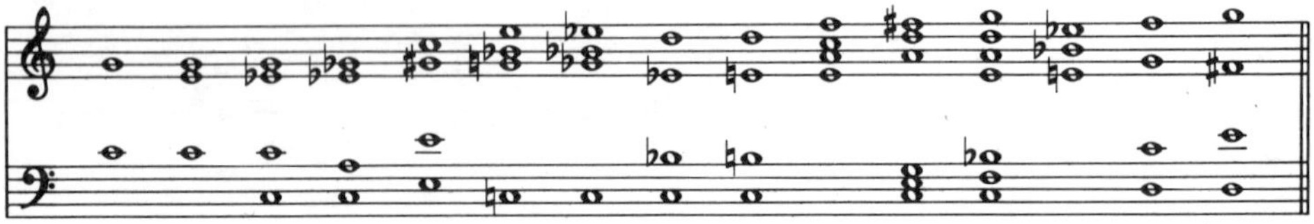

Chord doubling is influenced by many different factors, but most often it is the chord root that is reinforced, or doubled, particularly when the triad is in root position. First-inversion triads often occur with either the third (the bass note) or the root doubled. In second-inversion triads the chord fifth is usually doubled. However, certain factors, such as chord function, the occurrence of a specific tone in the main voice, the prevailing texture, spacing, the position of the chord in the phrase, or the rhythmic prominence of the chord, may influence chord doubling. Study Example 8-18, observing the details of spacing and chord doubling.

Example 8-18

J. S. Bach, *Meine Augen schliess' ich jetzt* (Chorale)

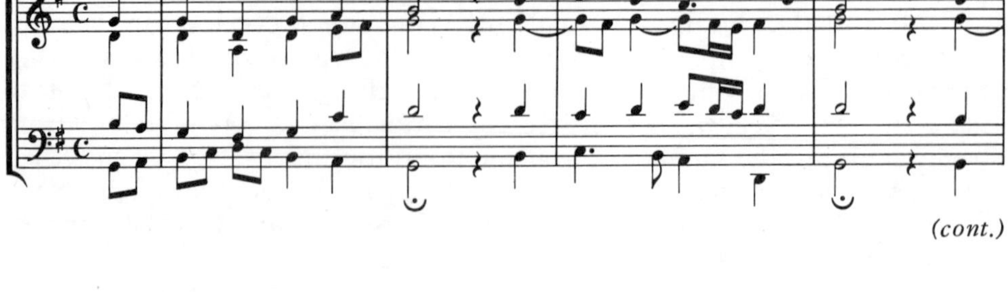

(cont.)

Example 8-18 (continued)

In Example 8-19 the doubling of members of triadic chords occurs as a logical consequence of the employment of five voices. Perform the passage and note the doubled tones. Consider each doubled note in the light of the considerations cited in the previous paragraph.

Detailed study of chord progression, spacing, and voice leading lies beyond the scope of this book. However, the following rules of thumb apply in varying degrees to most traditional and much current music composed of discrete musical parts, or voices, such as works for chorus, string quartet, brass choir, orchestra, or keyboard:

1. Each voice remains for the most part in a set register corresponding to its range capabilities. However, sometimes two voices *cross,* that is, exchange positions; for example, the tenor voice may be higher than the alto for a measure or so.
2. Upper parts are usually spaced more closely than lower parts. In many vocal compositions the span between adjacent upper parts rarely exceeds an octave, whereas the span between lower parts is limited only by range capabilities.

Example 8-19

Gesualdo, *Arditta zanzaretta* (Madrigal)

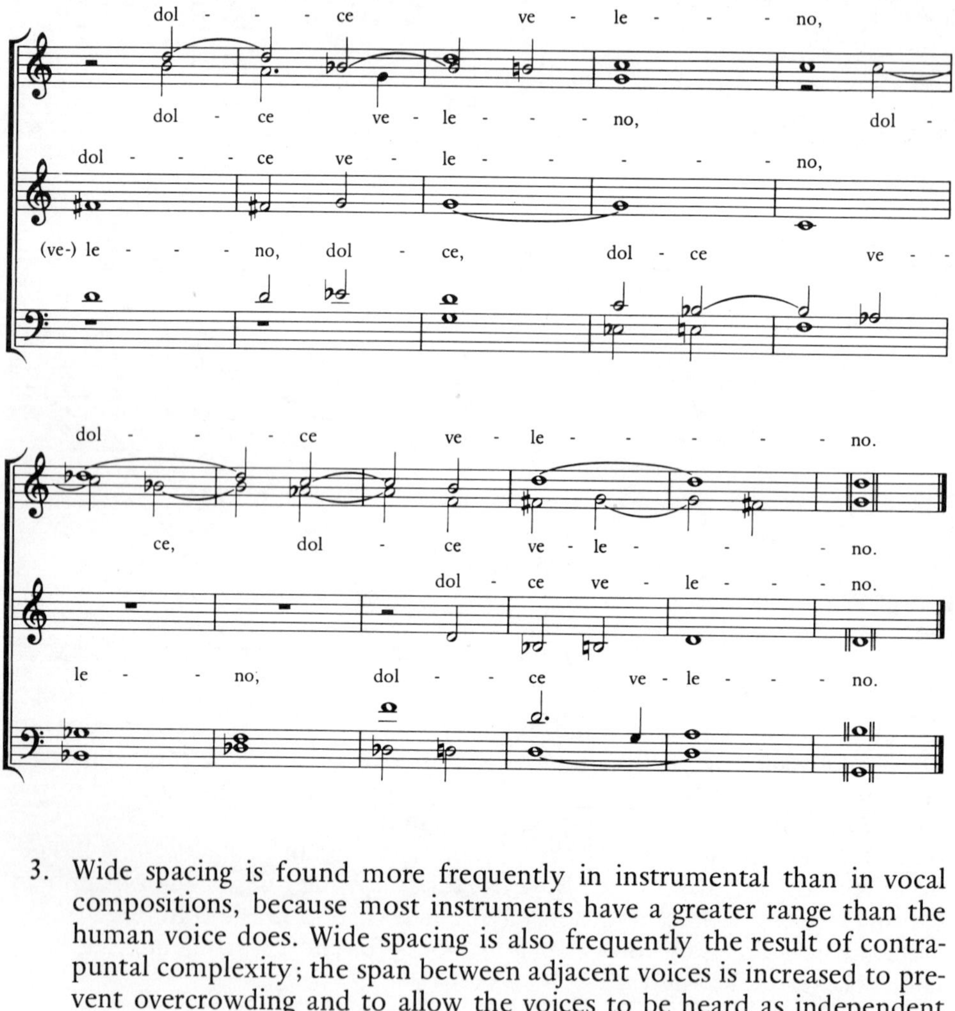

3. Wide spacing is found more frequently in instrumental than in vocal compositions, because most instruments have a greater range than the human voice does. Wide spacing is also frequently the result of contrapuntal complexity; the span between adjacent voices is increased to prevent overcrowding and to allow the voices to be heard as independent parts.
4. Most passages reveal considerable variety of motion (directional relations) between parts. Contrary or oblique motion tends to produce independence, whereas parallel or similar motion more often produces tandem effects.
5. Parallel motion involving successive octaves, unisons, or perfect fifths between any pair of voices tends to reduce part individuality, and is therefore avoided in much traditional music. However, such consecutive

octaves, unisons, and perfect fifths are by no means rare, especially in twentieth-century music.

6. Chord roots, the tonic, and less often the dominant are the most frequently doubled notes in triadic music.

Determine the applicability of these statements to Example 8-20. Note exceptions to these rules of thumb in Example 8-21.

Example 8-20

Scheidt, *Chorale Prelude*

Example 8-21

Hindemith, *Twelve Madrigals,* No. 8, "Judaskuss"

MUSICAL SCORES AND THEIR REALIZATION

Access to reading acquaintance with or study of much music is denied to anyone who cannot interpret scores. Musicians began recording compositions in score form, that is, in the form of vertically aligned parts for all instruments and voices, as early as the twelfth century. A score reveals the activity of all participating performers at any point in the performance.

There are three commonly encountered types of score. The first, *open,* or full score, has a separate stave for each instrument or voice. In orchestral scoring wind instruments, such as the flutes, oboes, or brasses, are sometimes notated in pairs, a pair to a stave. In *closed* score, the high (treble) and low (bass) parts are arranged on two staves, usually in the treble and bass clefs, as is the case with keyboard notation. These arrangements are commonly called piano scores, even though in some instances their rendition on the piano presents rather formidable problems. A third score format is the so-called *"conductor's" score,* which is usually a distillation of the total activity into two or three staves, with abbreviated indications of the instruments represented by each stave. Such scores are most frequently used for band compositions, which, because of the large number of transposing instruments, can be unwieldy to read in full score.

The formats of scores are determined partly by convenience and partly by tradition. In most scores the instruments are grouped so that those with high registers are at or near the top of the score, those with low registers at or near the bottom. For example, in a string quartet score, the instruments are arranged as follows:

First violin
Second violin
Viola
Cello

This is comparable to the arrangement of voices in open score:

Soprano
Alto
Tenor
Bass

The latter arrangement is normally abbreviated S. A. T. B. Example 8-22 shows a page from a string quartet and a page from a four-part (S. A. T. B.) vocal composition. Compare them, noting the alignment of parts and the comparability of roles (first violin and soprano, second violin and alto, and so on).

Example 8-22

a) Haydn, *String Quartet in G major,* Op. 74, Finale

(cont.)

Example 8-22 (continued)

b) Brahms, *A German Requiem,* Op. 45

Observe that violin parts are always written in the treble clef, as are soprano parts. Viola parts, however, are usually noted in the alto clef, though a switch to the treble clef is often made to avoid ledger lines when the viola plays in its upper register (roughly above c^2). Alto parts, surprisingly enough, are not notated in the alto clef, but in the treble clef. Cello parts are normally written in the bass clef, as are bass voice parts. However, when the cello plays in its upper register (above c^1) the clef changes to either tenor or treble.

Example 8-23 shows two score representations of the same passage. Study them and note their respective advantages and disadvantages.

An economical compromise of the current era, designed by publishers, is the so-called "pocket score," a miniature reduction, though a little too large for most pockets, of the full-score version. Although frequently difficult to read because of the small engraving necessary to get everything on the page, the miniature score, like the paperback book, is a sign of the times, serving a most useful purpose and making available much music that would otherwise be prohibitively expensive.

Example 8-23

Haydn, *Symphony No. 84,* Finale

a) Open score

(cont.)

Example 8-23 (continued)

b) Closed score

Scores for compositions using small orchestras or chamber ensembles of various single instruments or choirs usually reflect the full-score layout. The standard format is generally used, in which the instruments are grouped as follows:

Woodwinds
Brass
Percussion
Strings

If a vocal or instrumental solo part is to be employed, it is written on the stave immediately below the percussion and immediately above the first violins. Study Example 8-24, a song for voice (male or female) and orchestra.

TRANSPOSING INSTRUMENTS

A glance at Example 8-24 reveals that some instruments, such as clarinets, French horns, and trumpets, are notated in keys other than the concert key (actual sounding key) of the composition. Instruments whose parts are written in keys other than the concert key are called *transposing instruments.* To interpret notation written for transposing instruments, it is necessary to adjust mentally the actual notation in order to arrive at the desired concert pitches.

The principle of transposition itself is considerably simpler than the reasons for its continuance as a notational device, some of which are historical,

Example 8-24

Mahler, *Des Knaben Wunderhorn,* "Revelge (The Dead Drummer)"

based on tradition, and some practical, related to instrument construction and tone quality. The note name of the instrument—B♭ trumpet, French horn in F, clarinet in A, etc.—tells the reader or conductor the actual sound, in concert pitch, that results when the given instrument plays the written note *c*. Thus when a trumpeter using a B♭ trumpet plays the note *c* in his score part, the sound he produces is that of *b*♭:

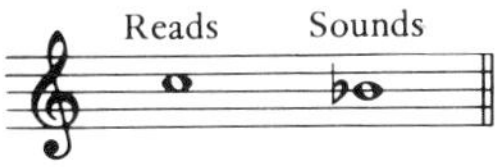

Return to Example 8-24 and look at the trumpet part. Note that B♭ trumpets are specified. Since B♭ trumpet parts are written one whole step above the desired sounding pitches, the E minor triad in the score will sound as a D minor triad:

The note name of a transposing instrument indicates only the note, not the precise octave registration, of the actual sound in concert. Most transposing parts sound *below* the written pitch; this is true of trumpets in B♭, horns in F (which sound a perfect fifth below the written pitch and are therefore written a perfect fifth above the intended concert pitch), clarinets in B♭ or A, and others. A small number of instruments sound *above* the written pitch; these include the E♭ clarinet, the C piccolo (which sounds an octave above the written pitch), and others. A comparison of the score and the written part with the range of the given instrument will usually reveal the direction of the transposition interval.

Determine the actual pitches produced by the other transposing instruments in Example 8-24. Note further that the contrabasses (string basses) sound exactly one octave below the written pitch. Were it not for this convention, string bass players (like piccolo players) would be forced to read numerous ledger lines most of the time.

TRANSPOSED SIGNATURES

In effect, transposed parts are written in keys different from the concert key. A symphony written in the key of F major, for example, will necessitate B♭ trumpet parts in the key, and utilizing the key signature, of G major. However, transposed parts, particularly those for brass instruments, belonging to compositions written during the early period of ensemble music (approximately 1600 to 1850, and later in some cases) do *not,* as a rule, use key signatures. The reason is that the trumpets and horns of that period, lacking valves, were drastically limited in the number of notes they could play; in fact, they were limited virtually to the first six pitches of the overtone series, which, as you will recall from Example 6-4, contain only three different notes. As a result, the parts for such works contain virtually *no* chromatic tones, indeed, no notes other than those of the fundamental triad of the key in which the instrument was originally built to sound. Thus, since the composer knew in advance that the part could utilize few notes other than *c, e,* and *g,* he did not use a key signature. The construction of the instrument and its limitations excluded other notes, those that might have been signaled by a signature, from the composition's notation.

A vestige of this historical circumstance can be observed in Example 8-24. Note that the trumpet parts have no key signature. However, since B♭ clarinets were specified, the trumpets should theoretically have the same F♯ signature as the clarinets, which corresponds to one flat in the concert key of D minor. The clarinets were not so limited in note production as were the trumpets; consequently no tradition of notating their parts without key signatures ever developed.

Since most published scores contain transposed parts, it is obvious that the student of music is in a sense denied access to a large segment of printed music if he is not equipped to read transposed parts. Despite some attempts by publishers to eliminate transposed parts by producing "C scores," whose parts are all converted into concert pitches, music reading still demands and, because of the traditions of music writing and reproduction, will continue to demand acquaintance with and fluency in reading transposed parts.

A chart of transpositions, together with indications of the basic written and sounding ranges for the modern orchestra and band instruments, is given here for study and reference. A chart showing the traditional grouping of voice parts and their respective ranges follows.

RANGES AND TRANSPOSITIONS

The order of instruments here is the order of their appearance in an orchestral score. The practical range is defined by the black notes; the open notes denote extreme ranges.

Woodwinds	*Written Range*	*Sounds*
Piccolo		Octave higher
Flute	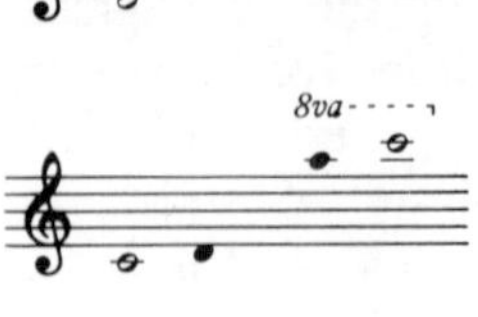	As written

Woodwinds (cont.)	*Written Range*	*Sounds*
Oboe		As written
English Horn		P5 lower
Clarinet		In E♭: M2 lower In A: m3 lower
Bass Clarinet		In treble clef: M9 lower In bass clef: M2 lower
Bassoon	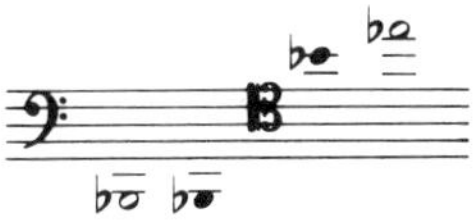	As written (uses bass and tenor clefs)
Contrabassoon		Octave lower

Brass	*Written Range*	*Sounds*
Horn		In F: P5 lower
Trumpet	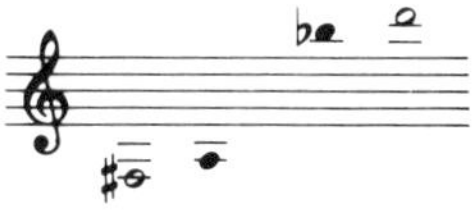	In B♭: M2 lower In C: as written In D: M2 higher

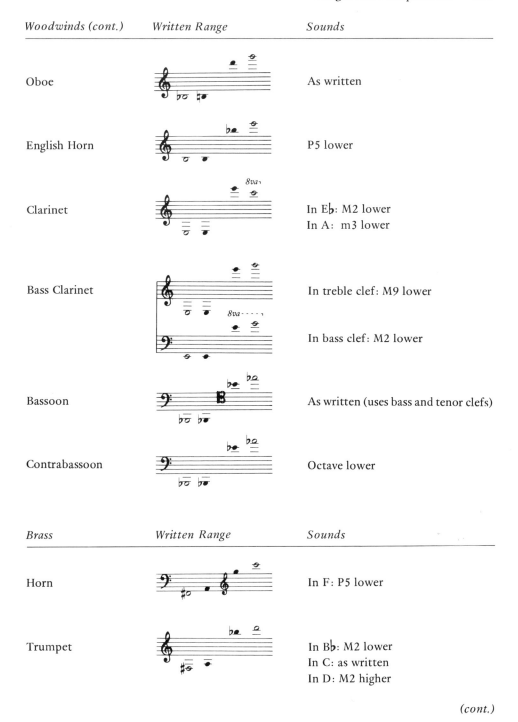

(cont.)

Brass (cont.)	*Written Range*	*Sounds*
Tenor Trombone	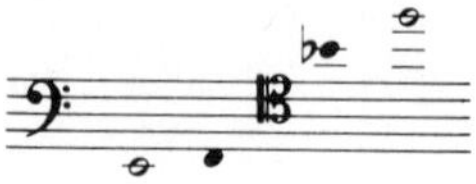	As written (uses bass and tenor clefs, occasionally alto)
Bass Trombone		As written
Tuba		As written

Percussion

Timpani, range from *F* to *f*, sound as written
Other nonpitched instruments
Xylophone, bells, celeste, harp, piano, etc., sound as written

Strings	*Written Range*	*Sounds*
Violin		As written
Viola		As written (uses alto and treble clefs)
Cello		As written (uses bass, tenor, and treble clefs)
Double Bass		Octave lower

Saxophones	*Written Range*	*Sounds*
Saxophone		B♭ soprano: M2 lower E♭ alto: M6 lower B♭ tenor: M9 lower E♭ baritone: octave plus M6 lower B♭ bass: 2 octaves plus M2 lower

Saxophones are not usually found in an orchestra. If they are notated in a score, they occur between the woodwinds and the brass (after contrabassoon and before horn).

Vocal Parts and Ranges (Normal)

Male Voices *Female Voices*

A practical rule of thumb for choral writing is to subtract one step from each end of the permissible range.

EXERCISES

1. Transpose the following melody for (a) B♭ trumpet, (b) F horn, and (c) E♭ saxophone (alto). Use appropriate key signatures for the trumpet and saxophone, but write in all needed accidentals for the French horn. Space for your answers is provided on page 164.

Chopin

Trumpet in B♭

a)

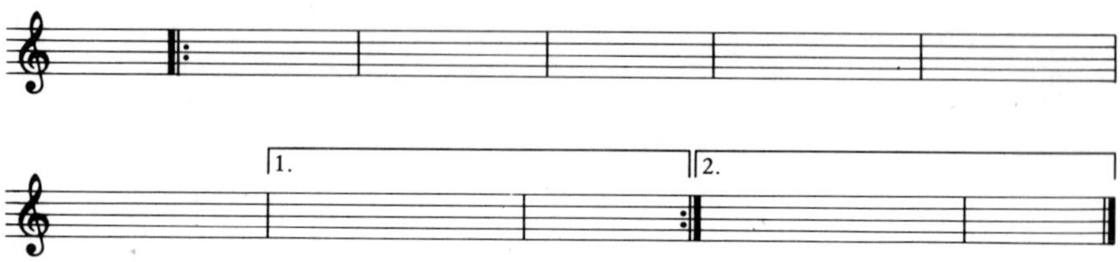

Horn in F

b)

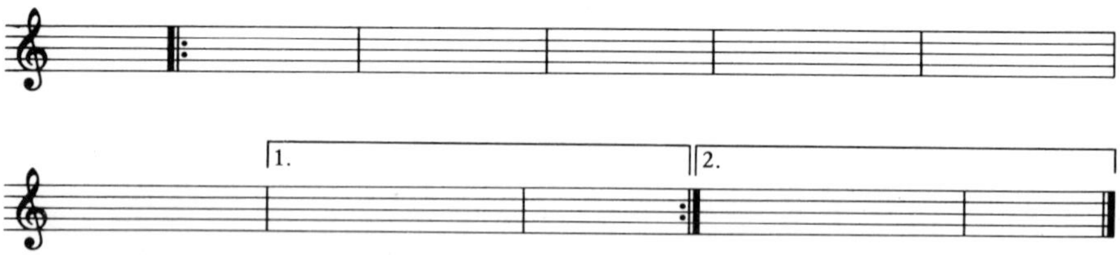

Alto Saxophone in E♭

c)

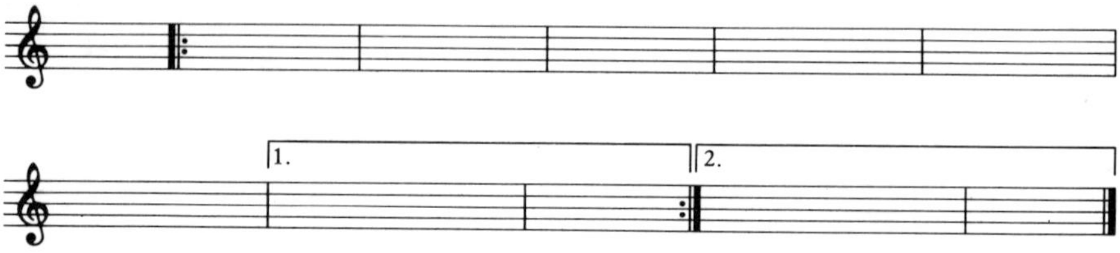

2. Transcribe the following passage for oboe, clarinet in B♭, French horn in F, trombone, and string bass. Write in open score. Each part should appear on the score exactly as it will in the player's part. If the appropriate players are available, copy the parts and perform your arrangement.

J. S. Bach, Passacaglia in C minor for Organ

(cont.)

Transcription

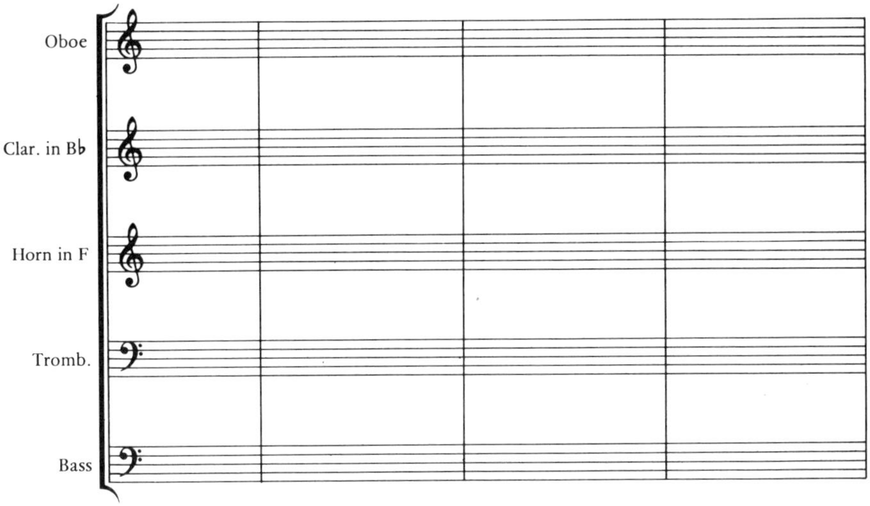

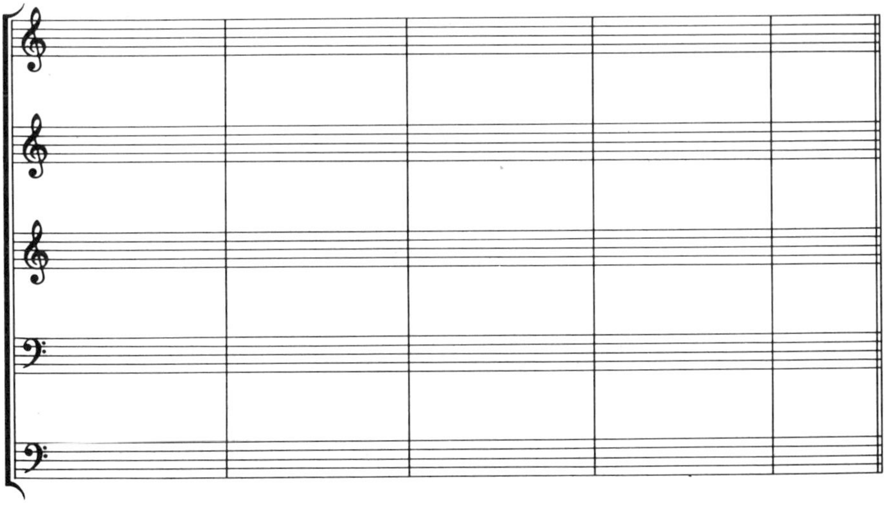

Mendelssohn, "Wachet auf, ruft uns die Stimme"

3. Locate one example of each of the following items in the musical example by Mendelssohn on page 166. Write the letter of each item at the precise point of its occurrence in the piece.

   a) root of triad doubled

   b) contrary motion between outer voices

   c) leading tone resolved normally

   d) parallel motion between inner voices

   e) tonic doubled

   f) oblique motion

   g) close-position spacing

   h) doubling of the chord fifth in second-inversion triad

   i) open-spaced chord

   j) typical doubling in first-inversion triad

(optional)

4. Make a new setting of the first three phrases of the example given on page 166, retaining only the upper voice from the version by Mendelssohn. Label all harmonic functions and nonchord tones that occur in your setting; then evaluate your setting by checking your work against the summary of rules for voice leading given in the text. Write for soprano, alto, tenor, and bass. Use closed score.

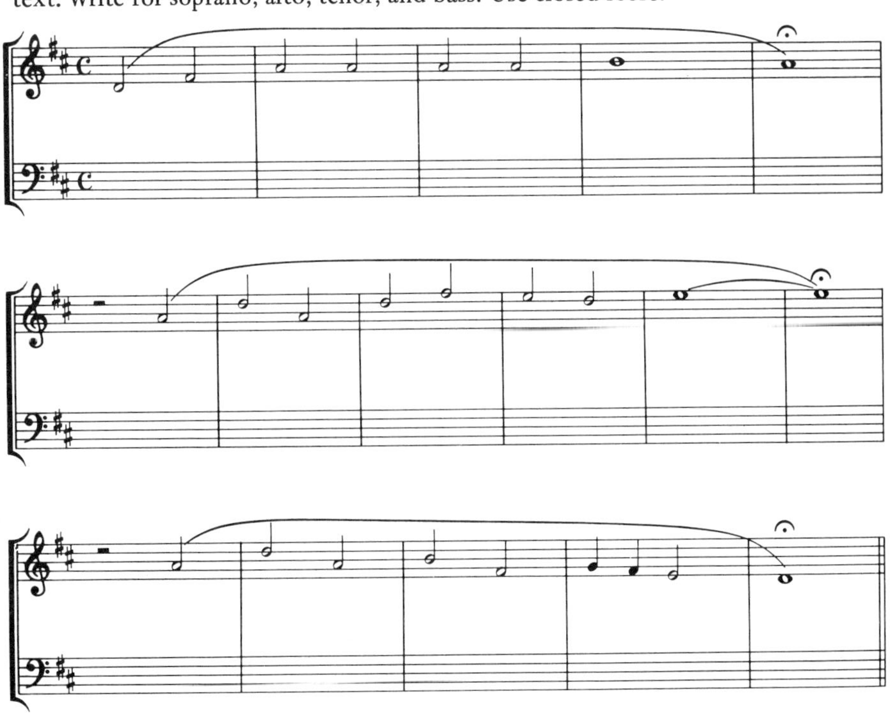

(optional)

5. Make a setting of the following melody by Corelli for a string group made up of first and second violins, violas, cellos, and basses. Use the chords indicated under the melodic line and apply the principles of chord connection discussed in the text. It is quite permissible in settings such as this for the cellos and basses to play in octaves (i.e., for the bass part to be identical with the cello part but notated one octave lower). However, avoid other parallelisms, such as fifths.

   No chords are indicated for the closing eight measures of the setting. Choose chords on the basis of the style and materials used in the opening section and on the basis of your acquaintance with normal harmonic progressions. It is suggested that you work out the setting in closed score before committing it to open score. Space is provided on pages 169–171 for your final version.

Corelli

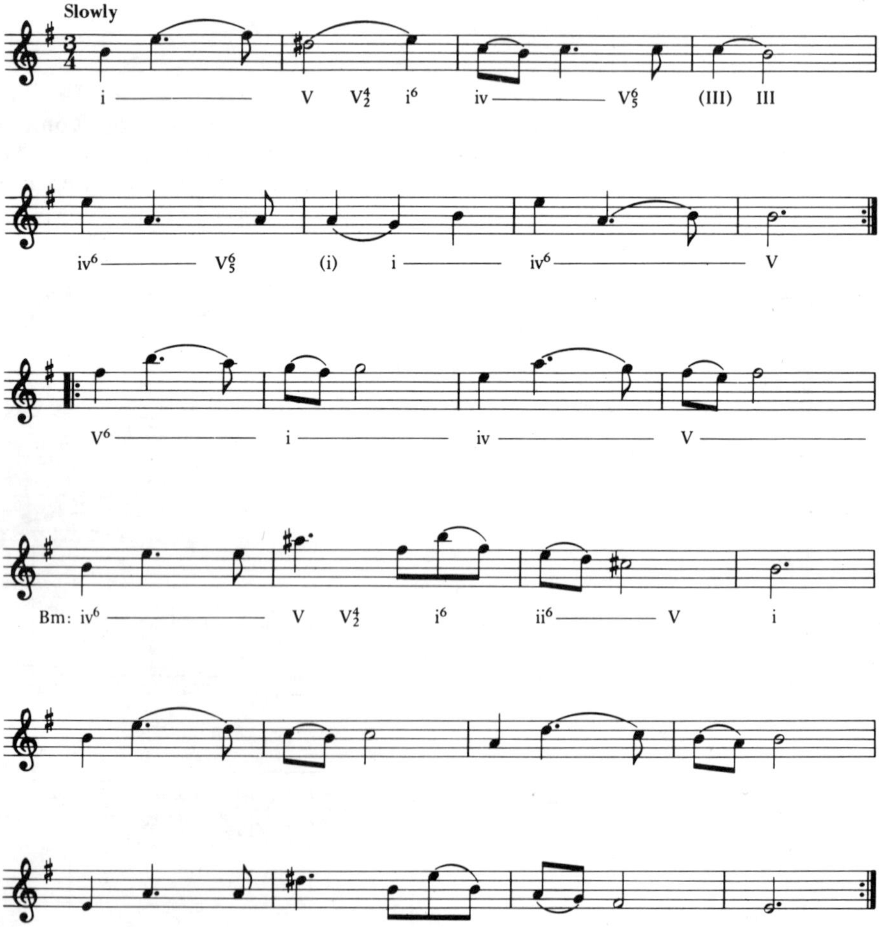

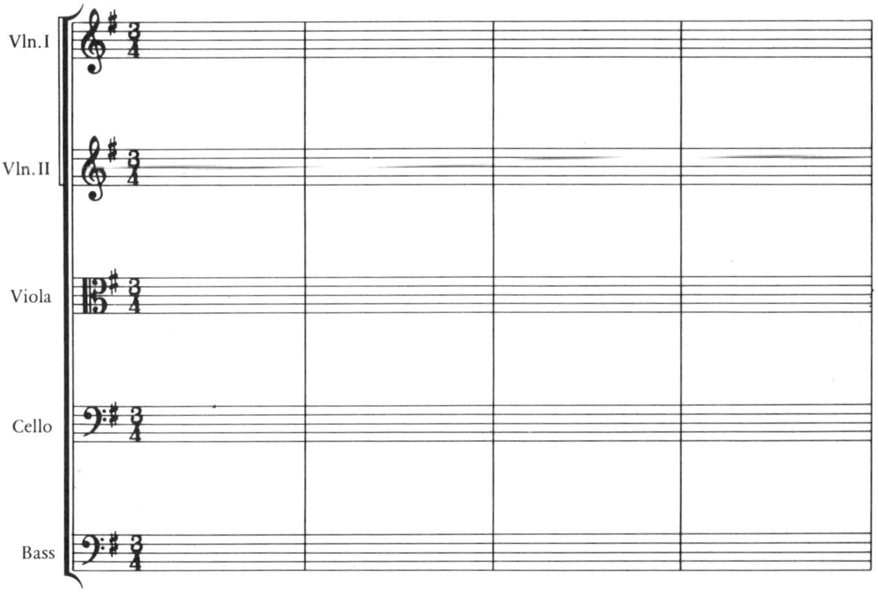

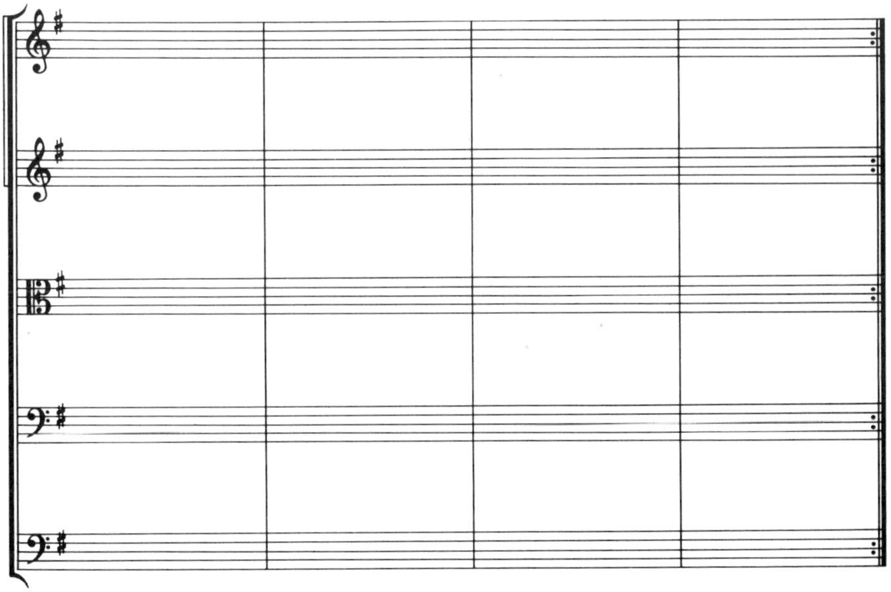

(cont.)

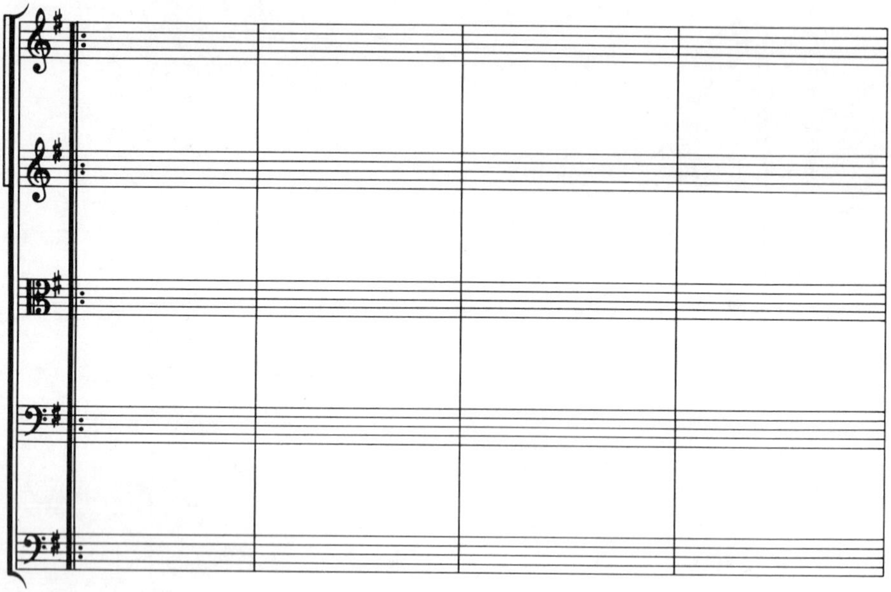

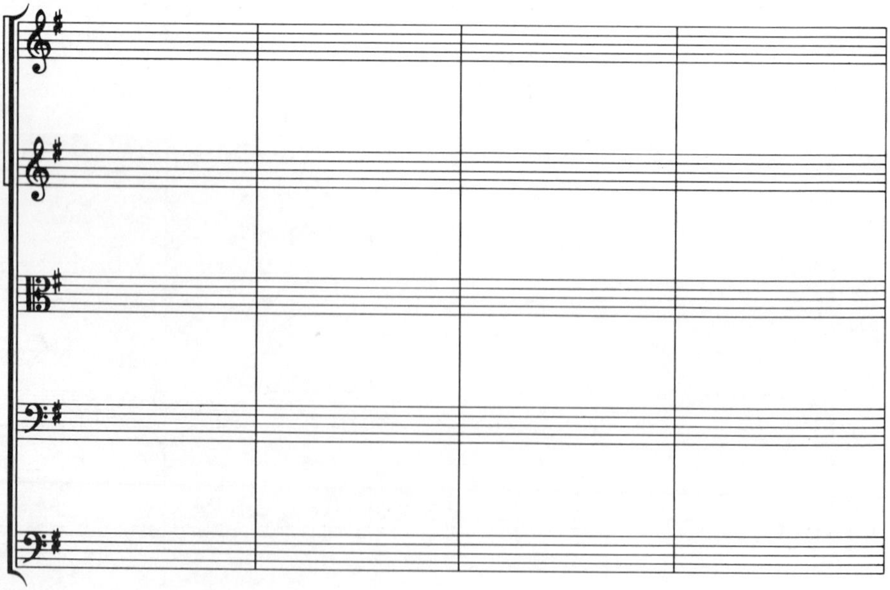

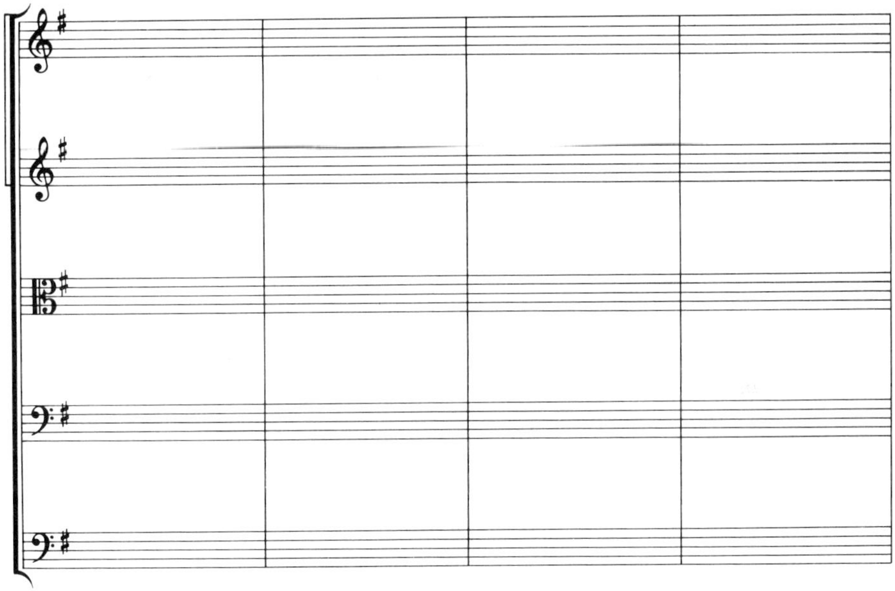

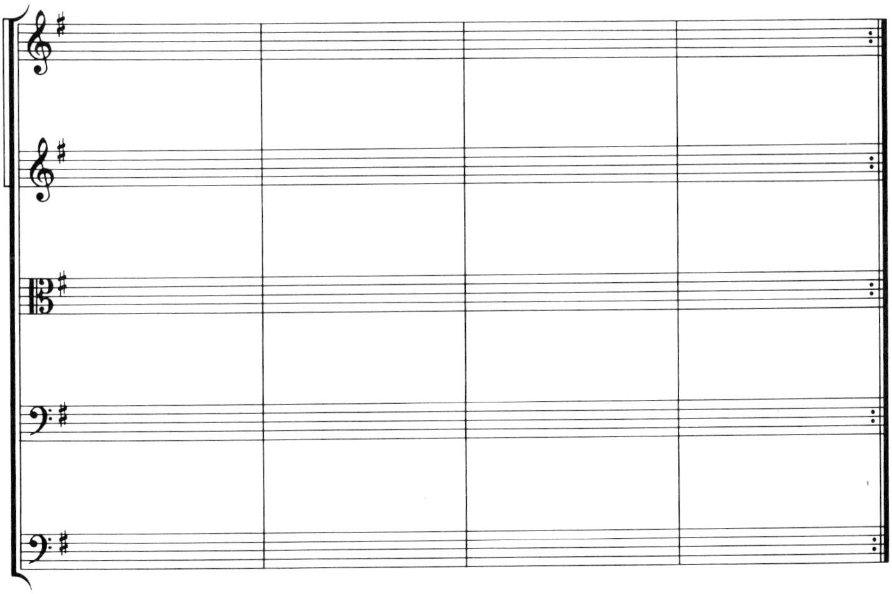

(optional)

6. Study the short passage by Handel that appears below. Continue each of the four alternative settings of the melody that have been started. Each setting represents a particular solution to the problem of casting the melody and its supporting harmonic progressions in an appropriate texture, contrapuntal or homophonic.

Handel

a)

b)

c)

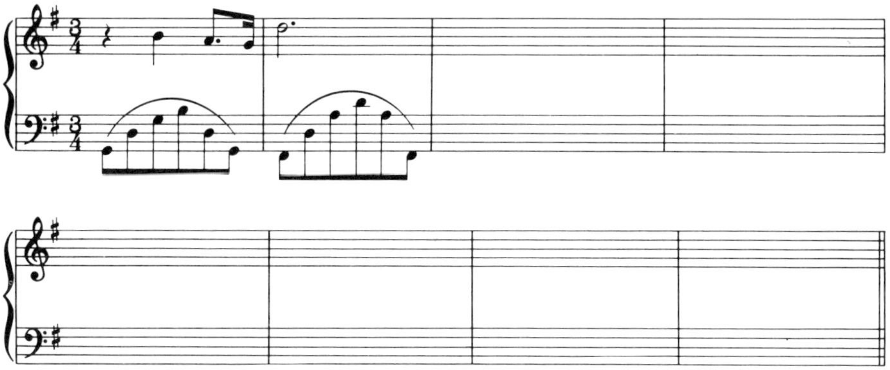

d)

Chapter 9

MUSICAL FORM: GENERAL CONSIDERATIONS

Form means shape or design. We can readily discern design in architecture, painting, or in the impression of a visible or tactile object; visual design is a product of color, line, and spatial distances. Musical shape, however, is more difficult to grasp, since it is perceived aurally through a series of successive musical events. Form in music is most easily understood as a product of musical *time.* That is to say, proportion and structure in music become "visible" to us through an awareness of the temporal spans or lengths in time of the successive events that constitute a composition. We do not actually clock each of the events (pitches, rhythms, phrases, chord patterns, etc.) heard in a piece of music and mentally record their durations in seconds or minutes. What we do is picture a composition's shape as a succession of uniquely related tonal and rhythmic patterns that proceed logically in time and that have a beginning and an end.

Musical form occurs within both large and small scopes. Let us consider a small-scale form, a recorded performance of a hit song by a rock group. Such a performance might consist of an instrumental beginning or introduction, a solo rendition of the song, a vocal ensemble treatment of the song, and an instrumental close. The result would be a four-section composition whose major events might have the following durations:

Instrumental introduction	45 seconds
Vocal solo	60 seconds
Vocal ensemble	60 seconds
Instrumental close	15 seconds

Such an arrangement clearly contains two elements of form that are basic to virtually any artistic design: *unity* (similarity of events) and *variety* (contrast of events). In this instance, unity is achieved by the use of the same medium or instrumental texture for both the introduction and the close of the arrangement. Variety results from the inclusion of both instrumental and vocal presentations of the material; in addition, such a composition would probably include a great deal of variety in its details—melodic contour, tonality, harmony, rhythm, and so on.

Virtually every detail or feature of a musical composition affects its form. In studying musical form, one usually begins with small units of a composition and then proceeds to progressively larger segments in the same way that one studies a prose work in terms of its phrases, sentences, paragraphs, and chapters. In doing so, it is important to keep in mind that a convincing musical design, large or small, is always a product of the interaction of broad outlines and significant details.

PHRASES

The basic unit of musical design is the *phrase,* a unit of melodic (or harmonic) materials constituting a more or less continuous thread of activity, terminated by a slackening or complete cessation of activity. The point of slackening or

Example 9-1

a) Beethoven, *Sonata in C minor for Piano,* Op. 13, 3rd movement

b) Vivaldi, *Concerto in D minor for Violin, Strings, and Cembalo*

(cont.)

Example 9-1 (continued)

c) MacDonald-Hanley, *Back Home in Indiana*

d) Schoenberg, *Pierrot Lunaire,* Op. 21, No. 21

cessation of activity is known as a *cadence.* There are no limitations on the length of a phrase. However, most traditional music is fashioned from phrases consisting of between two and eight successive measures, the number of measures depending on tempo, meter, and the prevailing beat divisions. Present-day music reveals much greater variety in phrase structure and phrase length. Example 9-1 contains four phrases typical of phrase construction in traditional music. Each passage unfolds an essentially continuous thread of activity which is clearly terminated by a cadence; the cadences are marked by both rhythmic relaxation and tonal stability in the form of a clear delineation of the prevailing tonality.

The harmonic effect of the cadence helps define the tonal meaning of the phrase. We studied cadences in Chapter 6 and noted three main types: terminal, progressive, and transient terminal. In Example 9-2 the same melodic phrase is given three different tonal "meanings" by the use of three different cadences. Sing the melody and play (or have someone else play) the accompanying chords. Example 9-2(a) has a terminal cadence; such a cadence

Example 9-2

a) Terminal cadence

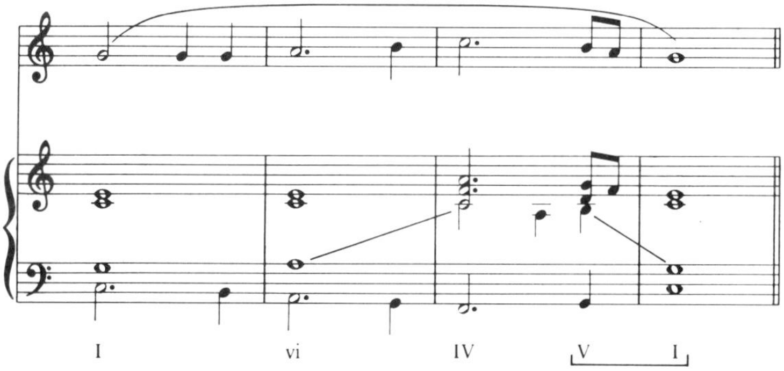

b) Progressive cadence

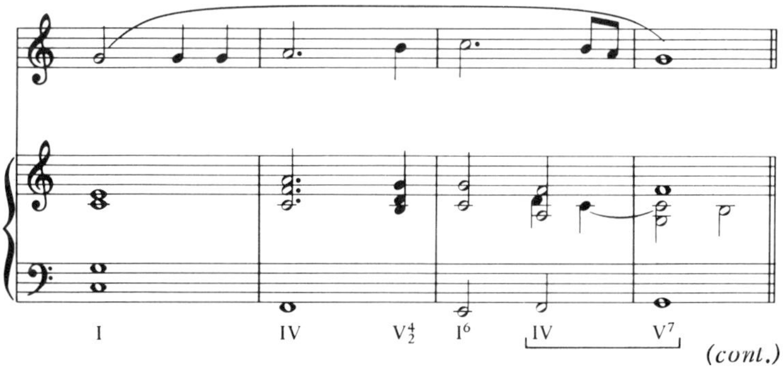

(cont.)

Example 9-2 (continued)

c) Transient terminal cadence

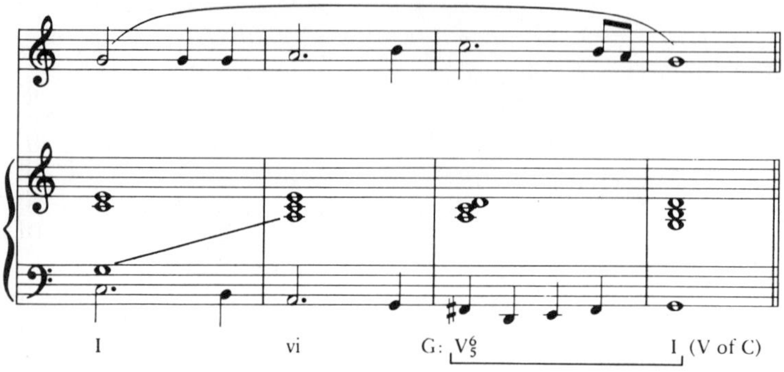

sounds "psychologically complete." Example 9-2(b) illustrates a progressive close; a phrase ending with such a cadence is somewhat analogous to a question in that it calls for an answering statement. In Example 9-2(c), which has a transient terminal ending, there is clearly a temporary shift of tonal focus.

Of considerable importance to cadence and phrase delineation is the rhythmic placement of the cadence tone (or chord). Compare the rhythms of the cadence notes in measure 7 of Example 9-3(a), (b), and (c).

The convincing terminal effect of Example 9-3(a) (which shows the rhythm that Mozart actually wrote) can be attributed to the placement of the cadential note f^1 (tonic) on the strong beat of the last measure. Note also that the arrival of the cadence pitch coincides with the beginning of a strong *measure*. In this composition the measures are clearly grouped in pairs, each pair having a strong-weak pattern.

Example 9-3 (Mozart)

a)

b)

c)

The rhythm of Example 9-3(b) produces a rather hesitant, uncertain close. This is the result of the arrival of the cadence note on a weak beat. Rhythmically weak cadences are sometimes called *feminine endings;* accented (strong) cadences are often called *masculine.* (These expressions seem rather inappropriate to many of today's musicians.)

Example 9-3(c) has the least convincing of the three rhythms. Besides occurring on a weak beat, the cadential note also occurs in a weak measure, disrupting the recurrent accents of the pairs of measures and thus weakening the accentual basis of the broader temporal units of the composition.

Clearly the impact of a cadence is related to the duration and metrical placement of the cadence note. A study of the cadences in a piece of any length will reveal much variety in both rhythmic and tonal treatments of cadence notes. The rhythmic placement and relative duration of the cadence note (or chord) often reflect the position of the cadence in the form of the composition; thus final or sectional endings are often of greater rhythmic strength than endings of phrases or shorter formal units. Locate and compare the treatment of the cadences in the passages shown in Example 9-4.

Example 9-4

a) Handel, *Rinaldo*

(cont.)

Example 9-4 (continued)

b) Ravel, *Pavane for a Dead Princess*

Cadence is not the only way of marking phrases for the listener. Quite commonly the beginning of a new phrase is signalled by the repetition of material just stated, as in Example 9-5. Sometimes only the rhythm is repeated to mark the beginning of a new phrase, as in Example 9-6. Note in the latter example that the pitches of the second phrase and the resulting contour differ markedly from those heard in the first phrase.

Example 9-5

Beethoven

Example 9-6

Bartók (Hungarian Folk Song)

Example 9-7(a) illustrates the use of contrast in both rhythm and melodic contour at the beginning of a new phrase. At measure 5 a new phrase begins which contrasts clearly with the phrase of measures 1 through 4. Note the characteristic rhythm () of the second phrase and the continual rise in the melodic contour.

The effect of cadence is minimized in Example 9-7(a). The phrase markings are dovetailed, suggesting that the cadential note of the first phrase *(a*[1]*)* is also the initial note of the succeeding phrase. The compositional technique of creating such a phrase juncture is called *elision.* It is the element of *change,* or contrast, that produces the phrase division in this passage, rather than rhythmic pause. In Example 9-7(b) rhythmic pause is introduced to create a more decisive cadence at the end of measure 4; the resulting loss of rhythmic continuity is quite apparent.

Example 9-7 (J. S. Bach)

a)

b)

MOTIVES

Many phrases are constructed from smaller units called motives. A *motive* is a short and distinctive musical pattern used as a formal or structural device. Most frequently it is distinctive in its rhythm and can thereby easily be recognized whenever it appears in a composition.

Study Example 9-8. The rhythm  constantly recurs in this passage, although the pitches which accompany this rhythm are continually changing. This technique of motivic development is basic to a great deal of musical composition; it combines the processes of repetition (of rhythm in this example) and change (of pitch here).

The passage reproduced in Example 9-8 has a highly unified organization. As can be seen at a glance, this unity stems from almost constant reiteration of the figure  . Heard in conjunction with a reiterated pitch sequence:

and given a characteristic articulation, the figure takes on significance as a melodic fragment. Melodies made up of repetitions (either strict or varied) of such motives are often called *motivic melodies.* In Example 9-8 the repetitions of the motive are punctuated with periodic harmonic cadences.

As has been said, motives are usually of rhythmic interest primarily, though frequently contour is also an important feature. A motive nearly always reveals some memorable characteristic, some easily recalled component

Example 9-8

Mozart, *Symphony No. 40 in G minor,* K. 550, 1st movement

Example 9-9 Several motives from music literature

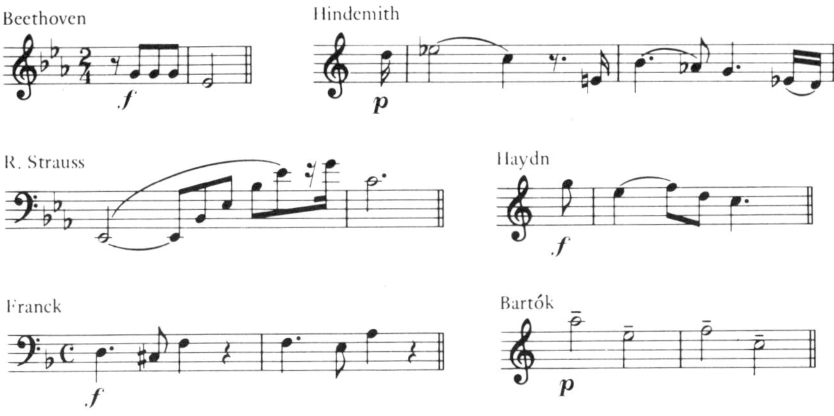

such as a particular rhythmic device, a particular sequence of pitches, or some type of performance articulation such as the slurred pair of notes followed by an unslurred note in Example 9-8. Each of the motives in Example 9-9 reveals some special feature that marks it for recollection.

Example 9-10 is another example of a motivic melody. The passage is evolved primarily from the opening figure:

This figure recurs in all but a few measures of the example. Despite the highly repetitive rhythm of the piece, variety is achieved by means of changes in pitch configuration, contour, and implied harmonic pattern, along with changes of register, dynamics, and articulation (legato, staccato, slurred notes, etc.). The treatment of cadences in this piece differs, however, from that in Example 9-8. The phrase structure is quite difficult to discern at first glance. The passage seems to show little evidence of the periodic phrase construction and cadencing that we are accustomed to; it appears rather to be composed of an almost unbroken, continuously spun-out rhythm. However, if one listens attentively to the melody, one will find that cadence points are suggested in measures 2, 4, and 10 through both rhythmic slackening and implicit harmonic patterns (mainly V-I).

The resources at a composer's disposal for varying the treatment of a motive throughout a composition are virtually endless. Repetition, variation, and contrast are organizing principles which are present in nearly all music. *Repetition* is the immediate reiteration of a musical utterance, long or short. *Variation* combines repetition with change in such a way that the reiteration of a pattern is modified. *Contrast* denotes the introduction of new materials or radically different treatments of previously used materials. It is important

Example 9-10

J. S. Bach, *Suite No. 1 for Unaccompanied Cello,* 1st movement

to note that there are no clearly defined boundaries between variation and contrast; variation, indeed, is based on the incorporation of contrasting elements into familiar materials.

A careful study of Example 9-11 will give some idea of how the processes of variation and contrast can be applied to a motive. Example 9-11(a) is the basic motive. Example 9-11(b) is a repetition of the rhythm of this motive with different pitches. Example 9-11(c) retains the contour and succession of intervals, as well as the rhythm, of the original motive, but begins one step higher; this is an example of *sequential repetition.* Note that the dynamic level of Example 9-11(c) contrasts with that of the original motive. Example 9-11(d) contrasts with the original motive in both dynamics and articulation, but it is still recognizable as a variant of Example 9-11(a) because of similarities in rhythm and contour. Example 9-11(e) is essentially a contrasted pattern, even though it is simply the reversal (retrograde) of the original motive. Both its profile and its rhythmic arrangement differ markedly from those of

Example 9-11 (Mozart)

Example 9-11(a), despite the retention of many common elements such as key, beat division, and dynamic level.

Example 9-11 merely scratches the surface of the subject of motive variation. This subject will attract our attention again when we study larger units of musical form. For the moment, Example 9-12 will serve to illustrate some additional techniques of variation. For the sake of simplicity one initial motive (labeled "Original motive") is used as the basis for the entire group of devices.

Example 9-12 Various techniques for elaborating a motive

(cont.)

Example 9-12 (continued)

Ornamental variation (embellishment)

Mutation

Sequence at the second above

PHRASE RELATIONS

As was said earlier, phrases consisting of two to eight measures occur most commonly in traditional music. Phrases consisting of an *even* number of measures—two, four, six, or eight—predominate; in fact, the deployment of motives, phrases, and other structural segments by twos characterizes the compositional layout, with its concomitant symmetry, of much traditional music.

Study Example 9-13, noting the pairing of successively larger formal segments. Each phrase consists of two measures. The first two phrases combine to produce a larger unit, as do the third and fourth phrases. These four phrases constitute the first half of the passage, eight measures. If we look at the second half. Thus the entire passage can be viewed as having two primary divisions, each of which can be broken into two secondary divisions, each of which can be further divided, and so on.

The term *period* could be applied to each eight-measure segment of this passage. This term does not have a precise meaning applicable to all compositions. It signifies a unit of structure larger than the phrase, and one which has a strong sense of closure. One will find that simple dance music, such as the Mazurka reproduced here, is often divisible into periods of eight measures each.

Note how the structure of Example 9-13 is *unfolded* as one listens to the passage. Hearing measures 1 through 4, the listener does not necessarily know that these two phrases constitute the first half of a formal segment. It is only when he reaches measure 8 that the formal significance of the first four measures becomes clear. Similarly, only at measure 16 does the pairing of the periods become evident. And it is only when the listener experiences the silence after the last chord that he knows there will be no further pairings, that the form is complete.

A study of Example 9-13 shows that phrase relations are established, on the whole, by the same processes that determine relationships between motives: repetition, variation, and contrast. The first six measures of each of the two periods are virtually identical; the periods differ only in their final cadence, which is progressive in the first period, terminal in the second.

Example 9-13

Chopin, *Mazurka,* Op. 68, No. 3

This phrase relationship is called *parallel structure.* There is also an element of contrast within each period. The first half of each period consists of two very distinct segments, the boundary being marked by a rhythmic pause in the second measure. This pause is missing in the second half; the result is a more smoothly flowing rhythm which binds the phrases more closely. Note also that the melodic contour of measures 7 and 15 differs from that of measures 3 and 11; the fact that the contour of measures 7 and 15 is a slightly varied repetition of the contour of the immediately preceding measures helps further to bind the second half of each period into a closely knit unit, and also adds an element of variety to the melody.

Example 9-14 illustrates a simple but effectively used phrase relationship, a statement followed by a varied repetition. Note the way in which rhythmic elaboration is used to vary the second phrase, which clearly retains the essential contour and harmony of the first. As in the previous example, the cadence of the first half of the excerpt is progressive, while the second half has a terminal cadence.

Example 9-14

Mozart, *Rondo in A minor for Piano*

Example 9-15

Wolf, *Mörike Lieder*

Example 9-15 reveals the continuation in the second phrase of a rhythm derived from the opening measure of the first phrase. The second phrase is not a variant of the first; it contrasts with the first in pitch contour, harmonic progression, length, and its use of immediate rhythmic repetition in the voice. Nonetheless its relation to the first phrase is derivative, rather than entirely contrasting. A passage such as this is representative of countless examples of phrase pairs which reveal contrast in one or more aspects while at the same time retaining a clearly unifying or common element. In more cases than not, the unifying element is rhythmic.

Example 9-16 contains two phrases which are essentially unlike, that is, contrasted. Note as many contrasting factors as you can.

Example 9-16

Mozart, *Piano Concerto in E♭*, K. 482, 2nd movement

A special type of phrase relationship is established by the use of *sequence,* which is one of the most common processes for combining repetition and change. Sequence involves the immediate repetition of a motive or phrase beginning on a different note, or pitch level. When a melodic (or harmonic) pattern is restated so that the content is unchanged but its beginning point is shifted up or down, as in Example 9-17, sequence occurs. The melodic motive in the violin in measure 1 is sequentially repeated in measures 2 and 3. Note that the repetitions are accompanied by sequential activity in the lower voices as well—the implied harmonies are also sequential.

Example 9-17

Corelli, *Violin Sonata,* Op. 5, No. 9, 2nd movement

Example 9-18

Wagner, *Tristan und Isolde*

Sequence is frequently used as the basis for relating successive phrases; indeed, throughout most of the history of musical composition, sequence has been one of the most essential repetitive devices in phrase construction. Example 9-18 shows a well-known nineteenth-century use of sequence.

Although, as we have said, phrases usually consist of an even number of measures, phrases consisting of five or seven measures, or some other odd number, are occasionally used to good effect. The second phrase of Example 9-15 consisted of five measures. Note also Example 9-19, which has five measures divided into two unequal segments, three measures followed by two. By leaving out measure 2 or measure 3 the example could be converted into a symmetrical but less interesting structure.

A phrase consisting of an uneven number of measures is often the result of *phrase extension.* Example 9-20 shows a simple example of phrase extension. By simply prolonging the cadence note of the second phrase by one

Example 9-19

Haydn, *String Quartet in F minor,* Op. 20, 1st movement

Example 9-20

Schubert, *Die Schöne Müllerin*

Example 9-21

Mozart, *Symphony No. 35 in D (Haffner),* 3rd movement

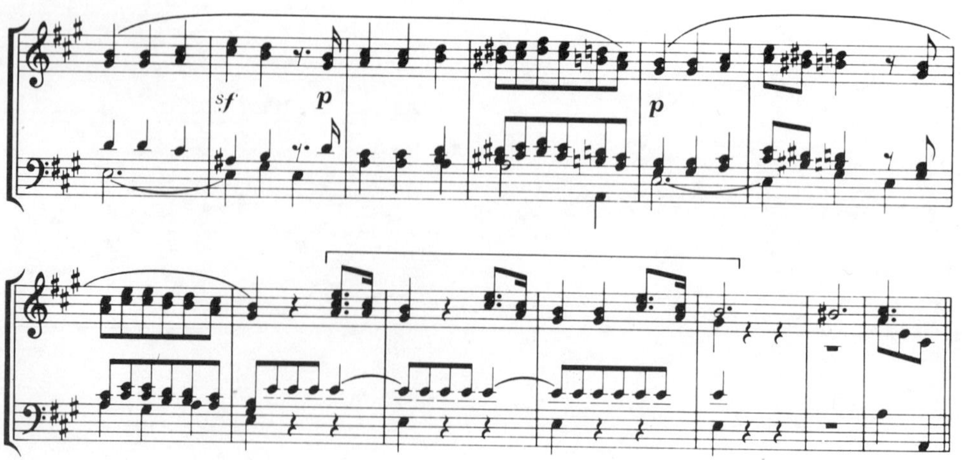

quarter note, the composer has extended this phrase to five measures; the result is an asymmetrical period, one that is composed of two phrases of dissimilar length.

Example 9-21 shows a different kind of phrase extension which is quite common in music of the eighteenth and early nineteenth centuries. This type of extension does not usually produce a phrase with an uneven number of measures; rather it delays the expected termination of the phrase as a means of producing formal variety and heightening interest. The second phrase of this example, which begins at measure 5, has a four-measure extension over a dominant pedal; the extension consists of repetitions of the motive introduced in measure 8.

It is clear that the means at the disposal of composers for treating and developing melodic materials and establishing relations among motives, phrases, and larger sections of a composition are almost inexhaustible. These "means" include various technical procedures for reshaping, extending, varying, and in other ways modifying melodic materials to create a unified composition based on the principles of repetition and contrast. The sample of such procedures given in this chapter is by no means complete.

EXERCISES

1. Sing the following example of thirteenth-century music and answer *from memory* (without recourse to the example) the brief questions about the song's structure.

Moniot d'Arras

a) Is repetition a factor in the piece's phrase organization?

b) Use lower-case letters to make a simple representation of the form of the song.

c) Name the *tonic* and the *meter-type* used in this song.

d) What is the general range of the song?

e) Name two scale degrees which serve as cadential points in the piece.

2. Familiarize yourself with the following melody; then answer the questions and complete the analytical problems.

Mozart

a) Mark all phrases in the melody.

b) Place a check mark over the cadential note of each phrase. Under each cadential note write the roman numeral that denotes the harmonic function implied by that note, as you interpret it.

c) Describe the formal relation of measures 9-16 to measures 1-8.

d) Where does phrase extension occur in this example?

e) Does this melody reveal phrase segments? If so, how long are they, in general?

3. Familiarize yourself with the following melody; then answer the questions and complete the analytical problems.

Vivaldi

(cont.)

a) Place a check mark after each of the following items that occurs in the melody by Vivaldi.

Sequence
Motivic phrase construction
Sharply contrasted phrases
Rhythmic repetition
Triad outlining
Modulation
Syncopation
Progressive cadence

b) Indicate on the music the keys (two) that shape the tonal organization of the melody.

c) Use roman numerals to indicate the implied harmonic changes of each measure. Assume that there is one chord per measure.

4. Familiarize yourself with the example by Schoenberg; then answer the questions.

Schoenberg, Concerto for Piano, Op. 42

a) How long are the melody's phrases?

b) What type of scale could be used to reflect the pitch materials of the melody?

c) What wide interval, used in ascending form, recurs and helps to unify the melody?

d) Cite three factors other than pitch that help to create unity in the passage. Write a brief essay, giving specific examples by measure number.

e) What factors help to create impressions of pitch focal points in the example? What pitches seem most to govern the tonal organization of the piece?

(optional)

5. Using the melodic phrase given below as a point of departure, invent various melodic materials as directed.

a) Invent a second phrase based on the rhythm of the above phrase but employing a different arrangement of pitches.

b) Rewrite the phrase given above so as to produce a progressive cadence.

c) Write a sequence based on the motive found in the first measure of the given phrase.

d) Write a variation in D minor based on the contour and rhythm of the given phrase.

e) Write the melodic inversion of measure 1 of the given phrase.

f) Illustrate an *extension* of the phrase given above.

(optional)

6. Show the susceptibility of the phrase given at the beginning of Exercise 5 to different harmonic settings by inventing three different harmonizations of it in D major. Write for the piano or organ.

a)

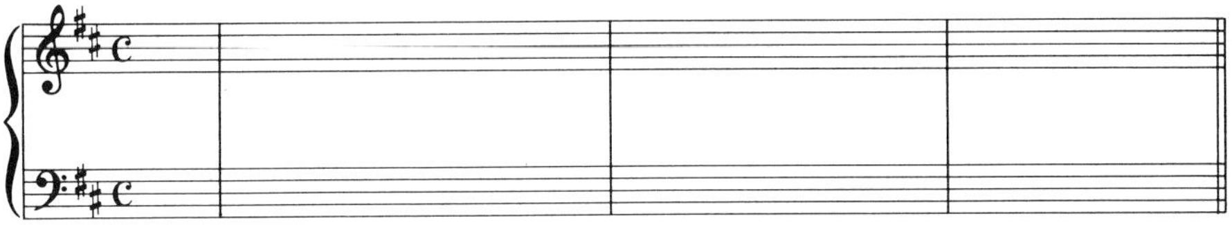

b)

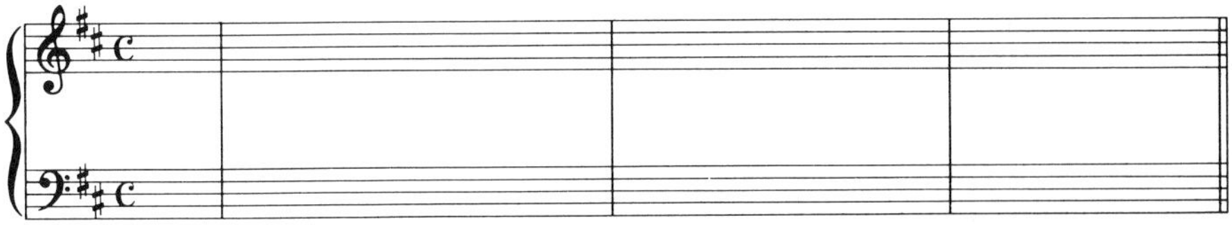

c)

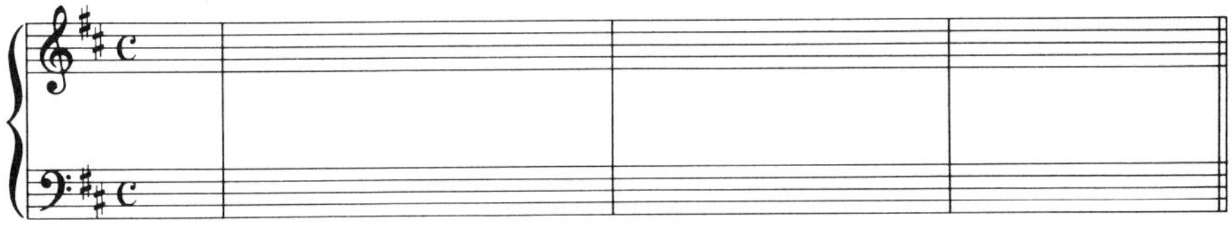

Chapter 10

TWO- AND THREE-PART FORMS; RONDO

Musical structure exists on three planes. One of these planes comprises the overall sweep of the totality of a composition from beginning to end. Another structural plane is that on which details of style—melodic figures, chord patterns, spacing, and the like—contribute to the design of a composition. Between these two planes lies the subject matter of this and the following three chapters. In these chapters we shall be concerned with the *main sectional divisions* of which a composition is comprised. Such divisions are a function of numerous interacting factors such as melody, tonality, texture, harmony, and rhythm. The present chapter will include a discussion of some of the most commonly encountered form types and of some of the factors which influence the various sectional arrangements of which such form types are made.

Sections vary in length, just as compositions do. For example, a piece composed of 18 measures might consist of two main parts, each clearly marked by a strong cadence; the two sections might be comprised of ten followed by eight measures of music. By the same token, a symphonic movement lasting eight minutes might similarly consist of two main sections, each terminated by a strong cadence, each section consisting of 70 measures or so. The point is that sectionalization is a relative factor and one that must be viewed in the light of the entire composition first, of details second.

The names of the various form types associated with traditional music represent general descriptions of the sectional divisions of a piece. These sections may in turn be subdivided to reveal subsections, periods, phrases, motives, etc. Although it is not really possible to treat large-scale sections and formal details as mutually exclusive, it is to the former primarily that we turn our attention here.

In this chapter we shall deal with *binary* form (two-part form), *ternary* form (three-part form), and *rondo* form. It should be understood that such terms are to be used flexibly. There is not always a clear boundary line between binary form and ternary form or between ternary form and rondo form; consequently there is no sense in trying to apply these terms in an unbending fashion to all musical compositions. There are few works of any significance that fail to lend themselves to more than one set of descriptive terms or to more than one formal interpretation. The recognition that one composition may be interpreted differently, but with equally cogent musical meaning, by two people is fundamental to an enlightened perception of art. The understanding that this condition exists is as basic to musical art as it is unscientific. Were it not so, music would be a dull proposition at best.

TWO-PART FORM

Compositions consisting of two main sections are usually called *binary,* or bipartite, which means simply "two-sectioned." Composers of the seventeenth and eighteenth centuries in particular made considerable use of binary formal schemes; see Example 10-1.

This piece, called a *sarabande,* is one of a unified group of pieces performed in succession; the entire group is called a *suite.* Suites consist of four (or more) somewhat stylized movements fashioned from well-known dance rhythms of the sixteenth and seventeenth centuries.*

Two factors in particular delineate the two-part design of this sarabande: first, the division of the piece into two four-measure units (periods) by means of a terminal cadence in G major in measure 4; second, the textural change—the use of only one voice—that signals the beginning of the second section. Note that the second part of this piece, which is a kind of answering state-

Example 10-1

Froberger, *Suite in E minor for Harpsichord,* 3rd movement

*This statement applies mainly to suites written during the eighteenth century by composers such as Bach, Buxtehude, and Handel. See Chapter 13 for a discussion of the dance suite as a multimovement form.

ment to the first, employs materials already introduced in the first. Note also the rhythmic figure (♩ ♩ ♩ ♩. ♪♩) common to both sections. The second part arises logically from the first and could be considered as a further continuation of the music in the first part. It is also important to note that both sections are intended to be repeated in performance. Such repetition, a common feature of the dance forms, further helps to impress the piece's binary division on the listener.

The first section of the sarabande closes with a transient terminal cadence in G major, the relative major of the movement's main key of E minor. The second section reinstates the key of E minor with a terminal cadence. This tonal sectionalization is characteristic of binary forms. Usually the main key is established at the beginning of a piece. Then there is a digression to a closely related key such as the dominant or the relative major or minor, this key being emphasized cadentially at the close of the first section. This digression is followed by a return to the main key during the second section of the piece. Thus the cycle

Main key ⟶ Digression ⟶ Return to main key

is embodied in the two main sections of many binary compositions. A schematic representation of the main sections and phrases of this sarabande might be made as follows:

Sections:	*A*	*A′*
Phrases:	*a, b*	*c, d*
Keys:	E minor, G	G, E minor

Capital letters denote main sections. (The use of *A* and *A′* reflects the similarity of the materials in the two sections; if the materials of the two sections were significantly different, we could label the sections *A* and *B*.) Lower-case letters denote phrases within sections.

Example 10-2

"The E-R-I-E" (Folk Song)

John A. and Alan Lomax

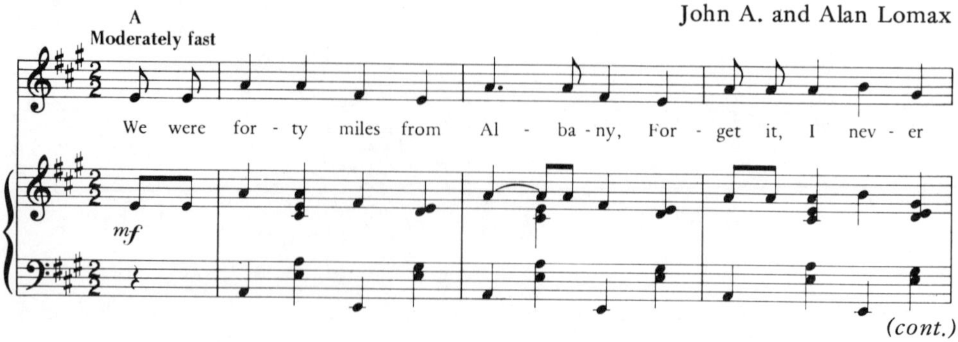
A
Moderately fast
We were for - ty miles from Al - ba - ny, For - get it, I nev - er
mf

(cont.)

Example 10-2 (continued)

Compare the form of the sarabande we have been discussing with that of the folk song reproduced in Example 10-2. The first section of the folk song closes with a terminal cadence (measure 8) on the tonic triad of A major. No tonal digression similar to that noted in Example 10-1 occurs here. A textural change in the form of accompanimental octaves marks the beginning of the second section, but both sections contain similar melodic materials and remain in the same key throughout.

This form could be described as either *AA′* or *AB.* If one regarded the similarity of materials in the two sections as a paramount feature of the piece, one could represent both sections by the same letter, *A,* affixing a prime to the second *A* to indicate that the second section is not simply a repetition of the first. If, on the other hand, one wished to emphasize the formal contrast and the difference in texture between verse and chorus, one could introduce a different letter, *B,* to denote the second section.

Examples 10-1 and 10-2 have in common a structural division into two main parts. In both examples the second part seems best described as a logical consequence of the first, rather than as a sharply contrasted counterstatement. The wide disparity of style between the two examples, and also the contrasting performance media, suggest that the basic two-part design crosses the boundaries between historical periods, styles, and performance media.

The term *rounded binary* is used to describe two-part forms containing a restatement, at the close of the second section, of thematic material stated in the opening section. The restatement, or brief return, sometimes restates the opening material in a slightly changed form, rather than literally. The effect, as the word "rounded" suggests, is to heighten the sense of closure by recalling material associated with the piece's beginning, thus producing a psychologically satisfying "rounding off" of the composition's form. This procedure is clearly evident in Example 10-3.

The interdependency of sections in this piece is due partly to the fact that the first section *(A)* closes on the dominant triad (V). The second section *(A′)* contributes to tonal continuity by starting out with the same V

Example 10-3

J. S. Bach, *Brandenburg Concerto No. 1 in F major,* Trio, 4th movement

(cont.)

Example 10-3 (continued)

chord and proceeding to reestablish the tonic before embarking on a modulation to G minor. The restatement of *A* (beginning at measure 21) is underscored by the fact that the beginning of the restatement coincides with the return to the tonic triad of D minor. It is through such essentially simple processes that tonality and chords are deployed to clarify formal arrangements and sectional divisions; frequently such clarification is achieved through the strategic placement of tonic and dominant triads. Study the movement and make a schematic representation of sections, phrases, and keys similar to that given for Example 10-1. Also pinpoint any motives that are common to both sections.

THREE-PART FORM

Three-part form contrasts sharply with two-part through (1) the use of a full-fledged restatement, or return, either literal or modified, of the first section of the piece, and (2) the inclusion of a contrasting section *(B)*. Three-part, or *ternary,* forms are commonly denoted by the letters *ABA*. Example 10-4 is a simple example of ternary form.

The form exhibited by this melody has been used in so many compositions, including many popular or folk songs, that one is tempted to conclude that composers have viewed it as an ideal form. In this brief example section *A* consists of a period made up of two identical phrases ending with a terminal cadence. The second section *(B)* begins with a change of register, exhibits a gradual descent in pitch from c^2 to $f\sharp^1$, introduces a change of rhythm from ♩. ♪♩ ♩ to ♩ ♩ ♩ ♩, and implies a new temporary tonic of *c*. The return of section *A* occurs at measure 13. The phrase that begins there is an exact restatement of the opening phrase. An outline of the form of the melody is given here:

Sections:	*A*	*B*	*A*
Phrases:	*a, a*	*b*	*a*
Keys:	G	C (implied)	G

The similarity of design between this song and the example of rounded binary (Example 10-3) is quite apparent. In some instances it is difficult, if not irrelevant, to distinguish between these two form types. Many musicians differentiate them on the basis of their tonal scheme, considering a cadence on the dominant at the close of section *A* to be the mark of a binary form. Note that Example 10-4 reveals a cadence on the tonic at the end of the first section. It is likely, however, that the complete, rather than partial, return of section *A* has a more pronounced psychological effect on the listener than the particular tonal scheme employed, since tonal schemes are a less readily discernible facet of form. To acknowledge the formal similarity of the two types seems of more consequence than to belabor a long-standing controversy.

Example 10-4

Traditional Melody

Example 10-5

Traditional Melody

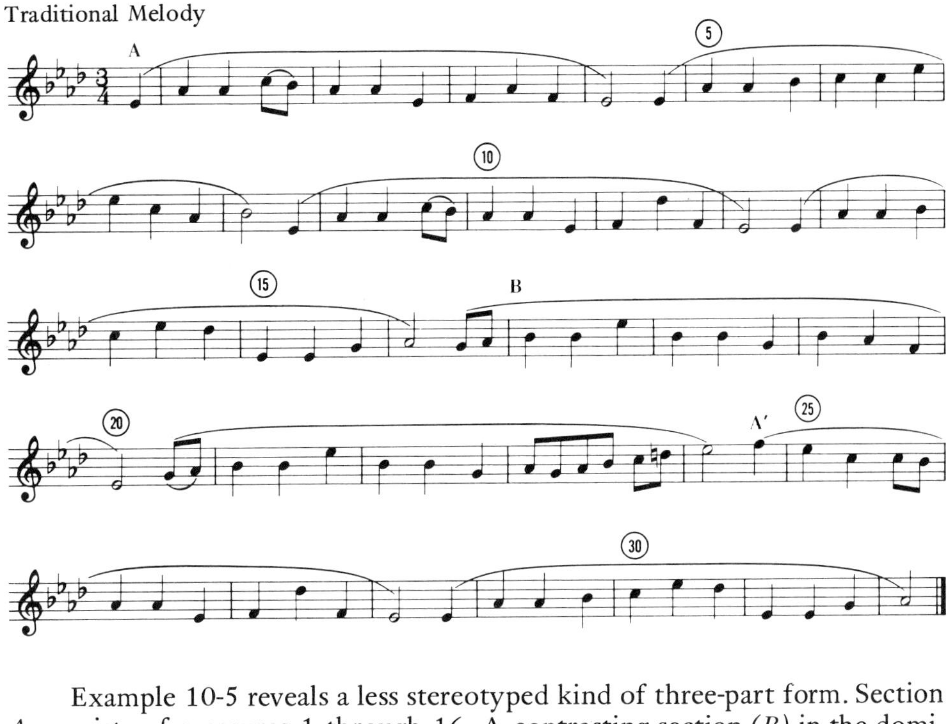

Example 10-5 reveals a less stereotyped kind of three-part form. Section *A* consists of measures 1 through 16. A contrasting section *(B)* in the dominant key of E occupies measures 17 through 24. The final section returns to the principal key of A♭, but the restatement of the melodic material is varied by means of changes of register and pitch. Note that there is also a small element of variation within the first section *(A).* This section consists of two periods arranged in the parallel structure discussed in Chapter 9. Note also that the second note in the third measure is different in the two periods. If we use the letters *a* and *b* to denote the two phrases which constitute each period, we could describe the phrase structure of section *A* as *aba′b′*, the primes indicating variation. Since section *B* consists of a new phrase and its varied restatement, we could indicate the phrase structure of this section as *cc′*. The final section *(A′)* could be denoted by *a″b′*, where *a″* is used to indicate that the final repetition of phrase *a* is somewhat different from either of its previous statements. The complete form could be represented as follows:

Sections:	*A*	*B*	*A′*
Phrases:	*a, b, a′, b′*	*c, c′*	*a″, b′*
Keys:	A♭	E♭	A♭

The variation in Example 10-5 is accomplished through changes in melodic organization and tonal scheme. *Texture,* however, is frequently of great importance, and in some compositions of primary importance, in differentiating sections. A contrasting statement, for example, often reveals a change of texture from that of an opening statement. This change may consist of the addition of parts, a change of parts, a change from simple homophony to counterpoint, or a change of instrumentation. Texture acts as an important

Example 10-6

Mozart, *Symphony No. 35 in D (Haffner),* 3rd movement

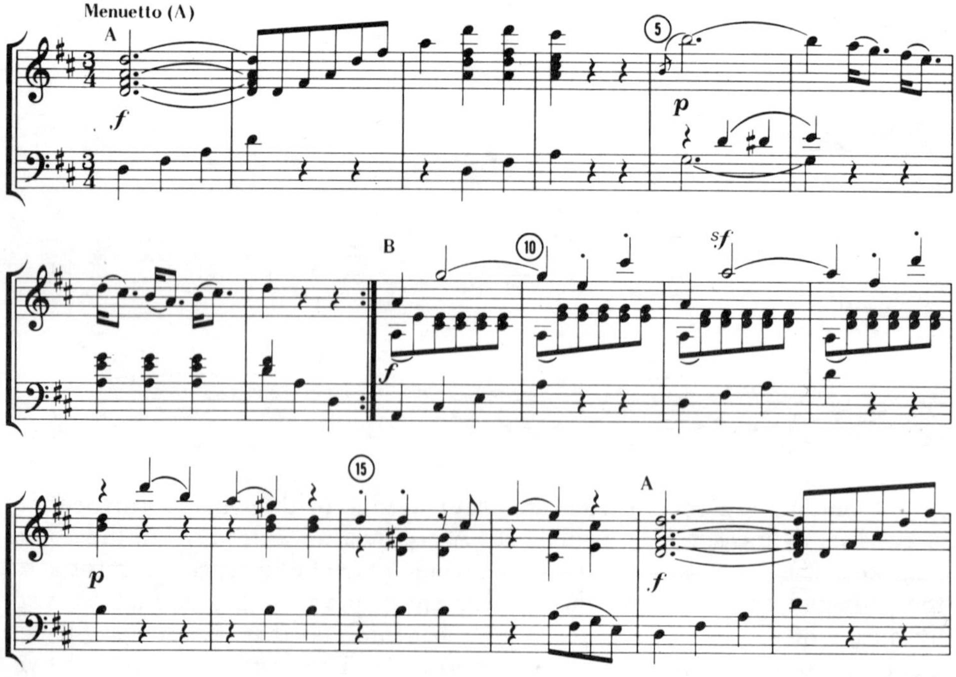

(cont.)

Example 10-6 (continued)

agent in delineating the three-part form of the movement shown in Example 10-6. Perform or listen to this example and note carefully the change of part deployment that occurs at the beginning of section *B*, the *Trio* section. The overall form of this movement is that of a *Menuetto* (minuet—measures 1 through 24) followed by a *Trio* (in this case a second, contrasting minuet—measures 25 through 52) and then a *da capo (D.C.)*, that is, a literal restatement of the opening minuet. This type of *ABA* form occurs very frequently in symphonic and chamber compositions.

The *Trio** of Example 10-6 is set off from the *Menuetto* through a change of key (from D to A major), a change in dynamic level to *piano* (soft), the introduction of a new melodic line, or principal part, and textural changes including both a reduction in the number of parts and a change of accompaniment through the use of recurring eighth-note motion in an inner voice and recurring quarter notes in the bass. Note also the more compact range of the *Trio*, in marked contrast to the wide range of the *Menuetto*.

If we turn our attention to the *Menuetto* section alone, we see that it is itself composed of a three-part arrangement of sections reflecting in miniature the formal design of the piece as a whole. Measures 1 through 8 constitute an opening section *(A)*. Measures 9 through 16 contrast with *A* in their emphasis on the dominant (V) of the key of D, in their melodic material, and in the prevalence of inner-voice eighth-note activity. The return of *A* is a literal restatement.

The *Trio* section *(B)* of the movement similarly exhibits a three-part design. Thus the principal sections of the movement mirror, in a way, the piece's overall design (although this is by no means the case in all ternary compositions). Study the *Trio* and note those factors which create contrast between the *A* and *B* sections. The following is a formal outline of the movement:

	Menuetto (A)			*Trio (B)*			*Menuetto da Capo (A)*
Sections:	*A*	*B*	*A*	*A*	*B*	*A*	As before
Phrases:	*a,b*	*c,d*	*a,b*	*a,b*	*c,c'*†	*a,b*	As before
Measures**:	1,5	9,13	17,21	25,29	33,37	45,49	As before
Tonal Scheme:	D	Dominant of D emphasized	D	A	Dominant of A emphasized	A	As before

RONDO FORM

Instead of designating a specific formal arrangement of a fixed number of sections, the word *rondo* denotes a formal principle of *alternation* of recur-

*The middle section of a minuet movement is commonly called a *Trio* even though it may be written for more than three parts, or voices. This use of the term *Trio* is a vestige of the eighteenth-century practice of writing such sections for three instruments, often two oboes and a bassoon.

†Note the phrase extension over a dominant pedal.

**The numbers indicate the measures in which the respective phrases begin.

rent statements of an opening passage with contrasting sections. The opening section is marked for recognition by the use of easily recalled melodic and textural materials. Interspersed between the restatements of the opening material are sections called episodes or interludes, which create variety, contrast, and formal interest while preparing for the eventual restatement of the rondo theme* (sometimes called *ritornello* or refrain). Tuneful display is a feature of many rondos.

The rondo principle predates many of the other form types associated with Western music. Theorists have distinguished several different types of rondos, but it is more important to recognize the adherence of each type to the basic formal pattern (statements of a principal theme alternating with episodes) than it is to know the details of sectionalization in the various types. In this discussion we shall be concerned primarily with the way in which the basic rondo principle operates. This principle can be abbreviated very simply as *RDRDR*. . ., where *R* stands for the rondo theme and *D* for the episodes or digressions.

The number of recurrences of the rondo theme in alternation with episodes providing contrast and variety is highly variable, although examples containing three or more statements of *R* predominate. The nature of the digression is similarly highly variable; it may be derived from *R*, or it may be a passage whose primary significance is to provide relaxation or create a sense of heightened expectation for a subsequent return of the rondo theme; it may occur only once in the composition, or it may recur at a later point.

The rondo principle is often employed for spirited movements which occur as finales (closing movements) in works of several movements, such as sonatas, suites, or concertos. Occasionally a slow movement of a contemplative cast is written in rondo form. It should be borne in mind that composers usually adopt formal plans that meet specific needs or aid in the solution of particular compositional problems; seldom do they write music to fit predetermined molds. For that reason the shape or design of a work rarely dictates its mood or expressive content.

Example 10-7 shows an entire movement based on the rondo principle. Listen to a performance of the piece. Its form is as follows:

Sections:	*R*	D_1	[Transition]	*R* (shortened)	D_2	[Transition]	*R* (extended and varied)
Measures:	1–25	26–38	39–45	46–53	54–61	62–69	70–97
Keys:	C	G	Based on dominant of C	C	C minor	Based on dominant of C	C

The rondo theme of this movement exhibits the light-heartedness of mood which often characterizes rondo finales of sonatas or concertos. Tempo, key,

*The term *theme* is commonly understood to mean primary or subsidiary melody, together with associated chords and accompaniment.

melody, and texture interact and coincide in such a way as to produce this mood.

Section *R* (measures 1 through 25) constitutes a small ternary design and spans about one-fourth of the total length of the work. Note the easily recalled and tuneful motive in measures 1 and 2, which signals and establishes the mood of the piece as a whole and whose rhythm is heard twelve times during section *R*. Repetition is frequently the simplest and most effective way of imprinting upon the listener's mind the rhythm and character of the rondo theme. The rondo statement ends with a terminal cadence (V^7-I) in the principal key of the movement, C major. This cadence establishes the separate and more or less *closed* character of the statement, emphasizing its importance as the main thematic material of the movement.

The first digression, beginning at measure 26, is clearly derived from the rondo theme. Note the constant references to the opening motive. The contrast between this digression and the opening statement is primarily one of tonality and rhythm. The key changes to G major, and a triplet figure is used to organize a counterline in measures 34 through 37.

The rondo theme returns, considerably shortened, at measure 46. Note that the passage used to link the episode with the restatement of the theme gives a preview of the main motive of *R;* it also hovers around the major triad on *g,* which, since it is the dominant triad of C major, acts as a pivotal chord in the modulation from G back to C major. Passages such as this are called *transitions;* it is the function of transitions to connect sections of a piece. Transitions are sometimes constructed out of thematic material derived from one or both of the two sections being linked; such is the case here. Transitional passages are often tonally unstable; they commonly create an impression of working toward a tonal goal, whose arrival is signaled by the harmonic enunciation of a tonic.

The second digression arrives without preparation. It unfolds a more smoothly articulated melody and a change of accompaniment in the form of a broken octave bass; it also contrasts tonally with the rondo theme through mutation to C minor, the parallel minor key to C major. Note the brief transition in measures 62 through 69 that reintroduces C major; this transition continues the eighth-note rhythm of the preceding digression, and prepares for the return of *R* by implying the dominant triad of C major in measure 68.

The final rondo statement parallels the first in length and design. Note, however, that the close (measures 86 through 97) reintroduces the triplet figure of the first digression to vary the final restatement of the rondo's opening period. Compare these measures with measures 17 through 25.

This brief discussion neglects many of the subtleties of design and detail that create form in the movement reproduced as Example 10-7. It should be clear, however, that formal elements such as repetition (or restatement), contrast, and variation work hand in hand in shaping such designs. The composer's manipulation of musical materials and our ability to interpret the signals projected by pitches and rhythms are mutually dependent.

Example 10-7

Haydn, *Sonata in C major for Piano,* Finale

(cont.)

Example 10-7 (continued)

65
cresc.
f
p
70
R (extended and varied)
75
f
80
p
f
85
3
p
90
f
95

EXERCISES

1. The piece shown below is from a suite by Bach. Play it, or listen to it played, on the piano and study its materials and their formal organization. Complete the analytical problems.

J. S. Bach, Overture in F major, "Bourrée"

(cont.)

a) Mark all phrases on the music.

b) Identify each cadence as progressive, terminal, or transient terminal.

c) Name the form of the piece, binary or ternary.

d) Cite three factors (details or general features) which create unity in the piece.

e) What factors produce contrast? Note that contrast is not a striking feature of the piece.

f) What devices contribute to the independence of the voices? Cite specific examples.

g) What factors limit part independence in this piece?

2. The excerpt shown below is the basis for a set of variations by Brahms. Play the passage and answer the questions that follow.

Brahms, Variations on a Theme by Handel, Op. 24

a) What form type does the piece represent?

b) Cite at least three factors that contribute to overall unity in the piece.

c) In what specific way does the tonal organization of the sections correspond to that of Example 10-3 in the text?

d) Which of the following does the formal segment heard in measures 1–4 constitute: a phrase, a period, a motive, a set?

e) Which measures contain chords whose general function is other than tonic or dominant?

f) What types of nonchordal activity typify the piece?

3. Consider the following group of questions *before* turning to the musical example by Schumann. After you have carefully read the questions, allow yourself about three minutes to read silently through the piece; then play it through once at the piano. Answer as many of the questions as you can without referring again to the music. After you have done this, complete your answers by referring to the music.

a) How many sections are there?

b) What form type does the piece apparently represent?

c) Which of the following helps to delineate the beginning of the second section: modulation, mutation, transposition, none of these?

d) Which of the following procedures organizes the first section: sequence, imitation, motive repetition in one voice?

e) Which of the following seems to best describe the overall texture of the piece: melody and accompaniment, counterpoint punctuated by implied harmonic changes, imitative counterpoint organized tonally by triadic chords and seventh chords?

Schumann, Album for the Young, "Kanonisches Liedchen"

(cont.)

10
15
cresc.
20
Im Tempo
rit.
fp
25
30
sf
35
pp
Etwas langsamer

(optional)

4. The complete movement from a piano sonata by Haydn that follows is to be made the basis of an extensive analytical project. Familiarize yourself with the piece through study at and away from the keyboard. Try to establish a mental picture of the sound materials of the work before exploring it at the keyboard. Consider the general topics listed below, each of which could be assigned to one or two members of a class as the basis for a class project. If the piece is to be dealt with by one person working alone, the various analytical topics given below should be spread over several class sessions.

Topics for Analysis

a) Overall tonal organization of the movement (keys used, sectional cadences, modulations, mutations)

b) Prevailing texture and texture changes (number of parts and their treatment—homophonic, contrapuntal, etc.—and texture changes between sections, accompanimental techniques)

c) Melodic materials (principal and subsidiary thematic elements of the piece)

d) Harmonic details (chordal materials, root relations, nonchordal materials)

e) Form (main sections and their divisions)

Haydn, Sonata in E♭ for Piano, Finale

(cont.)

35
p
f
sf
40
p
f
f
45
50
p
p
f

(cont.)

70
sf
75
p
80
p
sf
sf
85
p
3
90

95
100
105
cresc.
f
110
decresc.
p
p
115
f

Chapter 11

VARIATIONS

To vary is to modify or alter a musical theme or idea while retaining its substance or underlying structure. Variation is a fundamental aspect of musical form.

The process of variation is employed in various musical contexts. We have already observed that musical materials are restated in modified form—that is, varied—in numerous form types, such as binary, ternary, and rondo. Variation is also used in a large number of types of composition—theme and variations, passacaglia, chaconne, chorale variations, blues, and others—in which specific techniques of recurrence are employed as a means of creating unity. Varied restatements may occur immediately after the original statement, or a considerable time lapse may intervene during which other, less closely related materials are introduced.

VARIATIONAL PROCESSES

Few compositions exist which fail to reveal some variational techniques. The various means of modifying a motive discussed in Chapter 9 all constitute techniques of variation. However, as will become clear in this chapter, motivic variation is only one of many aspects of variation.

Example 11-1 illustrates a variational process already encountered briefly in Chapter 9, *rhythmic elaboration* of a figure or phrase through the addition of embellishments. Both Example 11-1(a) and Example 11-1(b) occur at different points in the same piece by Bartók. Example 11-1(b) derives its pitch contour, the predominant rhythmic figure (♩ ♫), and most of its accented pitches from Example 11-1(a). It differs from Example 11-1(a), however, in that sixteenth-note activity, often in the form of passing or neighbor tones,

Example 11-1 Rhythmic elaboration

Bartók, *Mikrokosmos,* Vol. IV, No. 28

enhances the melodic rhythm. The relation of Example 11-1(b) to Example 11-1(a) is one of varied restatement. The result is a considerably more interesting restatement than an unaltered repetition of Example 11-1(a) would have been.

Example 11-2 illustrates another kind of rhythmic elaboration. In this passage, *step decorations* are added to the bracketed figure when it is repeated. Note that all other factors remain unchanged in the restatement.

In Example 11-3 the bracketed figure at the beginning is subjected to varied repetition throughout the passage. In each of the five statements of

Example 11-2 Step decorations

Haydn, *String Quartet in G,* Op. 17, No. 5, 1st movement

Example 11-3 Modification of contour

J. S. Bach, *Mass in B minor*

this figure, the interval between the third and fourth notes is different. Despite the minor third in the third appearance of the figure, the overall effect of these varied restatements is to heighten interest by expanding the figure's contour. Note also that the direction of movement from the third to the fourth note of the figure is altered in the fourth and fifth statements.

Example 11-4 Contrapuntal elaboration

Buxtehude, *Auf meinen lieben Gott* (Chorale Prelude)

a)

(cont.)

Example 11-4 (continued)

b)

Example 11-4(b) is a *contrapuntal elaboration* of Example 11-4(a). Note that the basic contour of the upper voice is retained, together with the harmonic scheme of the original version. Rhythmic elaboration and contrapuntal play between voices are the main variational processes employed.

Measures 9 through 16 of Example 11-5 are a varied restatement of measures 1 through 8. The variation consists of thinning the texture, stating the main melody in the left hand alone, and inventing a figuration in triplets for the right hand. The right-hand figuration produces a counterline* against the main voice below. The variation in this example is produced primarily by *textural change.*

*In this case the counterline produces *heterophony,* that is, elaborated or embellished duplication, with the main voice.

Example 11-5 Change in texture

Beethoven, *Sonata in C major for Piano (Waldstein)*, Op. 53, 1st movement

Example 11-6 Change in harmonic accompaniment

Schubert, *Impromptu in C minor,* Op. 90, No. 1

In Example 11-6 the melody of measures 6 through 8 is repeated in measures 18 through 20, but with *altered harmonic accompaniment.* This technique is found quite frequently in music of the past 200 or so years.

Example 11-7 illustrates an extremely common process of variation in music of the eighteenth and nineteenth centuries: *mutation.* Measures 2 and 3 are repeated in measures 4 and 5 mutated from the major to the minor mode.

Example 11-7 Mutation

Mozart, *Sonata in B♭ major for Piano,* K. 333, Finale

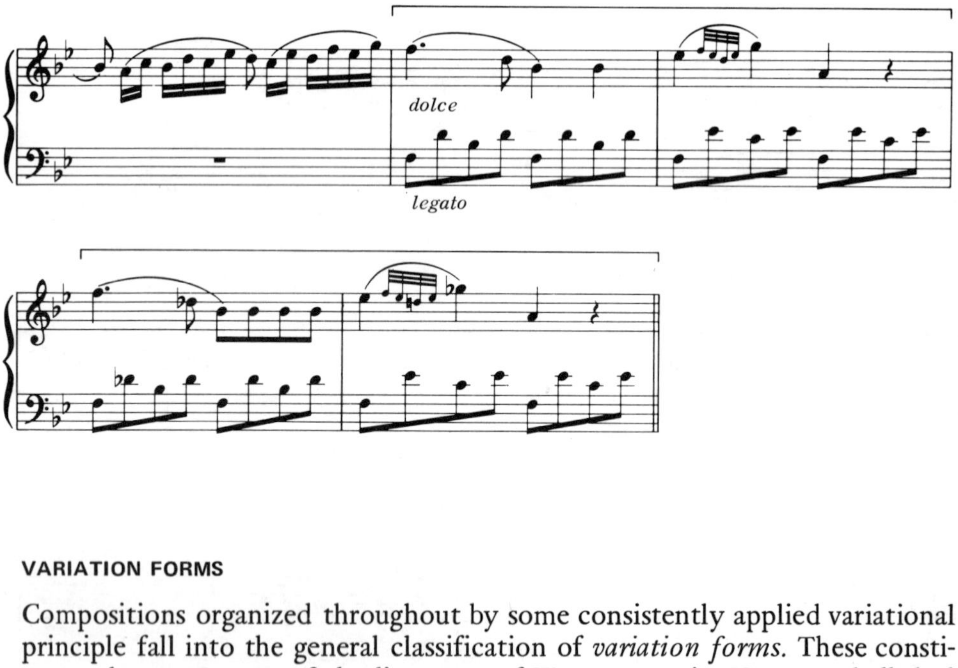

VARIATION FORMS

Compositions organized throughout by some consistently applied variational principle fall into the general classification of *variation forms.* These constitute a large segment of the literature of Western music. Here we shall deal with only a sampling of the many types of variation forms. All such forms have in common the principle of recurrence coupled with change. In some types, such as theme and variations, the retention of phrase structure and underlying harmonic scheme provides a rather transparent background for variations in texture and melody. Other variation forms, such as contrapuntal variations on a basso ostinato or some types of chorale prelude, tend more to conceal the recurring elements, thereby affording greater freedom of elaboration. The first of several variation pieces to be discussed appears in Example 11-8. The piece is represented by several brief excerpts showing the successive variations that occur.

This type of movement is commonly called *theme and variations.* It consists of successive elaborations of the theme statement; such elaborations usually retain the phrase structure, melodic contour, and basic harmonic changes heard in the theme. Note that the theme statement (Example 11-8a) is presented in a simple, unadorned texture, thus making the structural elements of the succeeding variations both easily comprehended and easily recalled.

The statement itself consists of a simple, almost march-like melody supported by on-the-beat chords. The middle part of the statement, measures 9 through 12, reveals smoother melodic articulation than does the first part. Other distinguishing features of the middle part include a change of register, transitory emphasis on the keys of F major and D minor (IV and ii, respectively, of C major), and a transient terminal cadence on V of C preparing for the return to the tonic key in measure 13. Note also the wider spacing of the four-note chords in the middle section. The return of the opening phrase occurs an octave above the first statement of that phrase; also note that the texture is thickened in measures 13 and 14. A four-measure codetta (ending passage) terminates the statement of the theme by reaffirming both the beginning tonality and register. Such a formal arrangement can be explained as either ternary or rounded binary.* Each variation will reveal a formal design identical to that of the theme.

The piece contains three variations, each of which unfolds its own unique elements while adhering to the structural basis of the theme. Listen to the opening two phrases of Variations 1 and 2 (Example 11-8b and c) and the opening phrase of Variation 3 (Example 11-8d).

In Variation 1 (Example 11-8b), the melody is repeated in the same register as in the theme, and is essentially unchanged. An upper part has been added which, with its note repetition, has the character of a pedal; occasionally it supplies counterpoint to the main voice. One of the most important factors in creating contrast in this variation is the syncopation in the upper voice. Note also that the accompanimental chords which support the main voice have been thinned out.

Variation 2 (Example 11-8c) also employs syncopation, but this time it is the result of displaced articulation in the main voice. The melody is now stated one octave higher than in the theme and in Variation 1. The bass line is made more active by the use of wide leaps in eighth notes; the bass line is in effect two parts—a pedal bass and a step "tenor" countermelody.

A four-measure transition based on a dominant pedal links Variation 2 to Variation 3 (Example 11-8d). In Variation 3 the texture is thinned to two voices. The theme is elaborated by a three-note motive which recurs in the upper part, the basic pitches of the theme falling on the second note of the motive.

---

*If it were regarded as a ternary design, it could be called an *incipient ternary* form.

Example 11-8 Theme and variations

Beethoven, *Sonata in G major for Piano,* Op. 14, No. 2, 2nd movement

a) Theme

b) Variation 1

c) Variation 2

(cont.)

Example 11-8 (continued)

d) Variation 3

Variations such as these exploit the possibilities of contrasting treatments of a set of compositional materials. The means of variation include modifications of texture, dynamics, and melody. Each variation involves the revamping of one or more aspects of compositional detail, but the underlying structure of the statement is retained.

Each of the variations in Example 11-8 is a separate section based on a self-sufficient theme and terminated by a V-I cadence. Many musicians would call these *sectional variations.* In contrast, Example 11-9 exemplifies *continuous variations.* Compositions of this type are based on the continuous repetition of a figure, harmonic scheme or chord progression, or bass melody *(basso ostinato).* This recurring material is often rather nondescript or neutral by itself; it merely provides a repetitive basis for the invention of compositions of a continuously unfolding design. Such works are usually less obviously sectionalized by marked cadences than are pieces consisting of sectional variations. Frequently the main variational process used in such compositions is contrapuntal elaboration; for this reason they are sometimes called *contrapuntal variations.*

The four-measure basso ostinato theme of Example 11-9 has little interest in its own right. It is nothing more than a descending chromatic scale passage:

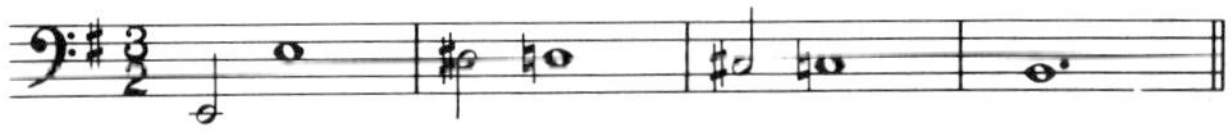

Example 11-9 Contrapuntal variations

J. S. Bach, *Mass in B minor,* "Crucifixus"

(cont.)

Example 11-9 (continued)

20
fi - xus e - - - - ti - am pro___ no - - - -
e - - - ti - am pro__ no - - - - bis, sub Pon - ti - o Pi -
no - bis e - - - ti - am pro___
- ti - am__ pro__ no - - - - - - - bis,
25
- bis sub Pon - ti - o Pi - la - to, pas - -
la - to, sub Pon - ti - o Pi - la - to, pas - -
___ no - - bis sub Pon - ti - o Pi - la - to, pas - -
sub__ Pon - ti - o Pi - la - - - - to, pas - -

(cont.)

Example 11-9 (continued)

40
- - ci - fi - xus e - ti - am pro no - bis
cru - - - ci - fi - - xus e - ti - am pro
cru - - - ci - fi - - xus
cru - - - ci -
45
sub Pon - ti - o Pi - la - - - to pas - -
no - bis sub Pon - ti - o Pi - la - - - to, pas - sus
e - ti - am pro no - bis,
fi - xus e - ti - am pro no - - - bis,

(cont.)

Example 11-9 (continued)

The ostinato is repeated unaltered throughout Example 11-9, creating counterpoint with and providing harmonic support for the polyphony which unfolds above it. The 13 statements of the ostinato which occur in the piece are concealed within the harmonic and contrapuntal activity which they support. The listener does not in all likelihood perceive 13 distinct sections in the piece. On the contrary, the movement is heard as consisting of two main sections, marked by the cadence at measure 36.

The vocal polyphony in both sections is based mainly on varied treatments of the motive introduced in measure 5:

A new figure is introduced at the beginning of the second section; it is obviously a derivative of the previous figure:

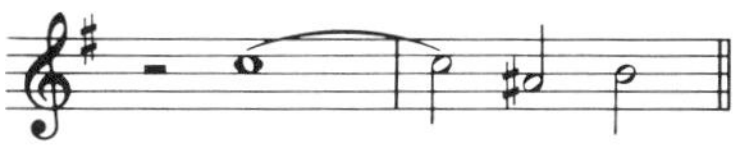

It is the elaboration of these figures that constitutes the leading thematic feature of the piece. And it is the composer's unique contrapuntal and harmonic treatments of these motives that obscure the repetition of the four-measure ostinato.

Several means of creating unity and variety while at the same time playing down the beginnings and ends of the ostinato statements are listed below. As you listen to a performance of the work, note as many of these and similar features as you can. Note also the continuity of mood (devout supplication) in the piece. Try to determine what musical elements are most effective in eliciting this mood.

1. Harmonic cadences (usually iv^6-V in E minor) in the third and fourth measures of the ostinato are minimized by maintaining rhythmic activity in the voice parts. For examples, see measures 7-8 and 15-16.

2. Changes in the recurring harmonic scheme occasionally suggest transitory key changes, as at measures 24-25, where the V-i progression in E minor is mutated so as to imply motion toward A minor. Tonal variety results from such harmonic devices.

3. Subtle increases in rhythm enhance the pace of the movement. For example, at measures 39-44, note the use of more or less continuous activity in quarter notes, shifted imitatively from part to part.

4. The procedure of introducing an imitatively treated figure within one phrase and continuing its imitation into the subsequent one helps to maintain the melodic continuity of the movement.

5. Changes in the number of voices contribute measurably to the textural interest of the piece by producing gradations in the density of the vocal texture; see measures 13-29. Note that texture changes of this sort seldom coincide with the beginning of a new statement of the ostinato; the placement of such changes thus further minimizes the ostinato's tendency to sectionalize the composition. An exception to this occurs at the midpoint of the work, at measures 36-37.

Listen several times to a recording of the movement, shown in piano-vocal score in Example 11-9. If possible, arrange to perform it. Doing so will add greatly to your comprehension of it as a model for further study of contrapuntal variations on an ostinato bass.

The agelessness of variation techniques can be seen in their predominant role in current music. Few formal principles have weathered the changes in musical style that have occurred in the twentieth century so successfully as has that of variation.

Example 11-10, by Stravinsky, shows the theme statement from the second movement of his *Octet for Winds,* one of the most significant works of the first quarter of the current century. The piece was written for flute, clarinet, two bassoons, two trumpets, and two trombones. Although the movement is clearly related to the type of variation illustrated in Example 11-8 (sectional variations), it reveals unique treatments of material that are of more importance to the student of music than mere comparison with earlier models would suggest. Study the thematic basis of the movement carefully (Example 11-10a).

The theme is divided into two units of unequal length, *A* (measures 1 through 8) and *A'* (measures 9 through 14). The division is made clear through the occurrence of a modified restatement of *A*, beginning on a different note *(e)* and omitting measures 3 through 6. Note the relation between the final four measures of *A* and *A'*.

One of the most telling features of the theme, and one that is important to the subsequent variations, is its economy and unity of pitch and rhythm. Like the Beethoven theme statement studied earlier, it is melodically self-sufficient. The simplicity of its materials and its design make it ripe for elaboration.

The beginning of each variation is shown in Example 11-10(b). Note the formal outline of the movement on page 247. Of particular interest is the rondo-like recurrence of the first variation after Variations 2 and 4. The composer has designed a composite form by combining the variation principle with that of the ritornello. Note also that the final variation is a fugue. The design of this movement, while clearly based on preestablished models, has been arrived at through an imaginative adoption of earlier models rather than through literal duplication of them.

Example 11-10 A twentieth-century set of variations

Stravinsky, *Octet for Winds,* 2nd movement

a) Theme

(cont.)

Example 11-10 (continued)

b) Variations

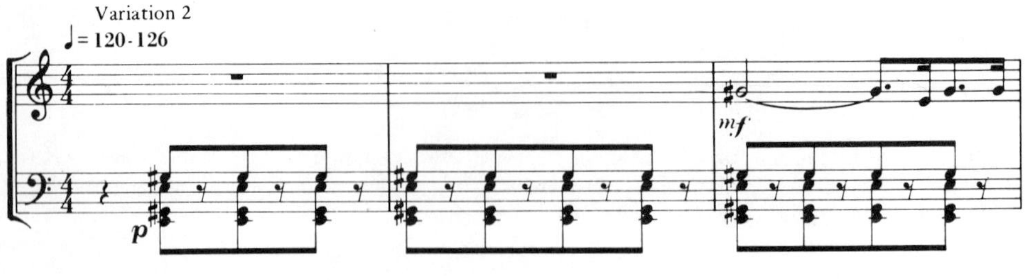

f
♩ = 63
5
Variation 1 repeated
Variation 3
♩ = ♩.
8va
(cont.)

Example 11-10 (continued)

Outline of the Variations from Stravinsky's *Octet for Winds*

Section	*Commentary*
Theme	Stated in woodwinds followed by brass; chordal texture
Variation 1 *(A)*	Theme in trombone, accompanied by rapid scale passages in woodwinds
Variation 2 *(B)*	Quasi-march with derivative and new melodic materials interspersed
Variation 1 *(A)*	As before, with cadential modification
Variation 3 *(C)*	Waltz-like derivative material (flute) staggered with complete statement of theme
Variation 4 *(D)*	Rhythmically broadened statement of theme accompanied by ostinati in bassoon and clarinet
Variation 1 *(A)*	Cadentially varied
Variation 5 *(E)*	Fugue whose subject is derived from the theme

The highly improvisatory art of jazz is based to a great extent on variation techniques. The improvised solos which typify jazz commonly involve the elaboration of a given (stated or implied) thematic or harmonic statement; the most obvious example is *blues.*

Pieces called blues, for example, "St. Louis Blues," "Blues in the Night," and "Swingin' Shepherd Blues," are built from recurring 12-measure chord patterns. Although the melodic lines (and words) of blues compositions are different, most blues compositions are built on similar, if not identical, chord sequences. In a sense, such pieces are variations on a harmonic scheme. One such scheme is shown in Example 11-11 with the notational shorthand commonly used to code such chord progressions for realization in improvisation.

One might compare such a pattern (a harmonic ostinato) to the ostinato used in the "Crucifixus" from Bach's *Mass in B minor* (Example 11-9). Such a pattern is not really self-sustaining or thematically self-sufficient; certainly it loses interest when repeated without elaboration. However, the blues progression is intended as an ostinato accompaniment for vocal or instrumental melody, composed or improvised, with or without words. It is the essentially simple plan of the blues progression that makes it so adaptable to solo improvisation and elaboration.

Listen to the harmonic pattern in Example 11-11 several times, to get it well entrenched in your mind. Then listen to several blues compositions, vocal or instrumental, identifying the progression as it occurs as the basis for successive "choruses" (12-measure passages featuring one type of solo or ensemble presentation). Note that such choruses often consist of repeated *riffs* (recurring figures somewhat comparable to motives), which form the basis of the melody. The riff of a blues composition usually gives way to solos after

Example 11-11 A blues progression

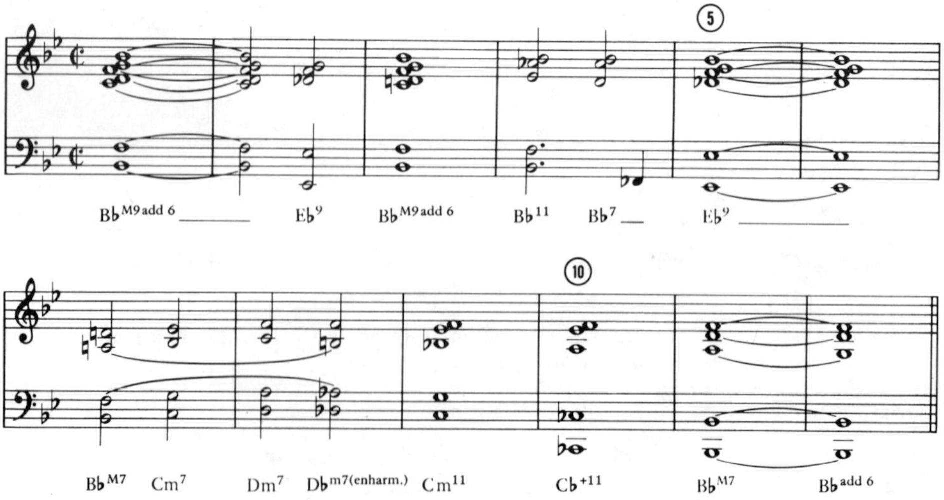

Example 11-12 A blues melody

an opening chorus, recurring as a prelude to closure. A blues riff, supported by the usual blues progression, is shown in Example 11-12. After you have performed the example, invent other riffs and use them to construct melodies to go with the blues progression.

One thing that should be obvious after studying this chapter is the timelessness of the variation technique, whether it is used to develop and elaborate a motive, as the basis for improvisation, or as the main formal element of an extended movement. Combining as it does elements of restatement and of change, variation is present to some degree in virtually all compositions.

EXERCISES

1. The following passage, the opening of the slow movement of one of Beethoven's piano sonatas, lends itself readily to variation.

Beethoven, Sonata for Piano, Op. 13, 2nd movement

a) Study the above passage carefully and then list at least five processes that could be employed as bases for varied restatements of it. Illustrate each process that you name by applying it to the opening four measures.

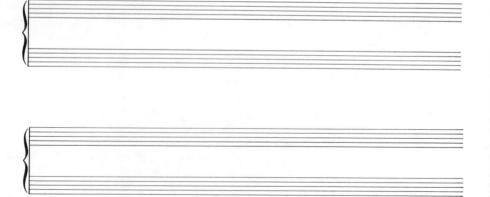

b) Invent a florid variation of the melody alone by retaining the original notes of the melody and adding figuration in the form of both step and skip activity. Be sure to preserve the basic contour of the original. Use the variation that you have written for practicing vocal reading.

2. This exercise is based on a theme statement and the first half of each of three variations on it. The eight measures of each variation correspond to the first four measures (repeated) of the theme. Study the excerpts carefully (pages 252-254) and complete the analytical problems on pages 254 and 255.

Handel, Theme with Variations for Harpsichord

Variation 1

Variation 2

Allegro

(cont.)

Variation 5

Presto

a) Locate one occurrence of each of the following items in the theme statement. Indicate the measure number of its occurrence.

Repetition of the rhythm of a phrase
Sequence
Transient terminal cadence
Modulation to F major
Cadence elaborated by a suspension
Syncopation
Secondary dominant
Tonic triad outlined by the melody
Motion in parallel tenths between outer voices
A measure in which all four parts have somewhat contrasted rhythms

b) Describe the relation maintained between the upper voice of the first variation and the theme.

c) Cite three ways in which the composer has modified the harmony of the theme in composing the first variation. Note particularly the bass voice as a basis for comparing the two settings.

d) What is the obvious unifying factor between Variation 1 and Variation 2?

e) The texture of the theme is clearly chordal. How does the texture of the first two variations compare with that of the theme?

f) How is the original melodic line (upper voice of the theme) preserved in Variation 5?

g) How does the upper voice of Variation 5 maintain the harmony of the theme?

h) Write on the music the implied harmonic changes of Variation 5.

(optional)

i) Invent a final variation in which the main voice is found in the tenor part of a four-voice keyboard setting.

Chapter 12

CONTRAPUNTAL TECHNIQUES AND FORMS

Counterpoint is often regarded as a basic element of the craft of composition. The acquisition of technique by a composer is usually considered to consist largely of gaining facility with counterpoint, the invention and combining of melodies. Counterpoint is brought to bear in inventing satisfactory voice leading and convincing chord connections, in creating a bass melody rather than just a bass part, or in writing a countermelody for the trombones to oppose the trumpets' theme statement in a composition for band. These uses of counterpoint, as well as others, exemplify a composer's application of the skills and tools that he has acquired as a basis for manipulating musical tones. Such basic skills and tools are as necessary in the craft of musical composition as they are in any other creative activity.

Counterpoint can be employed in various types of texture. We saw in Example 8-3 that it can be present by implication even in a monophonic composition. In homophonic textures it is frequently introduced to add linear interest to what might otherwise be a rather dull succession of chords supporting a melodic line. The most extended and elaborate use of counterpoint usually occurs in so-called "contrapuntal forms." Such forms—canon, fugue, motet, chorale prelude, and others—owe their organization to contrapuntal techniques. Counterpoint does not merely elaborate them; it gives them their basic form.

In this chapter we shall look first at a few examples of the use of contrapuntal techniques in textures which are not primarily contrapuntal. We shall then study some of the "contrapuntal forms."

CONTRAPUNTAL CRAFT

Example 12-1 consists of a melody with an accompanying bass line. The bass line is clearly subordinate to the upper part; yet it does have a certain degree

Example 12-1

Handel, *Sonata for Oboe and Continuo,* Op. 1, No. 6

of independence and rhythmic flow, achieved primarily through the use of step motion. An interesting relation between the two voices is set up by the predominant use of *contrary motion.*

Contrary motion is one of the techniques of *voice leading* which is basic to contrapuntal writing. Example 12-2 illustrates voice leading in a fuller texture than that of Example 12-1. Each of the four lines of this composition is acceptable as melody, although the primary melodic interest lies in the top voice. Note how the quarter-note chords are given a sense of logical succession by the step movement that is employed to connect them. Such step movement is basic to effective counterpoint.

Example 12-2

Stravinsky, *L'Histoire du Soldat,* Great Chorale

In Example 12-3, *imitation* provides a basis for the sharing of thematic interest, in this case by all four members of a string quartet. The movement's overall texture is homophonic, but the composer employs imitative entries (measures 5 and 6) as a means of restating yet shifting to different voices the main melodic content of the movement.

Example 12-3

Haydn, *String Quartet in G*, Op. 17, No. 5, 1st movement

Example 12-4

Hindemith, *Mathis der Maler (Symphony)*, 3rd movement (piano reduction)

The texture of Example 12-4 is essentially chordal; all voices move together in tandem. However, the composer has produced independence of motion in the outer voices by systematically employing contrary motion between them. Note further that the two parts mirror each other by employing similar melodic intervals while moving in opposite directions. This technique is commonly called mirror writing. Each voice is, in effect, a melodic inversion (directional opposite) of the other.

Example 12-5 is another example of compositional skill in the use of contrapuntal techniques in a work which is not a display of "learned" counterpoint. The four-part writing in this piece is characterized by the use of imitation and canon. In measures 1 through 7 the "alto" and "bass" parts treat the rhythmic figure  imitatively; the "bass," by inverting the figure used in the "alto," produces a mirror image of it. The "soprano" and "tenor" outline the main melody in octaves. In measures 7 through 12 the "soprano" and "tenor" engage in canon at the octave, with a distance of one beat separating them. Voice-leading principles are applied to the "alto" and "bass" parts to create a rich contrapuntal texture.

Examples such as those discussed in this section underscore the importance of counterpoint as a basic component of composition and musical craft. It is through melodic and rhythmic interchange of the type that counterpoint makes possible that much music is imbued with a sense of vitality and continuity, while maintaining a unified thread of motion.

Example 12-5

Brahms, *Intermezzo,* Op. 118, No. 4

CANON

The term "contrapuntal forms" is no more informative than its counterpart, "homophonic forms." Forms cannot be classified according to texture, since texture is only one of many factors that create form. The "forms" to be discussed in the remainder of this chapter merely represent a group of piece types which typically employ contrapuntal textures and are organized on the basis of contrapuntal techniques. One such type is canon.

Canon is both the name of a device and, when it is employed throughout a composition, the name given to the form of a piece. The word "canon" means law; applied to music, it denotes a strict imitative relation between two voices, a leader *(dux)* and a follower *(comes). Rounds,* for example, "Row, Row, Row Your Boat," are simple examples of canonic pieces. As in other types of imitation, the pitch interval and rhythmic distance separating the voices are variable. The duet in Example 12-6 is canonic.

Example 12-6

Bizet, *Suite Arlésienne No. 2*

Example 12-7

Reger, *Canon in D minor for Organ*

Example 12-7 is the first section of a movement called *Canon in D minor.* Sing the example and note the canonic relation maintained by all three voices. Note especially the various pitch and rhythmic distances that are employed. Such pieces are, of course, highly unified. At the same time, they risk being tedious in the hands of composers who slavishly adhere to the exact imitation of a leading voice *(dux)* for prolonged spans of time. Consequently, many canonic pieces reveal both rhythmic and pitch modifications of the imitating parts. Such deviations are most common at cadences, where harmonic formulas tend to predetermine melodic movement to some degree.

MOTET

The motet is one of a number of forms that we shall discuss which have largely disappeared from the compositional scene. Having originated in the thirteenth century, the motet underwent centuries of development and modification, and had considerable impact on the development of Western litur-

Example 12-8

Victoria, *O Magnum Mysterium* (Motet)

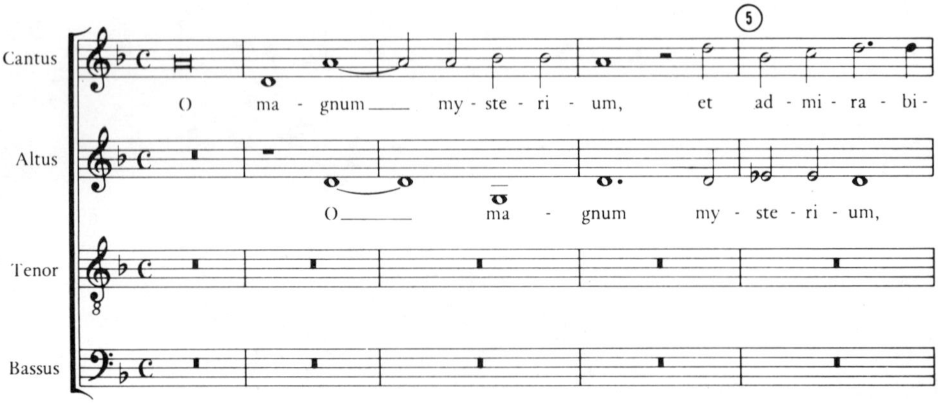

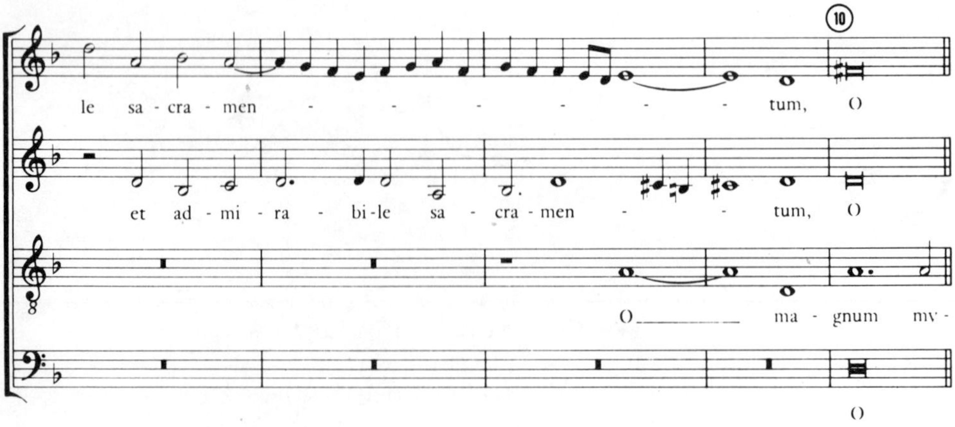

gical music. It reached its peak of importance during the Renaissance (about 1450 to 1600).

The motet is difficult to define as a specific form. It is essentially a sacred work* for voices, or voices and instruments, based on a Latin sacred text and designed for performance in the Roman Catholic Church service. Motets often reveal a formal structure called *through-composed* (a translation of the German term *durchcomponiert*). In through-composed compositions no large sections of the work recur; each line or stanza of the text is set to new, somewhat contrasted music. (The term "through-composed" is also applied to songs and other vocal or instrumental pieces containing no sectional return.) Many motets have two main sections, the second of which proceeds at a somewhat faster pace than the first.

The melodic basis of motets of the Renaissance was often a pre-existent melody *(cantus firmus)* borrowed from the vast fund of Gregorian chant melodies originally designed for unaccompanied performance in the church in accordance with the church calendar. Chant melodies were written without specific metric or durational indications, but a polyphonic motet based on a chant melody demanded the use of specific note durations and meter indications, as in Example 12-8. In this example, the polyphony is fashioned from motives which in turn are derived from the chant melody, shown on the top stave of the setting. Motets are by no means always as contrapuntal in texture as the beginning of the one shown here; some, in fact, employ prolonged chordal sections. Nevertheless, imitation, canon, and independent voice movement are perhaps the most typical traits of the Renaissance motet.†

MADRIGAL

The madrigal is also of relatively early origin, like the motet, Mass movement, and other forms of polyphonic vocal ensemble music, and is usually treated unaccompanied *(a cappella).* The madrigal evolved from the ecclesiastical motet, and thrived in the sixteenth century. Madrigals were written to Italian or English texts dealing with such topics as love, grief, dejection, and exhilaration. At its peak, the madrigal represented a stunning artistic achievement in the setting of moods (affects) and emotion-laden words to music. Homophony and counterpoint were juxtaposed to explore as deeply as possible the implications of a poem. Five-voice textures were the norm for such compositions, a section from one of which is reproduced in Example 12-9. The madrigal represents a high point in the development of vocal ensemble music, a peak seldom since reached.

---

*However, many motets, such as those of Machaut, a French composer of the fourteenth century, were apparently written for and performed at both sacred and secular festive occasions.

†Example 12-8 exemplifies, both in texture and in the use of a cantus firmus, a mode of composition associated with liturgical music in general during the Renaissance. Masses, anthems, and other liturgical works were written in this same style.

Example 12-9

Monteverdi, *Cruda Amarilli* (Madrigal)

CHORALE PRELUDE

The term "chorale prelude" embraces a large variety of seventeenth- and eighteenth-century compositions for organ, written in a polyphonic keyboard style and based on a pre-existent melody from the Lutheran liturgy. The chorale prelude served the function of prefacing (for the congregation) a hymn melody to be sung during the service.

Chorale preludes are variations on or elaborations of hymn tunes. Some are quite simple and direct, merely presenting straightforward statements of the hymn tune in the top voice, accompanied by smoothly articulated accompaniments of mainly chordal texture. The beginning of such a setting is shown in Example 12-10.

Example 12-11 illustrates a more ornate style, employing a highly embellished statement of the chorale tune in the upper voice and considerable contrapuntal interplay between the parts. The notes of the cantus firmus (the

Example 12-10

Scheidt, *Chorale Prelude for Organ*

Example 12-11

Buxtehude, *Ein' feste Burg* (Chorale Prelude)

chorale tune), which constitute the nucleus of the setting, are indicated by arrows to facilitate the reader's recognition of "Ein' feste Burg" ("A Mighty Fortress").

Perhaps the most representative type of chorale prelude is illustrated in Example 12-12. The cantus is stated in long notes in the bass, providing a slow-moving foundation for the invention of intricate counterpoint above. The superstructures of such pieces are often fashioned from motives which are in turn derivatives of the cantus; this is clearly the case in Example 12-12.

Chorale preludes often begin by "previewing in imitation" the material of the chorale melody's first phrase. This device (often called *Vorimitation*) is in effect an imitative introduction of the cantus. Interludes occurring between statements of the successive phrases of the cantus are often similarly derived from the melodic content of the phrase to follow. Study Example 12-13 and note the "preluding" of the cantus.

Example 12-12

Scheidemann, *O Thou of God the Father* (Chorale Prelude)

Example 12-13

Scheidt, *In the Midst of Early Life* (Chorale Prelude)

FUGUE

The ultimate peak of contrapuntal procedure is represented by fugue. Fugue is in no sense a stereotyped musical form. On the contrary, a great variety of design, structure, and texture exists in the vast repertoire of compositions of the past 400 years called fugues. J. S. Bach is generally considered to be the master of the fugue "form"; but his fugues, too, show a great variety of procedures, length, style, and structure.

Onc can only attempt to define fugue by citing those elements that are common to fugues in general, while noting that many of the "best" fugues lack some of these elements. Most fugues reveal the following: (1) the monophonic statement of a theme, usually called the subject; (2) an accompanying or subsidiary motive or figure, often derived from the subject, which appears both with and separately from the subject; (3) a series of imitative presentations (expositions) of the subject at the interval of a fourth or fifth, usually involving more than one key; (4) the more or less strict adherence to a set number of parts (voices); (5) sections (usually called episodes or interludes, and often derived from the subject or the countersubject) during which the subject is not stated in its entirety; and (6) a continuity of rhythmic activity which minimizes strong cadential interruptions.

These elements all appear in Example 12-14. Listen to this fugue, and then study the formal outline on pages 271-272. Two terms used in the outline require some explanation. A *real answer* is an answering statement which is identical to (that is, has the same melodic intervals as) the original statement. (A *tonal answer* is an answer in which one or more of the pitches have been slightly altered to comply with the requirements of the harmony. Example 8-9 contains a tonal answer.) A *stretto* passage is one in which successive statements of the subject overlap—the second statement begins before the first ends, the third begins before the second ends, and so on.

Example 12-14

J. S. Bach, *The Well Tempered Clavier,* Book I, Fugue in D minor

(cont.)

Example 12-14 (continued)

(cont.)

Example 12-14 (continued)

Plan of the Fugue in D minor

Measures	*Treatment of Material*	*Keys*
1-2	Statement of subject	D minor (tonic key)
3-4	Answering statement in alto at the fourth below; this exact transposition of the first entrance is called a *real* answer Countersubject derived from the sixteenth notes of the subject occurs in the top part (soprano)	A minor
5	Brief transition back to D minor	
6-7	A third entry of the subject in the bass with the soprano and alto dealing imitatively with the countersubject	D minor
8-9	Modified entry of subject in soprano, with countersubject in the bass	D minor
10-11	Episode derived from countersubject	Sequence of secondary dominants in D minor
12	Segments of subject combined contrapuntally in alto and bass	D minor
13-15	Second exposition involving *stretto* and inversion of the subject in measure 14; bass segment of subject	D minor
15-16	Modulatory sequence based on countersubject	D minor to A minor
17-21	Subject stated in stretto in bass and alto, with extension of countersubject in soprano	A minor with cadence (V^6 to i) in A minor (measures 20-21)
21-24	Modified statements of subject in stretto and melodic inversion	D minor
25-26	Episode based on first segment of subject combined with derivative of the countersubject	D minor
27-29	Entries in stretto and contrary motion (melodic inversion) in soprano, alto, and bass	D minor
30-32	Episode based on rhythm of countersubject organized sequentially	D minor

(cont.)

Measures	*Treatment of Material*	*Keys*
33-39	Climactic section involving coupling of lower voices based on opening segment of subject with derivative of countersubject in upper voice	D minor
39-44	Closing entries of subject in stretto (bass and alto), with rhythm of previous climax dissolved in soprano	D minor
	Additional parts added in closure for harmonic effect	D major

This fugue is characterized by various modifications of the subject throughout. One should note that the mere restating of an initial motive throughout does not constitute a basis for creating a satisfactory and interesting formal design. On the contrary, the restatements of the subject, transferred from voice to voice, simply establish a recurring, unifying basis for a design which derives its interest from other devices and techniques. The episodes, passages which are free of complete statements of the subject, represent moments of contrast and relief, and contribute to the pattern of statement, digression, and return common to most musical forms. Changes of key, texture, register, and spacing, and other form-making processes, are usually evident in fugues.

Fugue is often used as a generic name for a collection of similar types of pieces having different names. A *ricercare,* for example, is a historical prototype of the fugue; a *fughetta* is a short fugue; a passage marked *fugato* is a fugue within or beginning or ending a nonfugal piece; the adjective *fugal* describes a movement or section written in the manner of a fugue. Many compositions employ *fugati,* or fugal passages, as bases for contrapuntal treatment and development of thematic materials. Fugues sometimes occur as vehicles for intensifying closure in essentially homophonic works; listen to a recording of the Finale of Mozart's *Jupiter Symphony* for an example.

A good picture of the variety of style and design that exists in the literature of the fugue may be gained by listening to and comparing any Bach fugue with the fugue in Beethoven's *Sonata in A♭ for Piano,* Op. 110, or the first movement (Fugue) in Bartók's *Music for Strings and Percussion.*

POSTSCRIPT

Most of the contrapuntal forms discussed in this chapter have virtually ceased to function as bases for musical composition since the eighteenth century. It is true that Poulenc has written motets, that Brahms ended his career as a composer with a set of chorale preludes for organ, and that Hindemith has been a noted twentieth-century practitioner of the art of fugue; but such compositions are no longer common. The purpose of studying contrapuntal forms is to investigate their role as determinants of the style and structure of past music, music which represents part of the tradition from which current composition and performance have emerged. Although composers have largely discarded the motet, the chorale prelude, and the fugue as specific modes of composition, the formulative effect of these form types on compositional technique and craft in general can be easily recognized in present-day music. The composition quoted in Example 12-15 exhibits clearly the incorporation of contrapuntal techniques which originated centuries ago. This piece was written in the early 1950's.

Example 12-15

Stravinsky, *In Memoriam Dylan Thomas,* Dirge

EXERCISES

1. The selection below is from a large work by J. S. Bach which contains various examples of contrapuntal craft. Read the example carefully before answering the questions.

   J. S. Bach, "The Art of Fugue"

   a) The subject of the piece is first stated in the alto voice, from measure 1 through the first beat of measure 5. Cite the measures in which each subsequent statement of the subject occurs, and name the voice in which it occurs.

b) The material heard in counterpoint with the second statement of the subject (measures 5–9) is clearly contrasted with the subject. State three ways in which this contrast is established; consider such factors as rhythm, motion, and direction.

c) The second entry of the subject is a *tonal* answer. Why?

d) Rhythmic independence of voices is frequently accomplished by the use of rhythmically displaced (syncopated) accents in one of the parts. What type of nonchordal activity commonly results (in the example) from such displacements? Cite several examples.

e) Which two keys predominate in the passage? What relation do they represent?

(optional)

2. Complete the following writing tasks. Use the first statement of the subject of the example in Exercise 1 as a given voice (cantus).

a) Add a lower voice (below the cantus) that moves predominantly in eighth notes and uses mostly step motion.

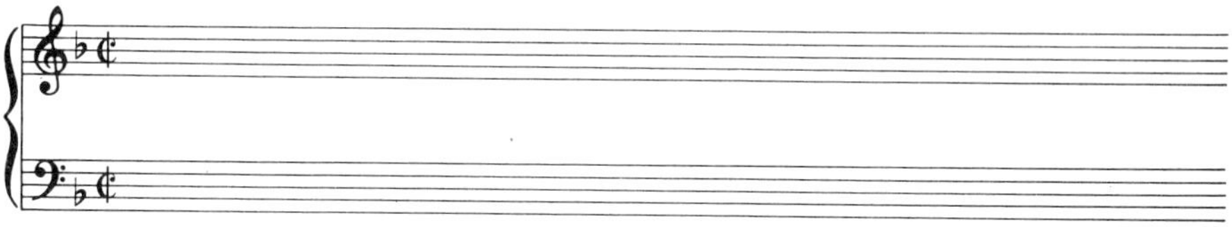

b) Assign the cantus to the lower of two parts and supply a soprano that moves predominantly in eighth notes and uses mostly step motion.

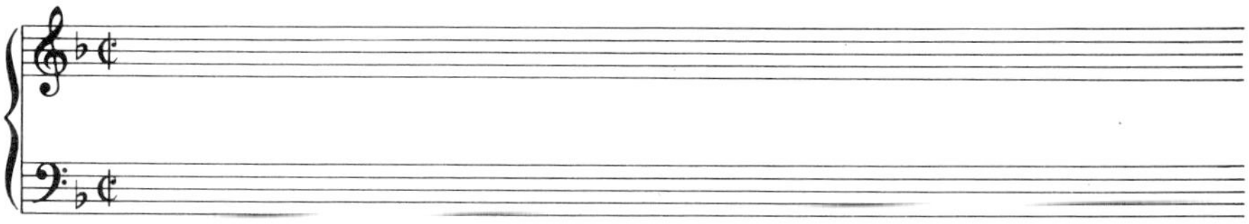

c) Invent an imitative lower part that enters in stretto at the octave on the second beat of measure 2.

d) Invent an imitative variation of the first ten measures of the example in Exercise 1. Write for two voices.

3. After you have familiarized yourself with the following chorale fugue by Pachelbel, make an analysis of the piece modeled after the analysis of Bach's *Fugue in D minor* that appears in the text. Be sure to account for *statements* of the subject and various *treatments* of it, episodes or transitions, and keys and key changes.

After you have completed the analysis, write a paragraph or make an outline in which you compare Pachelbel's chorale fugue with Bach's *Fugue in D minor.* Consider such factors as (a) treatment of the subject, (b) independence of parts, (c) tonal variety (e.g., cadences, variety of keys), and (d) texture.

Pachelbel, "O Lamm Gottes Unschuldig"

10
15
20
25
30
[tr]

4. Listen to a recording and read the score of the extended excerpt from Beethoven's *String Quartet in F minor,* Op. 95, and then answer the questions on page 282. The movement is in ternary form, and its middle section is a fugato. The opening section *(A)* and about half of the fugato are given here.

Beethoven, String Quartet in F minor, Op. 95, 2nd movement

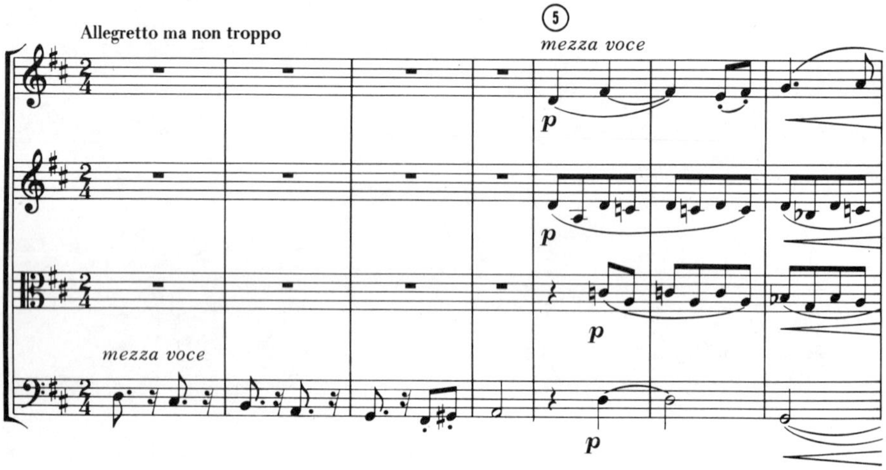

15
20
cresc.
cresc.
cresc.
cresc.
25
p
p
p
p
30
cresc.
cresc.
cresc.
cresc.

(cont.)

35
p
40
45
cresc.
sf
p

50
f
p
55
cresc.
60
sf

a) Although the texture of the opening section *(A)* is mainly homophonic, there is some independence of the string parts. Cite at least three aspects of the texture of measures 1–41 that reflect this independence. Be as specific as possible and give measure references.

b) Several progressive cadences occur in the *A* section. Cite three by measure numbers. Which cadence involves emphasis on V? What kind of cadence closes the *A* section?

c) Measures 13–22 reveal considerable melodic interplay between two of the four voices. Which two parts seem most important between measure 13 and measure 16? Why?

d) Tonal variety is achieved partly through mutation. Cite several examples of mutation in the *A* section where the parallel minor of D major is suggested.

e) The fugato is begun at measure 35 by the viola. Is the answer in the first violin tonal or real?

f) How does the fugue subject relate to the opening cello solo?

g) Cite at least three treatments of material in this movement that are similar to treatments found in the *Fugue in D minor* by Bach discussed in the text.

h) Does this fugato contain an episode? If so, where does it occur?

i) Indicate in order of appearance the keys that are found in the fugato. What is the interval relation of the key that terminates this excerpt to the tonal center of the movement?

Chapter 13

MULTIMOVEMENT COMPOSITIONS

Compositions made up of more than one movement constitute the most significant part of music literature. Composers began to write extended polyphonic works consisting of two or more contrasted yet related movements as early as the fourteenth century. Later centuries have seen the rise of various types of multimovement composition—dance suite, sonata, concerto, symphony, oratorio, cantata, and opera, to name only the most important.

It is not always possible or essential to make a clear distinction between *movement* and *section.* One can only say that the term "movement" is applied to large segments of a composition which are to some degree independent, whereas a "section" is a smaller unit which is closely related to the immediately preceding and following music and is not self-sufficient. The various movements of a long composition are often written in different keys and separated in performance by a pause. In many works written since the latter part of the nineteenth century—for example, Liszt's *Sonata in B minor for Piano*—the distinction between movement and section has been purposely obscured in the interest of creating new form types.

In this chapter we shall note some of the organizational schemes of multimovement compositions. We shall not attempt to deal with all of the various compound forms.

DANCE SUITE

The eighteenth-century dance suite was written primarily for the various keyboard instruments of the time—the clavichord, the harpsichord,* and the organ—although suites for ensembles of several players do exist. The rhythms

*The clavichord is a keyboard instrument which produces a very soft tone. When a key is depressed, a small piece of metal strikes the appropriate string. The clavichord is capable of slight gradations of dynamics. The harpsichord has a light, lucid tone produced by devices which pluck the strings when the keys are depressed. Because of its lack of sustaining power, the harpsichord is best suited to the performance of contrapuntal music, rather than music involving sustained chords.

of the various movements of the suite were derived from popular dances of that time and earlier. Most keyboard suites (they were also called *partitas*) consisted of four more or less standardized movements—*allemande, courante, sarabande,* and *gigue*—with an optional movement sometimes included after the sarabande.

Dance suites usually began and ended with a quick movement. The tempos of the various movements frequently conformed to the following pattern: *fast, moderately fast, slow, quite fast.* Thematic unity was sometimes achieved by the use of similar motivic materials and parallel harmonic plans in the various movements. Each movement was usually in binary form, and all the movements in a suite were usually in the same key.

Four movements of a keyboard dance suite by Froberger are shown in Example 13-1. Note the similar motivic materials used in the four movements:

Allemande (measures 1–2)

Courante (measures 4–7)

Sarabande (measures 3–5)

Gigue (measure 1)

Each movement makes use of the rhythmic patterns and the meter of the dance which gave it its name. Note the variety of texture, rhythm, meter, melody, and keyboard writing found within the suite.

The suite had practically disappeared from the compositional scene by the close of the eighteenth century. However, some composers of the nineteenth and twentieth centuries, such as Grieg, Tchaikovsky, Debussy, and Schoenberg, have revived interest in the suite as a vehicle for music of a

Example 13-1

Froberger, *Suite in G minor for Harpsichord*

(cont.)

Example 13-1 (continued)

(cont.)

Example 13-1 (continued)

nationalistic flavor, for ballets, and for sophisticated adaptations of the stylized eighteenth-century dance suite.*

Contemporary American composers have often turned to the suite in compositions for the peculiarly American medium of the college or high school wind ensemble, a medium that has attracted many young composers and which seems to hold much promise for the future. Among such composers are Gunther Schuller, Vincent Persichetti, William Schuman, and others. Another significant contemporary development is the jazz suite, which has attracted many Americans steeped in the traditions of jazz.

---

*See Grieg's *Peer Gynt Suite* and *Holberg Suite,* Tchaikovsky's *Nutcracker Suite,* Debussy's *Petite Suite,* or Schoenberg's *Suite,* Op. 25. Many nineteenth and twentieth-century suites resemble the Baroque suite in name only.

SONATA

The meaning of the word *sonata* (from *sonare,* meaning "to sound," as opposed to *cantare,* meaning "to sing") varies somewhat from one historical period to another. In the Baroque period (about 1600 to 1750) the term was applied so loosely that any attempt to pin down its various meanings would involve a great deal of effort. In general, sonatas written before the advent of Viennese Classicism (about 1730 to 1830) were multimovement or multisectional pieces for one, two, three, or four players, with the movements or sections commonly arranged in the following pattern: *slow, fast, slow, fast.* Such works often reveal the influence of the stylized dance rhythms associated primarily with the suite. These pieces fall into two general categories, the *chamber sonata (sonata da camera)* and the *church sonata (sonata da chiesa).* The former was akin to the dance suite; the latter, the more significant of the two from a historical point of view, was noteworthy for the inclusion of movements of an abstract nature, not based on dance rhythms or any other preestablished musical materials.

An outstanding feature of the Baroque sonata was the accompanimental support supplied by a *continuo bass.* Example 13-2 shows an example of a continuo bass. The composer indicated merely the bass line and, by means of numbers and accidentals, the chord progressions that were to be used in the accompaniment.* The accompanist, playing a harpsichord or an organ, filled in the upper parts as he went along, using appropriate chord spacings and doublings, melodic lines, and embellishments. The bass line was often reinforced by a low stringed instrument such as the viola da gamba, cello, or bass viol.

Not all Baroque sonatas called for a continuo accompaniment; many were written for solo instruments alone, without accompaniment. Those that did call for a continuo part were frequently written for three performers—two main players and the keyboard accompanist. Because of their three-part texture, such works were known as *trio sonatas.* Trio sonatas are the most characteristic type of preclassical sonata composition.

There is no doubt that the most important musical form to evolve in the course of Western musical development was the *classical sonata.* This form emerged during the eighteenth century as a product of changing patterns in the musical and social structure of Europe, the rejection of many preestablished forms, and the advent of an unprecedented amount of participation in music by amateurs.

The evolution of the classical sonata was in effect an amalgamation of several diverse formal elements into one compound form. The old form types of the Baroque era, such as the *aria da capo.* the French and Italian overtures, the trio sonata, and the canzona, were largely abandoned in favor of this new compound form.

---

*The code for abbreviating the accompanying chords is called *figured bass;* an explanation of figured bass symbols is appended to this chapter.

Example 13-2

Vivaldi, *Sonata da Camera in D minor,* Corrente

The compositions written in classical sonata form consist of three main groups: (1) *solo* or *duo* sonatas, that is, sonatas for single instruments (for example, piano or organ) or pairs of instruments (violin and piano, flute and piano, cello and piano, etc.); (2) sonatas for *small ensembles* of three, four, or as many as eight players, for example, piano trios (for piano, violin, and cello), string quartets (for two violins, viola, and cello), and wind quintets (for flute, oboe, clarinet, French horn, and bassoon); and (3) sonatas for *orchestra,* commonly called symphonies.

The piano supplanted the harpsichord as the mainstay of keyboard accompaniment not long after its invention about 1722, and the continuo bass was discarded in favor of written-out piano accompaniments. During the period of Viennese Classicism, most composers regarded the piano as better suited than the harpsichord to the prevailing homophonic textures (for example, in the music of Haydn and Mozart).

Sonatas usually consist of three contrasting movements in the following order: *fast, slow, fast.* Two important modifications of this scheme are frequently found. The first is a four-movement arrangement *(fast, slow, rather fast, fast)* resulting from the interpolation of a *minuet* movement (or a *scherzo* in works by Beethoven and some of his successors). The second modification is the occasional use of an *introductory* passage in slow tempo, preceding the beginning of the first movement proper; Haydn used this modification quite frequently. Beethoven's Seventh Symphony contains both of these modifications of the basic pattern of tempos.

It is no exaggeration to say that the sonata has served as the vehicle for much of the most durable and profound music of the past 200 years. Despite many internal changes, the sonata principle continues to thrive in some current music as a remarkably flexible formal pattern.

SONATA ALLEGRO FORM

The initial movement of the compound form called sonata is most often composed in a formal pattern called *sonata allegro form.* The pervading character of the work as a whole, notwithstanding the changing moods and varied materials of the other movements, is usually enunciated in the first movement. Sonata allegro form (often called simply sonata form) consists of three main sections: *statement* (exposition of materials), *digression and development* (elaboration and development of materials introduced in the first section), and *return and close* (restatement of materials introduced in the opening section, followed by a closing passage).

Despite the apparent similarity between sonata allegro form and ternary form—both have the same number of main sections, and both include a restatement of the opening material—the comparison should not be overstressed. Whereas ternary form consists of two contrasted sections followed by a return of the first, the second section being composed primarily of *new* materials, the middle section in sonata allegro form is devoted primarily to a development and elaboration of thematic materials stated in the exposition, rather than the introduction of new materials.

Exposition

The function of the exposition section is to give a clear and logically ordered presentation of materials (melodies, textures, chord patterns) in the framework of a specific relationship between two (or more) tonalities; frequently the materials are arranged in two large groups, one stressing the principal key of the movement, the other stressing the dominant or some other related key. Expositions vary in length, in the variety of the content, and in many other ways. As a rule, the two tonally related groups of material unfold statements of contrasted thematic ideas, usually called *themes.* It is important to note that themes do not necessarily consist of songlike melodic materials. Quite often, themes are passages constructed out of motivic materials; such themes may seem open-ended and lacking in self-sufficiency, as if they "need" further exploitation in the development section (and elsewhere).

The first movement of Beethoven's *Sonata in E♭ for Piano,* Op. 31, No. 3, reproduced in Example 13-3, illustrates sonata allegro form. Listen to a performance of the exposition (measures 1 through 88), noting particularly the differentiation of materials in the sections marked Theme 1 and Theme 2. Note also the passage marked Transition, which links Theme 1 with Theme 2 while bringing about a change of key from E♭ to B♭. The contrast between Theme 1 and Theme 2 is apparent in the thematic profiles, rhythms, registers, keys, and accompaniments. The easy motion and rather relaxed pace of Theme 1 contrasts with the more outgoing, active lyricism of Theme 2. In both thematic groups, the basic materials are stated and then immediately restated. This exposition is characterized by simplicity of design and uncomplicated projection of materials. Such simplicity of presentation helps mark the various elements heard in the exposition for recognition in subsequent sections.

Development

When musicians speak of *development,* they are referring to the numerous techniques for manipulating, reshaping, varying, and in general elaborating materials stated in the exposition. It is in the development section of a movement in sonata allegro form that the composer's craft (or lack of it) becomes most evident. The development section is a test of the composer's imagination and his capacity to solve the problem of sustaining musical continuity and interest while dealing anew with previously stated materials. Only a handful of composers have been able to write convincing musical developments.

Study the development section in Example 13-3 (measures 89 through 136). Two passages in this section deserve special attention. In measures 89 through 110, observe the fragmented treatment of the opening motive and the movement toward the key of C minor; note also the altered restatement of Theme 1 coupled with a mutation from C minor to C major in measures 101 and 102. The bass figure at measure 109 is derived from measure 20 of the exposition. Measures 122 through 136 are reminiscent of both the closing theme of the exposition (beginning at measure 65) and of the broken chords of the transition from Theme 1 to Theme 2 (beginning at measure 25). Try to find other relationships between the development section and the materials presented in the exposition.

We have already noted the importance of tonality in the exposition section. Tonal relationships are equally important in the development section. Most development sections reveal a dynamic treatment of tonality, a treatment which might be described as digressive and exploratory. The composer

(text cont. on page 306)

Example 13-3

Beethoven, *Sonata in E♭ major for Piano,* Op. 31, No. 3, 1st movement

EXPOSITION Theme 1

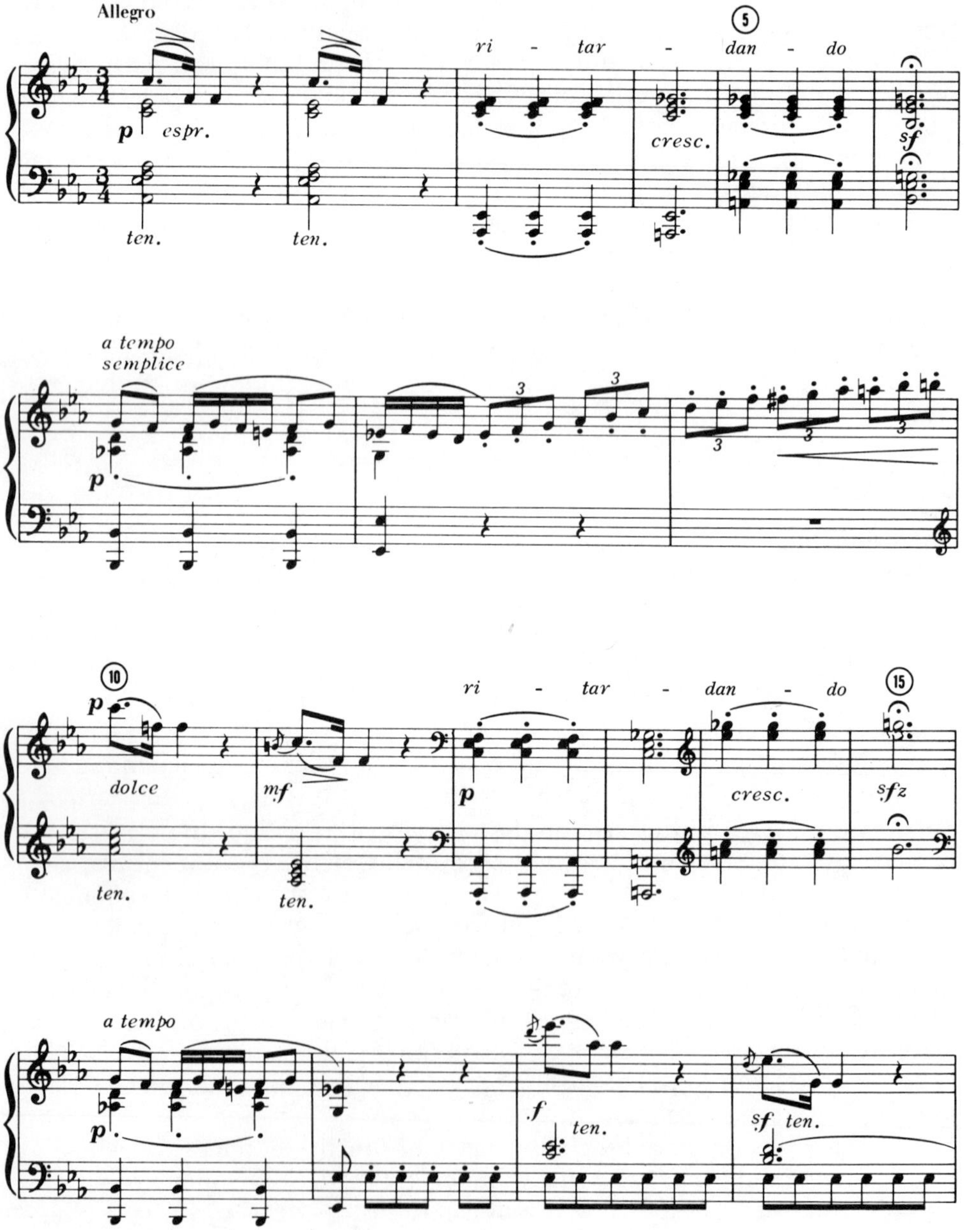

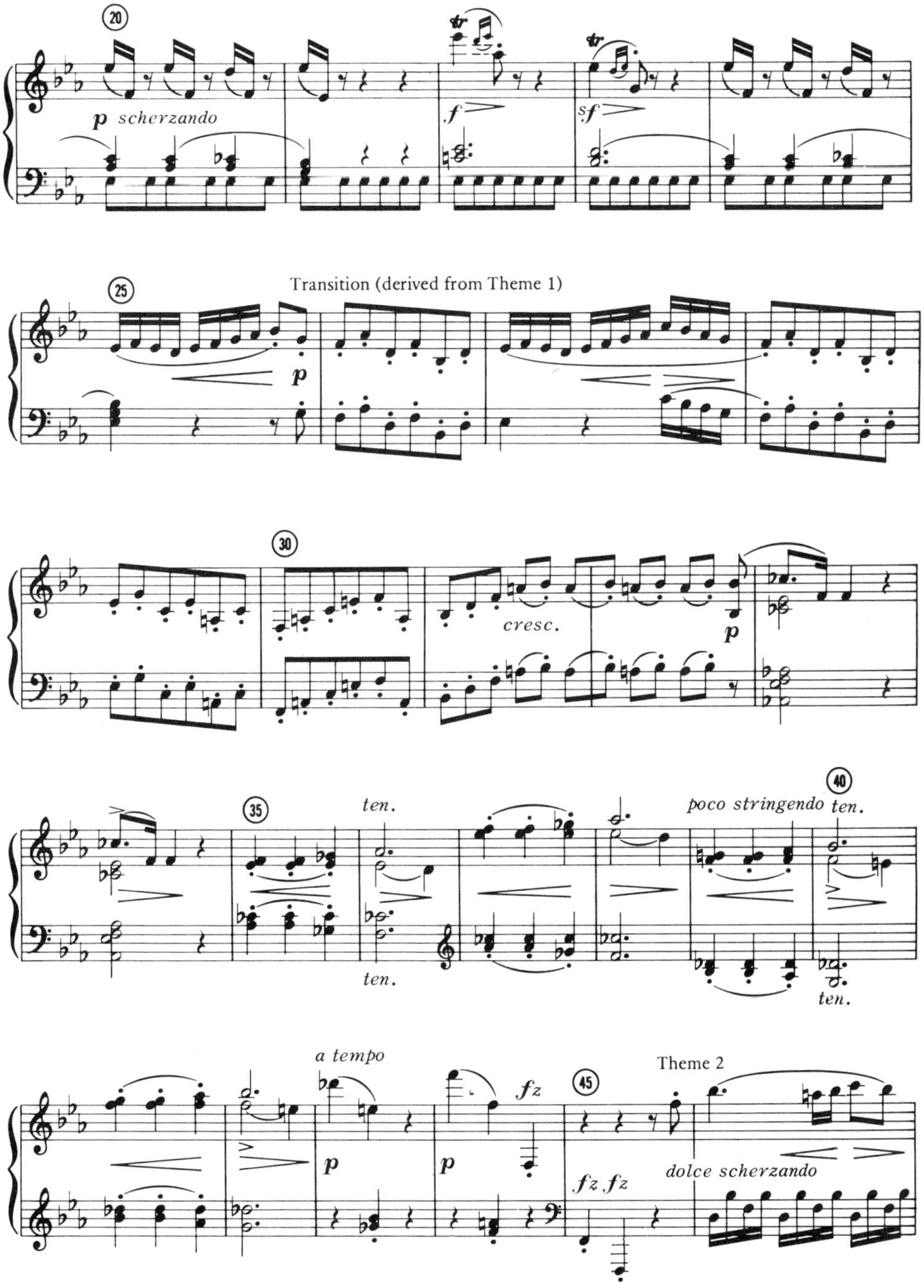
20
p scherzando
f
sf
25
Transition (derived from Theme 1)
p
30
cresc.
p
35
ten.
ten.
poco stringendo
40
ten.
ten.
a tempo
p
p
fz
45
Theme 2
fz fz
dolce scherzando

(cont.)

Example 13-3 (continued)

cresc.
espr.
mf
65
Closing material
ten.
mf
p
cresc.
70
sf
sf
sf
f p
cresc.
75
f
mf
f
f
80
p
p
cresc.
f

(cont.)

Example 13-3 (continued)

marc.
cresc.
f
115
ten.
sfz
f
pp
p
120
f
ten.
sf
ten.
125
sf
ten.
sf
Sempre forte
130

(cont.)

Example 13-3 (continued)

160
sf
sf
dimin.
Transition
p
p
165
cresc.
f
sf
Theme 2
sf
170
fp
f
p
cantabile
175
cresc.
dimin.

(cont.)

Example 13-3 (continued)

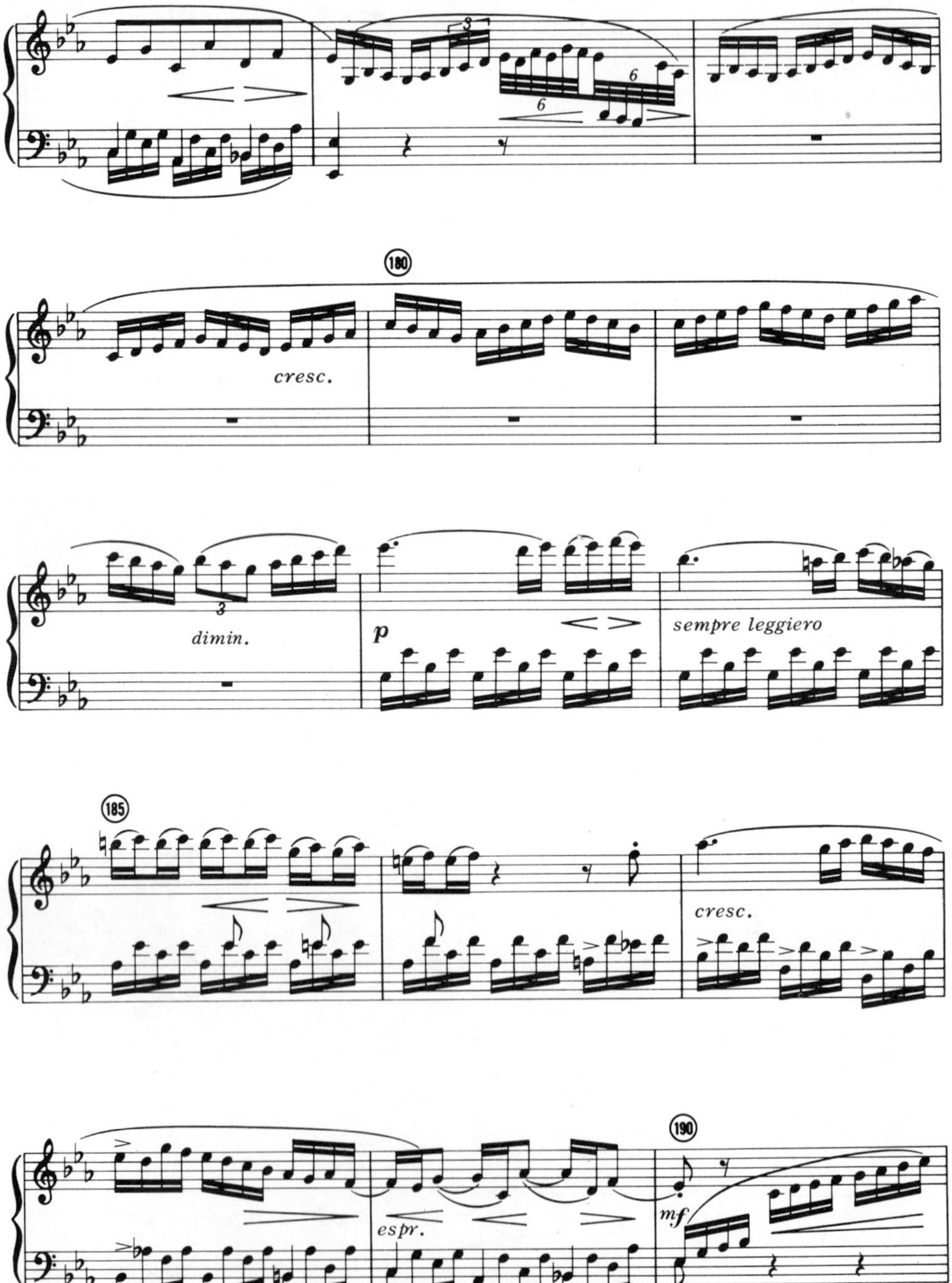

ten.
ten.
p
leggiero
195
poco a poco cresc.
200
f
p
f
p
f
205
f
mf
cresc.
f
fz p
p cresc.

(cont.)

Example 13-3 (continued)

p espr.
ten.
ten.
240
ri - tar - dan - do
a tempo
p
cresc.
245
p
p
p
250
p
ff
fz

tends to avoid strong cadences, with the result that there is little tonal stability in the sense of sharply defined key feeling. Sometimes the composer uses rapid shifts of key in an attempt to solve the problem of maintaining continuity while heightening interest, building a climax, and intensifying the sense of forward motion. In almost all development sections, the composer avoids any strong assertion of the principal key of the movement. By making the return to the tonic key coincide with the return of the original thematic material, he heightens the psychological impact of the return.

Return

The return, or *recapitulation,* of the original thematic materials is probably of greater psychological importance in sonata allegro form than in other forms. It is in the return, which coincides with the establishment of the tonic key, that the excitement and conflicts of the development section are resolved. After subjecting the listener to the tonal instability, polyphony, and dynamic tensions of the development, the composer rewards him by restating the original, familiar material with which the movement began. The return usually projects a sense of arrival, a confirmation of the opening propositions of the work.

In most sonata allegro movements, the original materials are modified in the return to avoid the possible monotony of literal repetition. More important, the tonic key is reasserted *throughout* the return, not only in the first thematic group; this emphasis on the tonic key reinforces the sense of arrival.

Listen to the return in Example 13-3 (measures 137 through 213). Note that Theme 2 is now in the key of E♭ rather than B♭ major. The transition passage linking Theme 1 to Theme 2 has been shortened, with the measures which produced the modulation to B♭ in the exposition omitted. Note also the passage leading up to the return (measures 131 through 136). The absence of important thematic materials in this passage helps to create a sense of anticipation, heightening the sense of arrival when the return begins.

Coda

A *coda* (the term comes from the Italian word meaning "tail") is a formal appendage, an extension of a composition beyond the termination of the form proper. A short coda is usually called a *codetta.*

Composers employ codas for various reasons: to allow more time for closure, to develop further the thematic materials of the piece, to reinforce the tonic key feeling, or even to introduce new materials which are better suited to closure than are those of the movement proper. The movement reproduced in Example 13-3 has been extended 40 measures beyond the point in the return which corresponds to the close of the exposition. The coda in this movement begins with materials closely derived from the exposition. It also begins with the tonic triad in E♭ major, approached from the dominant; thus, like many codas, it serves to reinforce tonal stability.

In some works the coda achieves the stature of a full-fledged section, comparable in length to the development section. Beethoven's Third Symphony (the *Eroica*) contains a first-movement coda that amounts to a second development section, occurring after the return. On the other hand, the codas in some of Mozart's symphonies (they should actually be called codettas) consist of nothing more than three or four repetitions of the V^7-I progression stated by the full orchestra. Codas are, indeed, highly variable in content and length, and the nature of a coda depends more on the individual composer's particular solution of the formal problem at hand than on observance of stereotyped models.

Other Movements

Sonata allegro form is usually found in the first movement of a sonata or symphony. The second movement is usually a slow movement in ternary or variation form. Frequently, however, slow movements are also cast in sonata allegro form, though sometimes with a very short or no development section.

In a four-movement sonata composition, the third movement is usually a minuet (or scherzo) and trio, a simple three-part form in which the minuet or scherzo is repeated after the trio is heard. This type of movement constitutes a point of relaxation in the overall design of the work. It usually contrasts markedly with the more profound character of the preceding slow movement. Occasionally the order of the second and third movements in a four-movement work is reversed, with the slow movement coming third.

Rondo form is frequently used in the final movement of a sonata or symphony. Sometimes, however, the composer returns to sonata allegro form in the last movement, or combines elements of sonata allegro and rondo to produce a movement in *sonata rondo* form. A set of variations or a fugue is occasionally found as the final movement. A famous example of the former is the last movement of Beethoven's Third Symphony. The same composer's Piano Sonata, Op. 101, has a fugue in the last movement.

CONCERTO

Like sonata, the word *concerto* has been used in many contexts during the past 400 years of Western music. Musicians of the late Renaissance and early Baroque (about 1550 to 1650) used concerto as a name for ecclesiastical compositions (sacred concertos) for both vocal and instrumental choirs. Such compositions featured the opposition of contrasted sound groups and explored rather boldly the rich potential of vocal-instrumental contrast. The term *concertato style* is an outgrowth of this textural procedure.

Instrumental concertos of two somewhat different types were written during the Baroque era. The *concerto grosso,* which thrived during the latter stages of the Baroque, pitted a special *group* of players, usually three to five, against the orchestra proper and the continuo. In such pieces the solo group was called the *concertino,* the other players the *ripieno,* or support. In some concertos, particularly those of Corelli and Handel, the concertini were composed of solo strings, rather than a collection of winds or of winds and strings. Bach's Brandenburg Concertos constitute the high-water mark of concerto grosso writing. In these works, particularly Nos. 1, 2, 4, and 5, Bach created an animated or, in the slow movements, intensely moving dialogue between the small groups of soloists and the orchestra. A dialogue of this type, from a concerto grosso by Corelli, is shown in Example 13-4. Note the role of the supporting continuo in providing a harmonic framework for the solo passages and for the contrapuntally combined melodies of the soloists and the orchestra. (The continuo part was not written out on a separate stave, but was read from the bass viol or cello part.)

The other type of instrumental concerto written during the Baroque period was the *solo concerto.* The solo concertos of Bach and his contemporaries featured a lively interplay between the orchestra, which contributed to formal unity by reiterating statements of a principal thematic section called a *ritornello,* or refrain, and a single soloist, who played materials of an episodic nature or freely derived from the ritornello. This type of interplay is called *concertato* technique. As in the grosso concerto, thematic and textural contrast, rather than motivic development as found in the later sonata, was the most compelling feature of the writing. The Baroque concerto became standardized as a three-movement form: *fast, slow, fast.* *

The development of the solo concerto of the Baroque era led directly to the subsequent perfection by Mozart and others of the classical concerto for solo player (such as the piano, violin, cello, or flute) and orchestra. This late eighteenth-century form evolved hand in hand with the development of the classical orchestra; the characteristic continuo of the Baroque orchestra, which played an essential role in the concertos of the Baroque period, was discarded. The evolution of the classical solo concerto from the Baroque concerto is a complex historical question well beyond the scope of this book. Of greatest significance is the adherence of the classical concerto to the concertante technique of *dialogue* and *opposition* between soloist and orchestra. It is the retention of this principle, together with the adoption of a modification of sonata allegro form (so-called concerto sonata allegro form), that constitutes the formal basis of the classical concerto. Recent composers such as Stravinsky have shown interest in reviving the spirit, if not the substance, of earlier concertos.

*The slow movement was often no more than a bridge between the fast movements; it frequently consisted merely of a Phrygian cadence—iv^6-V in minor keys, ii^6-III (with the third of iii raised to make it a major triad) in major keys.

Example 13-4

Corelli, *Concerto Grosso in C minor,* Op. 6, No. 3

(cont.)

Example 13-4 (continued)

(cont.)

Example 13-4 (continued)

(cont.)

Example 13-4 (continued)

55
60
65

Works in concerto sonata allegro form contain a *double* exposition. The orchestra usually presents the principal material of the movement in the tonic key, followed by an incisive cadence. The same materials, sometimes modified, are restated by the solo instrument, accompanied by the orchestra. The second exposition normally features at least two keys. Through such a procedure the composer indicates that the work is going to involve the staggering of material in dialogues between the orchestra and the soloist. An example of such a dialogue appears in Example 13-5.

Example 13-5

Mozart, *Concerto in C major for Piano and Orchestra,* K. 503, 1st movement

A special feature of the concerto, not associated with sonata allegro form *per se,* is the *cadenza.* This *unaccompanied* passage allows for virtuoso display of an improvisatory nature, often derived in part from the thematic materials of the movement. The cadenza usually occurs, heralded by a progressive cadence in the orchestra, at the end of the recapitulation, just before the coda. Example 13-6 shows part of a cadenza from a concerto by Beethoven. In the time of Mozart it was customary for the soloist to improvise the cadenza. Beethoven started the practice of writing out cadenzas, and other composers generally followed suit. In the later nineteenth century the formal cadenza virtually disappeared from the concerto.

Example 13-6

Beethoven, *Piano Concerto No. 4 in G major*, Op. 58, Cadenza

COMPOUND VOCAL FORMS

The expression "compound vocal forms" is more a convenient than a meaningful way of describing a group of types of large vocal composition. In this section we shall deal with no new forms, but rather ways of combining various forms into a composite work of considerable scope.

Mass Setting

Nearly all Mass compositions are settings of the Ordinary of the Mass, which consists of those portions—the Kyrie, Gloria, Credo, Sanctus, and Agnus Dei—which remain the same, for the most part, for all services of the liturgical year, as opposed to the Proper, which consists of those parts which vary from service to service throughout the church year. Mass composition began with monophonic settings in the form of unmetered modal melodies designed for performance by soloists or small male chorus. Such settings constitute the vast repertoire of Gregorian chant, contained in the *Liber Usualis,* portions of which are still sung in the High Masses of the Roman Catholic Church.

Much of the historical significance of Gregorian chant lies in its continued use in polyphonic Mass settings, which began to evolve in the ninth

Example 13-7

Binchois, *Sanctus* (from an incomplete Mass setting)

century. The polyphonic Mass flowered in the Renaissance. A twentieth-century Mass setting is Hindemith's, written in 1963. Example 13-7 is an excerpt from a fifteenth-century Mass movement. The cantus firmus used in this work is a Gregorian chant melody composed more than 1000 years ago.*

In this setting the composer has placed the cantus in the top part (often called the *superius*), shaping the melody in such a way that the cantus notes frequently coincide with the beginning of new words in the text. Note that considerable elaboration and invention occurs in the upper voice in the form of rhythmic interpolations of other tones between the cantus notes. This technique, called *paraphrase,* is fundamentally a variational process.

A complete Mass setting usually consisted of five movements: Kyrie, Gloria, Credo, Sanctus, and Agnus Dei. The cantus firmus chosen as the basis of the entire work usually appeared in each movement, though frequently there were sections within a movement where the cantus was absent. The cantus often migrated from voice to voice, and various techniques were used to elaborate it. In the fifteenth century, secular tunes began to be used as the cantus, weakening but not destroying the pervading influence of Gregorian chant. Sixteenth-century Masses were frequently based in part on preexistent secular or sacred pieces; they were called *parody Masses.* Palestrina, in particular, employed parody in many of his Masses.

Cantata

A *cantata* (from the Italian word *cantare,* meaning "to sing") is comprised of a number of contrasting vocal movements, usually four or more, including choruses, recitatives, arias, and duets. The greatest production of cantatas occurred during the Baroque period; at first they were based primarily on secular texts, but religious texts came to predominate in the later part of the Baroque era. J. S. Bach wrote about 200 church cantatas, many of which are called *chorale cantatas* because they use a Lutheran chorale tune as a basis for variation and thematic reference.

The chorale "Ein' feste Burg" ("A Mighty Fortress") serves as the basis for one of Bach's best-known cantatas. Example 13-8 shows an excerpt from this cantata, in which the chorale's first phrase is treated imitatively and richly elaborated by chorus and orchestra. It should be clear that this manner of dealing with a preexistent melody is an extension of techniques developed in earlier Mass and motet compositions. However, whereas the text of a Mass movement or motet was usually different from the words to which the original chant melody was sung, the text of a cantata based on a chorale tune was ordinarily the original chorale text, or an elaboration of it.

---

*The technique of basing a composition on a cantus firmus was discussed briefly in Chapter 12 in connection with the motet.

Example 13-8

J. S. Bach, *Cantata No. 80,* "Ein' feste Burg"

10
Ein' fe - - - - ste Burg ist
- - - - ste Burg ist un - ser Gott, ein' gu - te Wehr und Waf - -
gu - te Wehr und Waf - - - - - fen, ein' gu - te Wehr und

(cont.)

Example 13-8 (continued)

The instrumental accompaniment for a cantata typically ranged from continuo alone to an orchestra of somewhat limited resources, such as strings and a few winds. In more festive works, such as the one quoted in Example 13-8, a small orchestra consisting of a few members of each instrumental family was employed.

Oratorio

An oratorio is quite similar to a church cantata. The difference between the two lies mainly in the greater resources and display that are characteristic of the oratorio; an oratorio is usually scored for large orchestra, several soloists, and chorus, and often calls for sung narration. Considerable emphasis on the chorus is common in oratorios, the best known of which are Handel's *Messiah* and Bach's *Passion According to St. John* and *Passion According to St. Matthew.*

A characteristic feature of oratorios is the pairing of recitative and aria, the recitative preceding the aria and providing a narrative introduction to it. *Recitative* is a form of vocal narration based on the rhythms and inflections of speech; an *aria* is an explicitly musical and poetic elaboration of the implications of the narration. A distinction is usually made between two types of recitative: *secco,* which is unexpressive declamation supported by unobtrusive sustained chords; and *accompagnato,* which is closer to song than to speech, treats the text in an expressive and occasionally dramatic manner, and is supported by an accompaniment which contributes to the expressive treatment of the words. Recitatives are through-composed, whereas arias are often written in ternary form, with a literal repetition of the first section signaled by the words *da capo.* Example 13-9 shows, in piano and vocal score, a *recitativo accompagnato* and part of the following aria.

Example 13-9

J. S. Bach, *Passion According to St. Matthew,* "O Blessed Saviour" (Recitative) and "Grief and Pain" (Aria)

(cont.)

Example 13-9 (continued)

10
Alto Solo
mf
Grief and pain,
15
grief and pain
Rend re - pent - ing
p
p
20
hearts in twain,
f
25
cresc.
grief and
p ten.
30
pain,
grief and pain
rend re - pent - ing hearts in
35
p con espress.

The role of the accompaniment in this aria is clearly that of establishing mood, as well as heightening interset by the interplay of voice and instruments. The recurrence of the opening instrumental passage in measures 21 through 28 unifies the movement, provides variety of texture and timbre, and underscores the affective meaning of the material of the introduction, which is never duplicated exactly in the vocal line. One cannot help but note in this setting Bach's use of musical patterns and a vocal melody that project a vivid image of the text.

Opera

Opera combines solo and ensemble singing with orchestral backing, scenery, and acting. It is thus a unique composite art form embodying visual, theatrical, and musical modes of expression. Like oratorios (with which they are sometimes compared), operas typically consist of a succession of numbers, including instrumental overtures and interludes, vocal solos (recitatives and arias), duets, trios, and larger vocal ensembles, and choral numbers.

Opera originated in Italy in the seventeenth century. The earliest operas were typically based on subjects borrowed from legend and mythology; an example is Monteverdi's *Orfeo* (1607), set to a text by Alessandro Striggio. Since the seventeenth century, operas have been produced continuously by virtually every country that has shared in the development of Western music, Italy, France, and Germany being the most important contributors to operatic literature.

Composers usually organize an opera in such a way as to bring the vocal solos and small ensembles into prominence as the high points of musical interest. The chorus normally plays a subsidiary role (although there are certain operas in which the chorus is very prominent, such as Mussorgsky's *Boris Godunov* and Borodin's *Prince Igor*). In the early eighteenth century the standard form for the vocal solos was the *aria da capo* preceded by a recitative, which, we have seen, was also used in the oratorio. The practice of preceding an aria by a recitative continued into the nineteenth century, but the *da capo* form was largely abandoned in favor of a freer structure. In the early nineteenth-century operas of Rossini, Bellini, and Donizetti, and in the early operas of Verdi, many large vocal solos consisted of three parts: an introductory recitative, a *cavatina* (a slow, songlike melody), and a *cabaletta* (a fast concluding section calling for great vocal display). Since the time of Wagner (1813-1883), the formal aria has been an increasingly rare occurrence in opera, though it is still found in works which hark back to earlier styles, such as Stravinsky's *The Rake's Progress.* With *Lohengrin* (1847), Wagner introduced what he considered to be a new art form, the *music drama,* in which a string of successive, separate numbers is abandoned in favor of a continuously unfolding interplay of voice and orchestra.

Opera has made use of several forms associated primarily with instrumental music. Many operas, especially French operas, incorporate a ballet suite into one of the acts. Purcell used the passacaglia form as the basis for one of the arias in *Dido and Aeneas.* Mozart (for example, in *The Marriage of Figaro*) applied the techniques and tonal relationships of the classical symphony to opera. Richard Strauss employed the techniques and style of the tone poem in *Salome* and *Elektra.* Britten used the variation form as a structural principle in *The Turn of the Screw.* Opera has, in fact, participated in most of the major developments in the historical evolution of musical style since the seventeenth century.

The interested reader can formulate a good idea of the materials and historical evolution of opera by thoughtful study of the following operas: Monteverdi's *Orfeo* (1607), Purcell's *Dido and Aeneas* (1689), Rameau's *Hippolyte et Aricie* (1733), Handel's *Alcina* (1735), Gluck's *Orfeo ed Euridice* (1762), Mozart's *The Marriage of Figaro* (1786), Weber's *Der Freischütz* (1821), Bellini's *Norma* (1831), Verdi's *La Traviata* (1853), Gounod's *Faust* (1859), Wagner's *Tristan und Isolde* (1865), Mussorgsky's *Boris Godunov* (1874), Puccini's *La Bohème* (1896), Debussy's *Pelléas et Mélisande* (1902), Richard Strauss's *Salome* (1905), Berg's *Wozzeck* (1925), Stravinsky's *The Rake's Progress* (1951), and Argento's *The Boor* (1960). If time is limited, the reader might restrict himself to the works listed above by Monteverdi, Mozart, Verdi, Wagner, Berg, and Argento.

A complete number from Verdi's *Aida* is shown in Example 13-10 in piano and vocal score. Listen to a recording or sing the excerpt, which consists of a brief recitative and extended aria. What are its broad formal outlines? Are there places where the text seems to suggest the choice of musical material? What are the harmonic materials of the piece? Are there ways in which the orchestral accompaniment contributes to the dramatic meaning of the text? How does the composer create tonal variety? What kinds of texture are used?

Example 13-10

Verdi, *Aida,* "Se quel guerrier io fossi" (Recitative) and "Celeste Aida" (Aria)

(cont.)

Example 13-10 (continued)

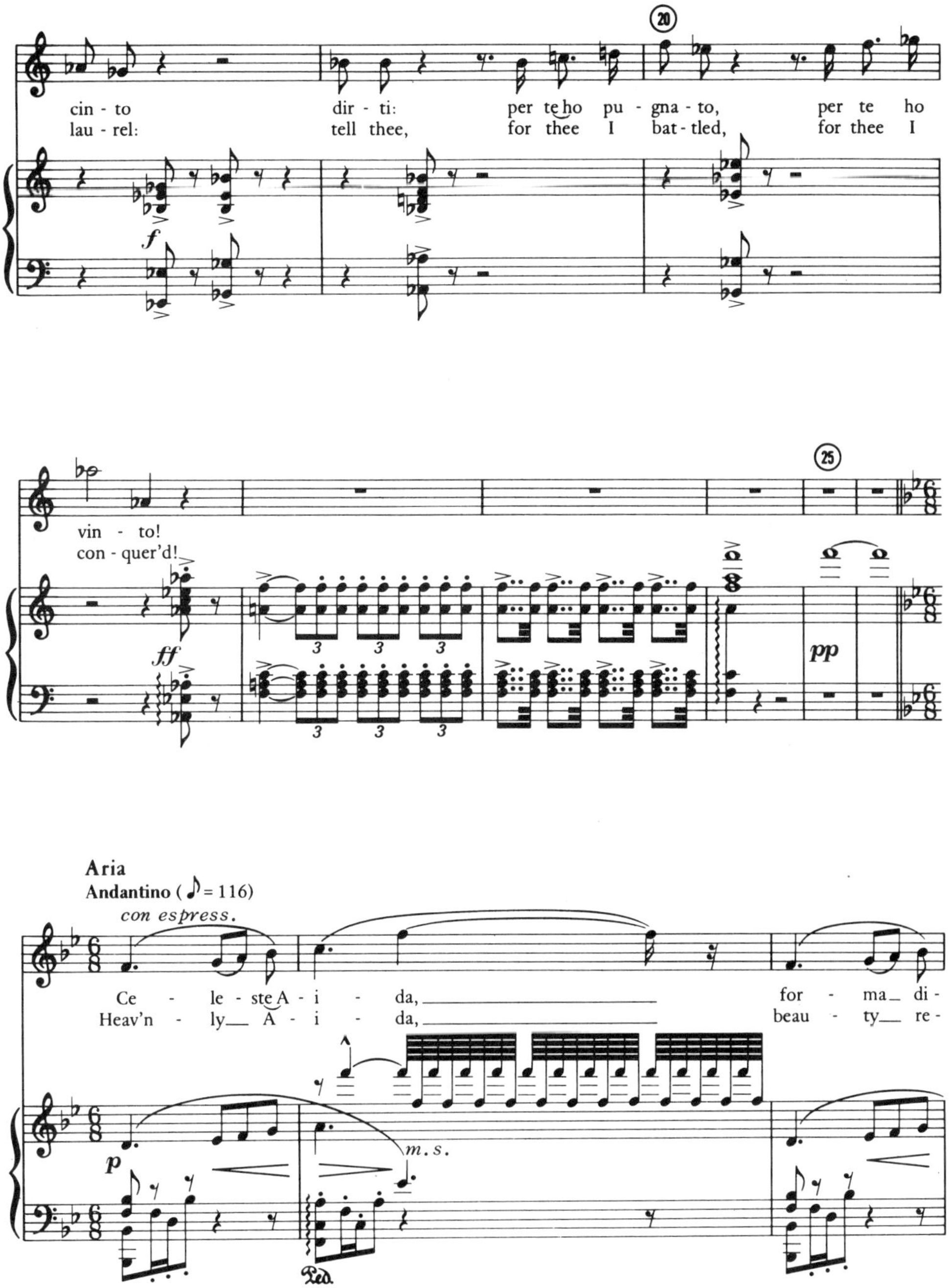
20
cin - to
lau - rel:
dir - ti:
tell thee,
per te ho pu - gna - to,
for thee I bat - tled,
per te ho
for thee I
f
vin - to!
con - quer'd!
ff
25
pp
Aria
Andantino (♪ = 116)
con espress.
Ce - le - ste A - i - da,
Heav'n - ly A - i - da,
for - ma di -
beau - ty re -
p
m.s.
Ped.

(cont.)

Example 13-10 (continued)

vi - ta sei lo splen - dor.
spir - it in beau - - - ty's light.
p espress.
m.s.
15
sempre dolciss.
Il tuo bel cie - lo vor - rei ri - dar - ti, le dol - ci
Would that, thy bright skies once more be - hold - ing, Breathing the
m.d.
m.s.
m.d.
m.s.
20
animando un poco
brez - ze del pa - trio suol· un re gal ser - to sul crin po -
air of thy na - tive land, Round thy fair brow a di - a - dem
m.d.

(cont.)

Example 13-10 (continued)

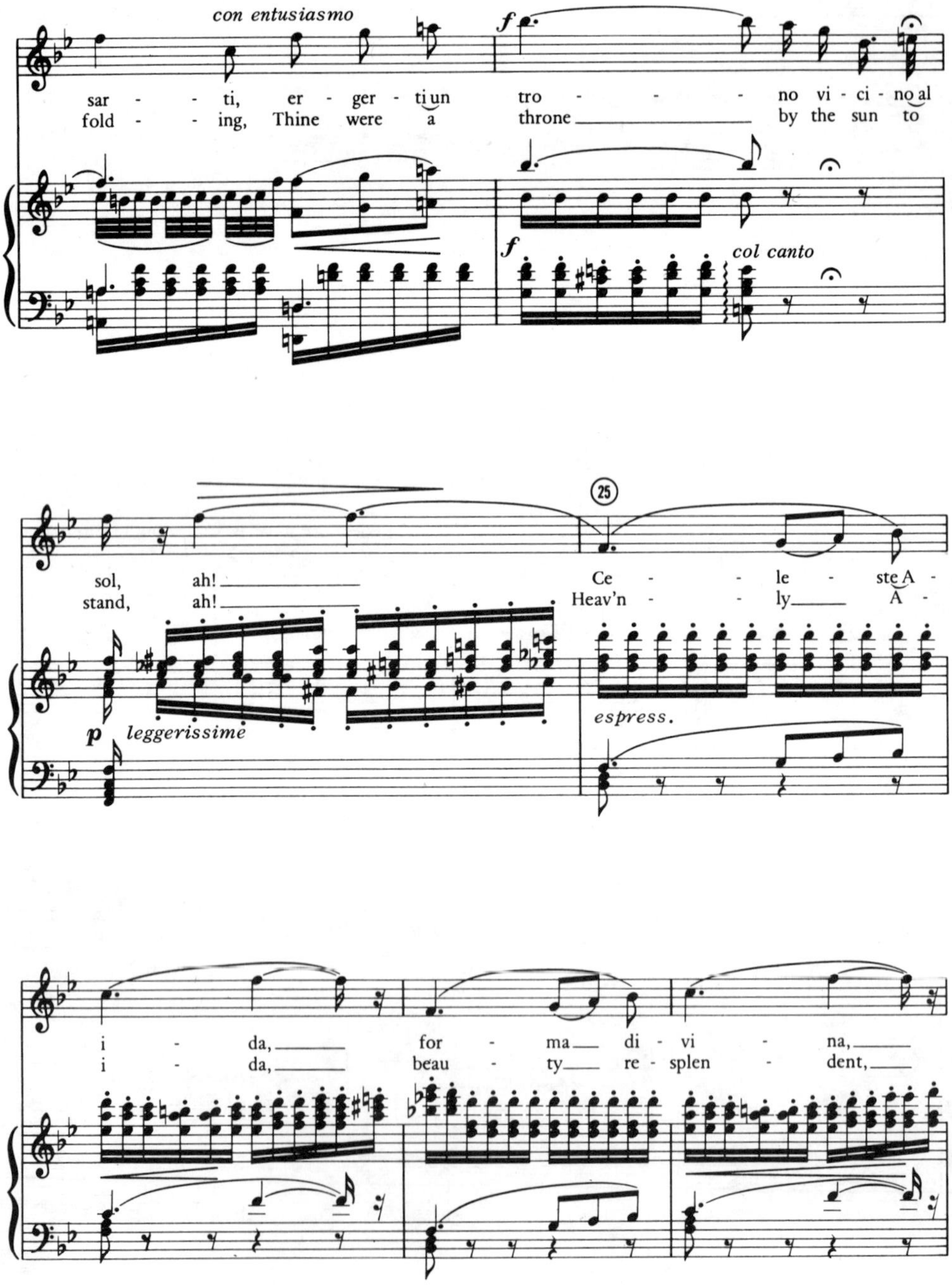

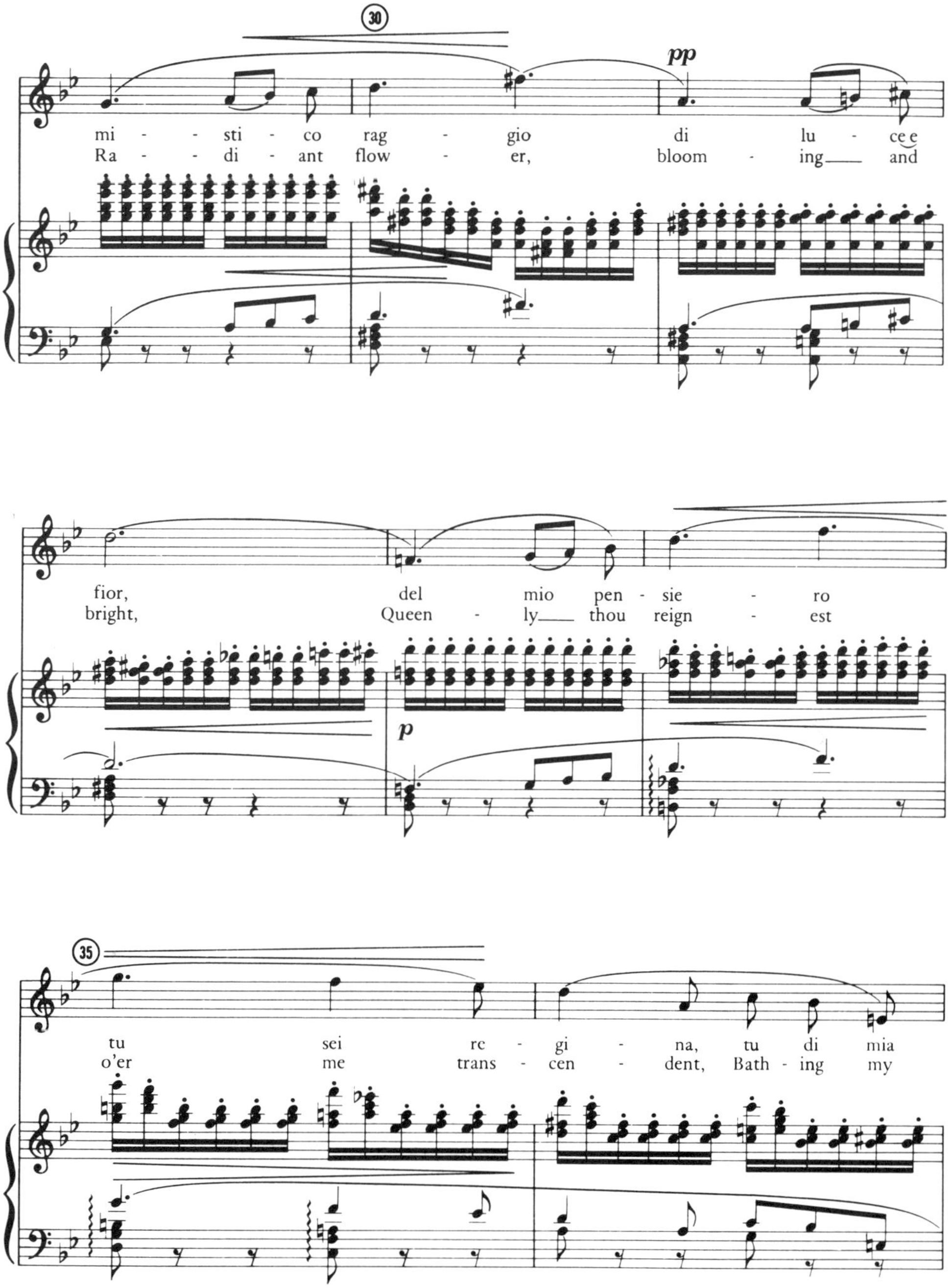
30
pp
mi - - sti - co rag - gio di lu - ce e
Ra - - di - ant flow - er, bloom - ing and
fior, del mio pen - sie - ro
bright, Queen - ly thou reign - est
p
35
tu sei re - gi - na, tu di mia
o'er me trans - cen - dent, Bath - ing my

(cont.)

Example 13-10 (continued)

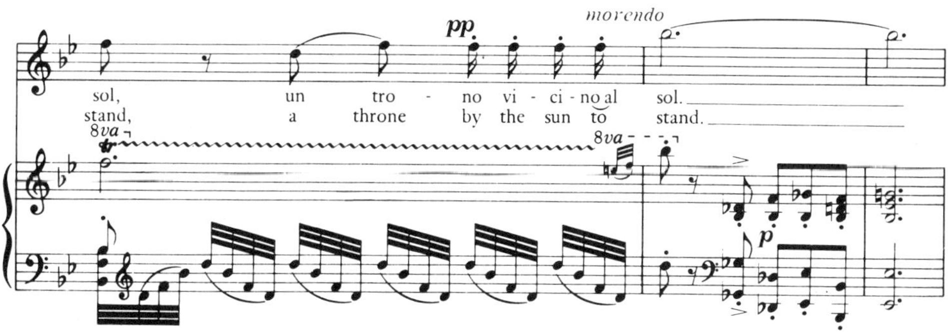

EXERCISES

1. A complete movement for string quartet, arranged in open score, is included here as the basis for a summary problem which involves many of the facets of musical materials and organization that we have dealt with. Familiarize yourself with the piece by silent reading and, if possible, keyboard realization. Then confirm your impressions of the piece by listening to a recording. When you feel well acquainted with the piece, complete the analytical problems below and on pages 346-348.

   a) Write down the principal melodic materials that constitute the basis for the movement. Identify each melodic figure with a letter of the alphabet for future reference.

Beethoven, String Quartet in F major, Op. 18, No. 1, 1st movement

(cont.)

cresc.
f
fp
p
ff
sf
90
100
110

(cont.)

150
sf
fp
160
170
cresc.

180
ff
ff
ff
ff
p
p
p
p
p
190
p
p
p
cresc.
cresc.
cresc.
cresc.
200
p
p
p
p
210
cresc.
cresc.
cresc.
cresc.
f
f
f
f
p
p
p
p
cresc.
cresc.
cresc.
cresc.
ff
ff
ff
ff
decresc.

p
p
p
p
cresc.
cresc.
cresc.
sf
sf
sf
p
p
p
p
cresc.
cresc.
cresc.
cresc.
f
f
f
f
fp
fp
fp
fp
cresc.
cresc.
cresc.
cresc.
f
f
f
f
fp
fp
fp
pp
pp
pp
pp
fp
fp
fp
fp
fp
fp
fp

(cont.)

b) List in order of occurrence the keys that represent important tonal areas in the movement. Indicate the measure in which each key first appears.

c) What do you find to be the most representative kinds of texture found in the movement? Use such relevant terms as homophonic, unison or octave (monophonic) arrangement, imitative dialogue, two-voice counterpoint, etc. Cite at least five part deployments that more or less typify the piece and indicate their occurrences by measure numbers. Indicate which of the melodic materials cited in (a) are associated with the textures that you enumerate.

d) You have probably reached the conclusion that the movement is in sonata allegro form. This conclusion is correct. Indicate the principal formal divisions of the movement, together with the keys that delineate them, by filling in the rough outline on page 347.

Exposition

	Theme 1	Transition	Theme 2	Transition	Closing
Measures	________	________	________	________	________
Keys	________	________	________	________	________

Development

Thematic materials ____

Measures ____

Keys ____

Return

	Theme 1	Transition	Theme 2	Transition	Coda
Measures	________	________	________	________	________
Keys	________	________	________	________	________

e) What characteristics of the opening material of the exposition (the motive in measure 1) are indicative of its *suitability* as the main thematic material of the movement?

f) Cite three distinct treatments of the opening motive that occur in the exposition (for example, octave statement in measures 1–4, sequence in measures 13–16).

g) Many analysts name measure 30 as the beginning of the transition to Theme 2. In what way would the role of the cello beginning at measure 30 support such an analysis?

h) Circle on the music *four* chords which best signify the harmonic movement of the transition from Theme 1 to Theme 2 as it moves from F major to C major.

i) Considering the second theme as beginning at measure 57, indicate at least three ways in which the textures of the first and second themes are contrasted.

j) Mutation heightens the close of the second theme area. In what specific chord is the use of mutation evident?

k) Explain why the closing material of the movement should *not* be regarded as discrete or separate (new) melodic material.

l) The development of the movement is compact but intense. This intensity is to some degree manifested by the rapidity of key changes. Write triads to represent the tonic of each key that appears in the development. Write the triads in the order of their occurrence as key representatives, and cite the measure of each key's arrival.

m) The development section is clearly the section of greatest intensity and excitement in the movement. Speculate about this statement and then consider measures 129–150 and measures 167–170 in relation to the statement. Indicate what aspect of the composer's treatment of *materials* and *texture* would, in each case, substantiate the statement.

n) The recapitulation provides a strong feeling of arrival. Why?

o) The coda reveals many of the characteristics of a second development section. Why is this so? From where does the composer draw the thematic and rhythmic materials used in the coda?

APPENDIX: FIGURED BASS SYMBOLS

1. Any bass note with no symbol has above it a triad in root position.

2. Any numbers appearing below a bass note refer to *intervals* above the *bass:*

$\begin{smallmatrix}5\\3\end{smallmatrix}$ or 5	root-position triad
6	first-inversion triad
$\begin{smallmatrix}6\\4\end{smallmatrix}$	second-inversion triad
7	root-position seventh chord
$\begin{smallmatrix}6\\5\end{smallmatrix}$	first-inversion seventh chord
$\begin{smallmatrix}4\\3\end{smallmatrix}$ or $\begin{smallmatrix}6\\4\\3\end{smallmatrix}$	second-inversion seventh chord
$\begin{smallmatrix}4\\2\end{smallmatrix}$ or 2	third-inversion seventh chord

Doublings can be indicated by numbers. Here are some examples:

Root-position triads

$\begin{smallmatrix}3\\3\end{smallmatrix}$ or $\begin{smallmatrix}8\\3\\3\end{smallmatrix}$ doubled third

First-inversion triads

$\begin{smallmatrix}6\\6\end{smallmatrix}$ doubled root (sixth above bass)

$\begin{smallmatrix}8\\6\end{smallmatrix}$ doubled third (octave above bass)

3. Numbers appearing under one another refer to intervals which sound *together* above the bass note, as in the inversions of the seventh chords (the largest number is always on top). Numbers appearing alongside one another refer to intervals which sound *successively* above the bass note, as in suspensions and other decorative pitches:

4 3	4-3 suspension above bass
8 7	octave moving to seventh above bass (both the octave and the seventh must be in the same voice)
7 6	7-6 suspension above bass

4. Chromatic alterations or mutations are indicated by various symbols:

a) An accidental by itself (♯, ♭, ♮, 𝄪) means that the *third* above the bass is to be altered in the way indicated by the accidental.

b) *Raised notes* are indicated by a line through the figure (6̸, 4̸, 2̸, 7̸) or by a ♯ or ♮ preceding the number (♯6 or ♮6, ♯4 or ♮4, ♯2 or ♮2, ♯7 or ♮7).

c) *Lowered notes* are indicated by a ♭ in front of the figure (♭7, ♭3, ♭6, ♭2).

5. These symbols can be put together in various ways to show activity above the bass. The following are a few possibilities:

7 ♮	seventh chord with a raised (natural) third
4 ♯	4-3 suspension in which the 3 is raised (sharp)
8 7 ♯	root-position triad with one voice passing to a seventh, with a raised (sharp) third

Chapter 14

OVERVIEW OF STYLE AND HISTORY

Style in music is the selection of and manner of ordering the materials of musical composition. Style cannot be considered in isolation from form, because style and form interact continuously. A musical interval, for instance, has little meaning and does little in the way of communication until it is placed in context with other intervals and interacts with other aspects of musical organization. In this chapter an attempt is made to view style as a dynamic, changing aspect of music, embracing both the selection of raw materials of composition and their structuring in time. The survey of music history presented here is necessarily brief, and should be supplemented by additional reading.

THE MIDDLE AGES

The first 800 years or so of Western musical development (up to about 800 A. D.) are best represented by the vast collection of monophonic melodies known as Gregorian chant. Western Europe—namely, Italy (the center of the Church of Rome), France, Switzerland, and Spain—fostered the composition and performance of Gregorian chant, mainly in church monasteries. Based to a great extent on preexisting Greek and Jewish chants, Roman chant, with its diatonic melodies, provided the tonal foundation for Western music. It also employed certain formal schemes and developmental techniques, such as sequence, variation, and elaboration, that were to play an important role in the evolution of later music. The significance of Roman chant in the development of Renaissance polyphony has already been discussed.

The chant melody shown in Example 14-1 illustrates the modal scale basis, the elusive sense of pitch focus, and the characteristic melodic design of chant. Note the essentially *conjunct* motion, which precludes, as a rule, inter-

Example 14-1 Gregorian chant (modern notation)

val leaps larger than fifths, thirds being the most characteristic skips. Note also the melodic cadences by falling or rising steps. Sing the melody at a moderate pace, letting the rhythm of the text determine the musical rhythm.

The Middle Ages witnessed the initial and tentative development of polyphonic music. The rhythm of this music, called *measured rhythm,* was based on the six poetic meters. The six rhythmic modes amounted to basic rhythmic patterns, reflecting the rhythms of the accented and unaccented syllables of poetry. They were as follows:

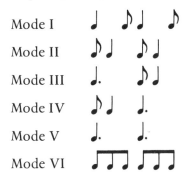

Mode I

Mode II

Mode III

Mode IV

Mode V

Mode VI

The harmony of early polyphonic music was characterized by the use of certain preferred consonant intervals—namely, octaves, fifths, fourths, and unisons.

Early polyphony consisted mainly of church compositions for two or three parts. Mass items and prayers were the sources of texts for such works. A passage from an early polyphonic work is shown in Example 14-2.

Example 14-2 Early polyphony, 13th century (modern transcription)

(cont.)

Example 14-2 (continued)

ARS NOVA AND RENAISSANCE

The period from 1300 to 1600 embraces the fourteenth-century *Ars Nova** and the Renaissance. This 300-year span embodies the greatest general flourishing of ensemble vocal music, sacred and secular, to date. Of particular significance to the development of musical style are the following general trends:

1. There was a predominance of triple meter, with duple meter becoming more common during the fifteenth and sixteenth centuries.
2. There was a reliance on consonant intervals, primarily octaves, unisons, fourths, and fifths, with increasing use of thirds and sixths as harmonic staples. Triads occurred with ever increasing frequency in music of this period as the result of three- and four-part combinations of voices using the harmonic intervals mentioned above. The triad was not acknowledged as a harmonic entity until the close of the Renaissance. The name triad was first introduced by the theorist Zarlino.
3. Compositions were to a great extent fashioned from preexistent melodies. Such melodies were of both sacred and secular origin. Some consisted of repetitive rhythm or pitch schemes and amounted to ostinati.
4. Musical form was based largely on the chosen text, rather than on any abstract design.
5. Tonal materials were based on the church modes, rather than on the more recent major, minor, and chromatic scales.
6. Secular compositions, that is, vocal works for various combinations of voice and instruments (usually not specified) or for voices alone or with instruments, based on secular texts, predominated during the fourteenth century and continued to appear in ever increasing varieties of forms, such as the ballade, virelai, and madrigal.
7. Most music revealed an essentially vocal orientation, since an independent instrumental style as such had not yet been evolved. No clear dis-

*The term *Ars Antiqua* is applied to music of the thirteenth century.

tinction was made between vocal and instrumental music; most music was designed for performance in either medium. Voice parts were commonly doubled by instruments such as strings or winds.

8. There was no meter in the modern sense; instead, there was a common temporal unit, the *tactus*, equivalent to about MM 72, or the human pulse rate. Duple and triple divisions of the tactus are roughly equivalent to the duple and triple meters of more recent music.
9. Melody, rather than harmony, constituted the main basis of composition; the result was a predominance of contrapuntal textures. Cadences consisted of certain recurrent harmonic formulas with simple consonant sonorities as goals.
10. The exploitation of chordal sonority and dissonance as vehicles of dramatic and poetic expression helped to establish chords and tonality as building materials of composition. A sense of tonality is found in secular music especially, which became free of the strict discipline imposed by the traditions of liturgical texts and melodic traditions.

The excerpts appearing in Example 14-3 illustrate the stylistic trends noted above. Perform each passage and note carefully which of the above characteristics occur.

Example 14-3 Five excerpts from the Ars Nova and Renaissance

a) Machaut (*ca.* 1300-1370), *Je puis trop bien* (Ballade)

(cont.)

Example 14-3 (continued)

b) Dufay (1400-1474), *Tu lumen, tu splendor patris* (Motet)

5
Tu lu - men, tu splen - dor pa - - tris, tu
10
spes per - en-nis, om - - ni - - - - um

c) Josquin des Prez (1450-1521), *Missa ad Fugam,* Agnus Dei

5
Superius
A - gnus De - - i, a - - gnus De -
Tenor
A - - gnus De - i, a - -
Bassus
A - gnus De - - - - i, a - -

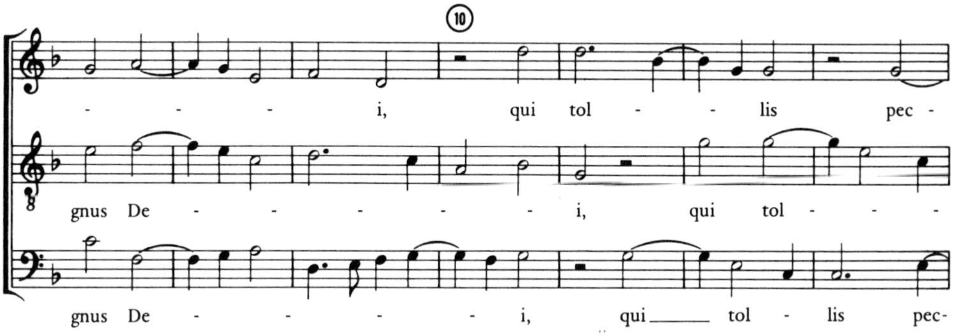

d) Claudin (1490-1562), Chanson (text omitted)

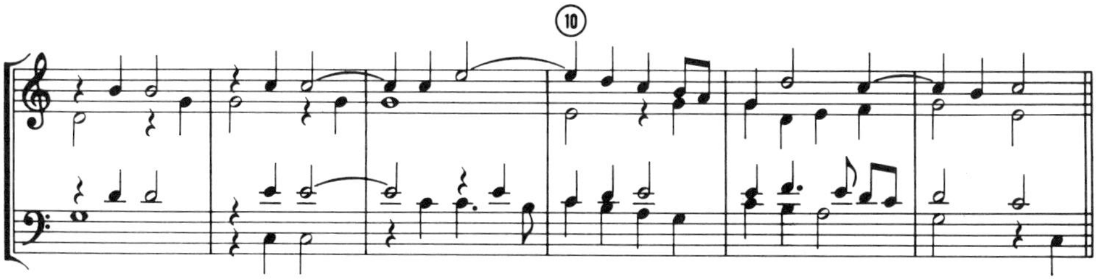

(cont.)

Example 14-3 (continued)

e) Marenzio (1560-1599), *O fere stelle* (Madrigal)

THE BAROQUE PERIOD

The Baroque period, from about 1600 to 1750 (the latter date is the death of J. S. Bach), saw a virtual explosion of creative activity. New musical forms and styles appeared in abundance, mainly in the four European countries of Italy, France, Germany, and England. The Baroque era unquestionably influenced the future course of musical development more than any other single period before the twentieth century. During this period the main focus of musical activity shifted from the church to the home, concert hall, and opera house. Although music, particularly choral music, continued to flourish in the Church of Rome, in the newly founded German Lutheran Church, and in the Church of England, composers rid themselves of the drastic limitations imposed by church domination and patronage. Instrumental music was established as a separate mode of composition distinct from vocal music, and many new vocal forms arose, such as opera, oratorio, and cantata.

Indigenous instrumental forms evolved during these 150 years, some of them reaching, within this period, their highest peaks of development. Several of these instrumental or keyboard forms, such as the chorale prelude, the fugue, the concerto grosso, and the suite, have since lapsed into relative obscurity.

The stylistic changes that occurred during the Baroque period are so many and so diverse that any attempt to "overview" them is necessarily an oversimplification. The following list describes some of the most salient features of style change:

1. The major-minor key system was established.
2. The triad was established as the main harmonic staple, together with the family of chords constituting diatonic tertian harmony.
3. A distinctively instrumental orientation to melody writing, texture, accompaniment, etc., was formulated.
4. The keyboard instrument became the standard means for realizing the harmonic basis of Baroque polyphony.
5. Musical rhythm became free of the dictates of textual rhythm.
6. The portrayal through such musical factors as dissonance, rhythm, melody, and harmony of moods, emotions, and feelings became an important part of musical composition, particularly early Baroque opera.
7. Melody and harmony were reconciled in such a way that melodies and counterpoint clearly reflected the harmonic materials from which they seemed to derive. By the same token, triadic harmonies often seemed to occur as the logical result of converging melodies. In a word, melody and harmony interacted mutually and became, to a great extent, one and the same. The peak of harmonic contrapuntal composition is found in the works of J. S. Bach.

8. In such instrumental forms as the concerto, sonata, suite, and keyboard toccata, where no limitations were imposed by a text, composers invented numerous formal bases for producing unity; examples include passacaglia, chaconne, ostinato bass, ritornello, fugue, and variations.

The six excerpts shown in Example 14-4 give an overview of stylistic development in several forms and media most characteristic of the Baroque.

Example 14-4 Six excerpts from the Baroque period

a) Monteverdi (1567-1643), *Orfeo*, Act II

Arioso

Ritornello

The Messenger announces to Orfeo the death of Euridice.

ORFEO
Don - de vie ni? O - ve vai? Nin - fa, che por - ti?
MESSENGER
A te ne ven-go Or - feo, Mes - sag - ge - ra in - fe - li - ce di
5
ca - so più in - fe - li - ce e più fu - ne - sto. La tua bel - la Eu - ri - di - ce.
ORFEO
Ohi - mè, che o - do?
MESSENGER
La tua di - let - ta spo - sa è mor - ta.

(cont.)

Example 14-4 (continued)

b) Frescobaldi (1583-1643), *Toccata Cromatica per l'Elevazione*

c) Pachelbel (1653-1706), *Suite in A♭*, Courant

(cont.)

Example 14-4 (continued)

d) J. S. Bach (1685-1750), *The Well Tempered Clavier,* Book II, Prelude and Fugue in A minor

FUGUE

Maestoso

(cont.)

Example 14-4 (continued)

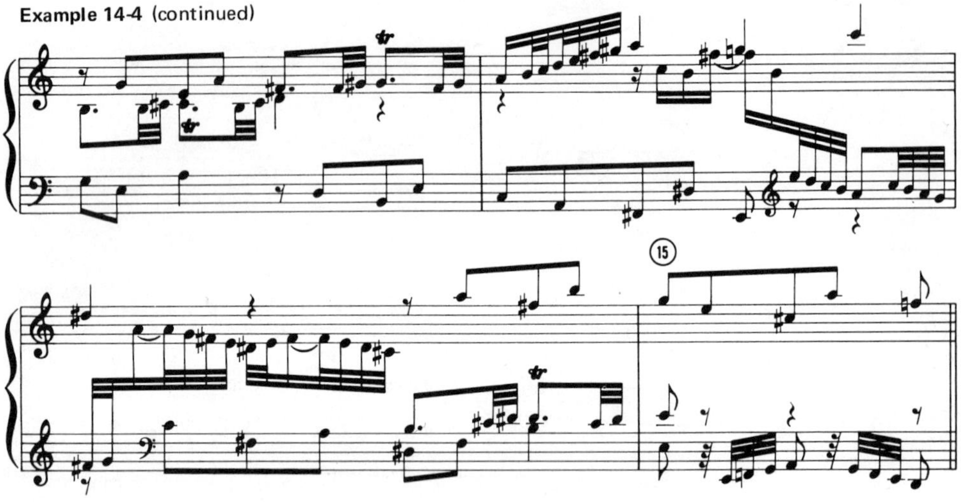

e) Vivaldi (1675-1741), *Sonata da Camera in D minor,* Corrente

f) J. S. Bach (1685-1750), *Passion According to Saint Matthew*, "He is of Death Deserving" (Chorus)

(cont.)

Example 14-4 (continued)

VIENNESE CLASSICISM

During the closing years of the Baroque period many composers, among them some of J. S. Bach's own sons, recognized that J. S. Bach and others had reached a peak of contrapuntal complexity in their works. These younger composers, reacting against the intricacies and subtleties of Baroque composition, turned toward musical styles and forms of a less contrapuntal, less demanding nature. This movement toward formal and textural simplicity and conciseness of statement, which culminated in the works of Haydn and Mozart and in Beethoven's early compositions, is known as Viennese Classicism. One of the most significant predecessors of Haydn and Mozart was C. P. E. Bach, the eldest son of J. S. Bach. An example of C. P. E. Bach's music appears in Example 14-5. Note in particular the relatively thin texture, the melodic expressiveness ("sensitive" style), and the homophonic simplicity of the passage.

Viennese Classicism fathered such significant musical *forms* as the sonata allegro, the minuet and trio, the scherzo, and the classical concerto for instrumental solo and orchestra, as well as most of the chamber *combinations,* such as the string quartet, piano trio, and wind quintet. A style of opera (best represented by the works of Mozart) made up of successive numbers, including instrumental overtures, arias, duets, choruses, and finales (climactic scenes or closing numbers involving as many as seven soloists, chorus, and orchestra), emerged from the sometimes stilted and stylized Baroque opera to create a captivating musical drama or comedy.

Classical music retained the diatonic tonal basis established during the Baroque, while employing a thinned-out homophonic texture, occasionally enlivened or elaborated by simple contrapuntal means. Objectivity toward composition replaced, to a great extent, the concern for "affective representation of the emotions" characteristic of the Baroque era.

Participation in music by amateurs, together with the underwriting and patronizing of music by the nobility, helped to bring about a popularization of music "for its own sake." The singing melodies of the classical period, articulated by the keyboard, chamber group players, singer, or orchestra, and supported by simple accompanimental patterns such as the Alberti bass (see Example 8-5b), are characteristic of a period of musical productivity and formal growth that led directly to the late works of Beethoven, to Schubert, and to the succeeding developments of the nineteenth century.

Some idea of Viennese Classicism can be gained from a study of the three chronologically arranged excerpts shown in Example 14-6. The peak of Viennese Classicism spans the years from 1770 to 1830, which coincide with the life of Beethoven (1770-1827).

Example 14-5

C. P. E. Bach (1714-1788), *Württemberg Sonata No. 1 for Clavier,* 2nd movement

Example 14-6 Three excerpts from the period of Viennese Classicism

a) Haydn (1732-1809), *String Quartet,* Op. 74, No. 3, 2nd movement

(cont.)

Example 14-6 (continued)

(cont.)

Example 14-6 (continued)

(cont.)

Example 14-6 (continued)

b) Mozart (1756-1791), *Piano Concerto in E♭*, K. 482, Finale

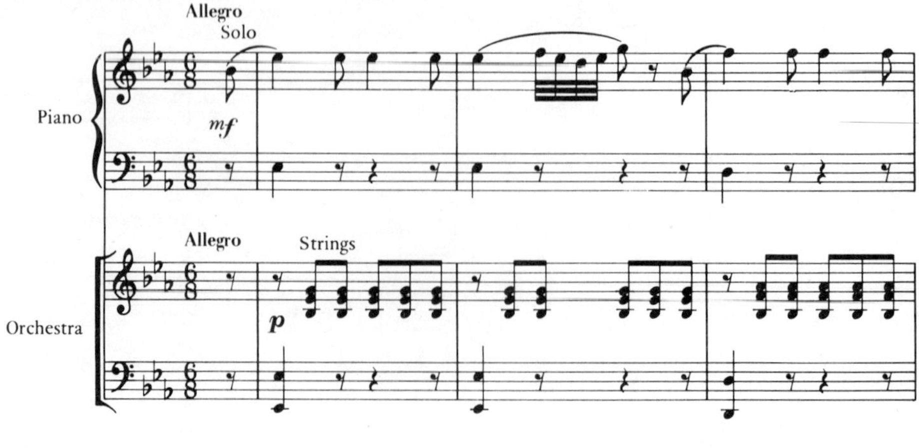

(cont.)

Example 14-6 (continued)

(cont.)

Example 14-6 (continued)

c) Beethoven (1770-1827), *Sonata in E major for Piano,* Op. 109, 3rd movement

ROMANTICISM

The Romantic era, which lasted from about 1830 to about 1900, is best viewed as exhibiting an extension of stylistic and formal practices initiated during the mid-eighteenth century, rather than as developing new or radically different modes of composition. Many of the trends associated with nineteenth-century Romanticism may be found in various "classical" works by Mozart (for example, *Don Giovanni,* the second movement of the *Piano Concerto in A major,* K. 488, and the *Quartet in D minor,* K. 421), Haydn (for example, *The Creation*), and especially Beethoven (for example, the Fifth, Sixth, Seventh, and Ninth Symphonies, the late piano sonatas, starting with Op. 101, and the late string quartets, starting with Op. 95). Concentrated at first in Germany and Austria, the Romantic movement gathered momentum and spread through all of the significant music-producing countries of Europe and America.

Some music historians regard the Romantic outlook as one which pervaded music, in lesser or greater degrees, from the mid-eighteenth century until the close of the nineteenth. In this view, Viennese Classicism represents but a brief departure from an overall movement which is first and foremost a Romantic one. Whatever one's view of the historical position of Romanticism, one must recognize its diversity. The various countries of the Western world, and various schools within these countries, developed their own peculiar brands of Romanticism. To list specific stylistic traits of a movement as diversified as Romanticism is a highly questionable procedure. Nevertheless, an attempt to distinguish Romanticism from the preceding Viennese Classicism is in order.

Musical romanticism may be said to involve a *subjective* approach to composition, interpretation, and performance. Emphasis is placed on such matters as mood, expression, originality of material and its treatment, and correlation of musical form with extramusical factors such as poetry, painting, folklore, plays, or even nationalistic movements. Romantic music often suggests a kind of self-consciousness of method in that the composer seems to regard the projecting of individualistic ideas or emotions, rather than the implementation of musical craft to solve specific formal problems, as the prime *raison d'être* of composition.

Two main branches of the Romantic movement in music are represented in Example 14-7. Schubert and Brahms represent the *conservative* group in the early and later parts of the nineteenth century, respectively. These composers adhered mainly to musical forms developed during the period of Viennese Classicism, choosing time-honored formal bases for compositions such as symphonies, sonatas, and concertos. Chopin and Wagner represent the *progressive* group. This group modified the existing formal schemes to create new types of composition. One such type is the tone poem, a symphonic composition based on extramusical material; examples are Liszt's *Les Préludes,* based on a poem by Lamartine, and Rachmaninoff's *Isle of the Dead,* based on a painting of the same name. The progressive composers were also interested in the exploitation of sonority. Chopin and Liszt explored the capabilities of the piano, while Berlioz, Liszt, and Wagner made greater demands on the orchestra than any previous composer had. With their tonal resourcefulness and imagination, the progressive composers contributed greatly to the exploration and expansion of traditional tonality and to the eventual dissolution of the key system.

A third group of composers may be referred to as *nationalists.* Nationalism developed mainly in those countries which did not already have well-developed traditions of musical composition, such as Russia, Czechoslovakia, Hungary, Poland, and the Scandinavian countries. Most of these composers employed the classical formal models, but imbued their music with the spirit of national folklore, heroics, and local color. They frequently used the melodic and harmonic materials, including modes other than major and minor, and rhythms of folk music. Smetana's opera *The Bartered Bride* is one of the best-known manifestations of nationalism.

The following list is a grouping of a few of the major nineteenth-century composers into the three categories that we have mentioned. Note that some composers appear in more than one category.

Conservatives	*Progressives*	*Nationalists*
Beethoven (1770-1827)	Beethoven (1770-1827)	Chopin (1810-1849)
Schubert (1797-1828)	Berlioz (1803-1869)	Borodin (1834-1887)
Mendelssohn (1809-1847)	Chopin (1810-1849)	Smetana (1824-1884)
Schumann (1810-1856)	Liszt (1811-1886)	Dvořák (1841-1904)
Brahms (1833-1897)	Wagner (1813-1883)	Rimsky-Korsakov (1844-1908)
Bruckner (1824-1896)	Mahler (1860-1911)	Grieg (1843-1907)
Sibelius (1865-1957)	Wolf (1860-1903)	Sibelius (1865-1957)
Tchaikovsky (1840-1893)	Richard Strauss (1864-1949)	Mussorgsky (1835-1881)
Fauré (1845-1924)		
Dvořák (1841-1904)		

Example 14-7 Four excerpts from the Romantic period

a) Schubert (1797-1828), *Heidenröslein* (Lied)

(cont.)

Example 14-7 (continued)

b) Chopin (1810-1849), *Prelude in E minor,* Op. 28

c) Brahms (1833-1897), *Symphony No. 3 in F major,* 2nd movement

(cont.)

Example 14-7 (continued)

d) Wagner (1813-1883), *Tristan und Isolde,* Act II

IMPRESSIONISM: DEBUSSY

The nineteenth-century composers explored and largely exhausted the resources of traditional tonal materials, extending to the breaking point the organizing rationale of the major and minor key system. Composers of the early twentieth century inherited a tonal language whose capabilities for further extension seemed seriously impaired.

Claude Debussy (1862-1918) created a unique musical language, often called Impressionism, whose materials were derived largely from previous practice but were deployed in a highly imaginative, entirely fresh way. More than any other composer of the late nineteenth and early twentieth centuries, Debussy, by inventing new ways of organizing pitch and rhythm, gave initial impetus to the redirection of the course of musical composition which occurred in the early years of the twentieth century. Instead of revolting against his inheritance, as he is often believed to have done, Debussy revealed to his successors new ways of organizing musical patterns while continuing to employ traditional harmonic and melodic materials. Example 14-8 is an example of Debussy's music.

Debussy's "method" in this piece consists of placing familiar tertian chords, such as triads and sevenths, in unfamiliar juxtapositions, so that a sense of key is only suggested rather than established. Melodies occur as brief, undeveloped fragments in harmonic parallelism, accompanied by ostinati, tremolos, or figuration. Registral differences are used to create form, not merely to project materials. Meter, in the sense of a recurrent pulse, is often obscured by novel and sometimes very subtle rhythmic arrangements.

Debussy abhorred the giant crescendos, enraptured strings, and thundering brass and timpani of Wagner, Liszt, and Strauss, even though he was admittedly fascinated by them. In developing an understanding of musical innuendo, Debussy created a precedent for the subtleties of much twentieth-century music, such as that of Webern. However, Debussy's music is best regarded as one of the last manifestations of Romanticism rather than as being inspired by the strong winds of change that one feels in the works of such twentieth-century masters as Stravinsky, Bartók, Schoenberg, and Webern.

Example 14-8

Debussy (1862-1918), *Préludes,* Book I, "Des pas sur la neige"

EXERCISES

Exercises 1 through 5 are based on Example 14-3, which contains excerpts by Machaut, Dufay, Josquin, Claudin, and Marenzio. Mark each statement true (T) or false (F). Answers are provided after Exercise 5. These exercises may be used for self-grading.

1. This exercise is based on Example 14-3(a) by Machaut.

   a) The upper line suggests a vocal performance. ______

   b) The use of a French text reflects the chant basis of the piece. ______

   c) The vertical span of the parts lies generally within a perfect fifth. ______

   d) The harmonic basis of the composition, as shown by the beginnings and ends of phrases, is clearly triadic. ______

   e) The pitch materials of all three voices are drawn from the major scale. ______

2. This exercise is based on Example 14-3(b) by Dufay.

   a) The prevailing parallel voice motion in this piece produces a more or less consistent arrangement of triadic sonorities in the form of successive first-inversion triads *(fauxbourdon).* ______

   b) It is entirely possible that the upper voice of this motet is based on the elaboration (paraphrase) of a Gregorian chant melody. ______

   c) The triple meter of the piece is typical of Renaissance music. ______

   d) Cadences are preceded by an acceleration of activity that commonly involves rhythmic displacement. ______

   e) Imitation is a recurring feature of the polyphony of this piece. ______

3. This exercise is based on Example 14-3(c) by Josquin des Prez.

   a) The use of duple meter is consistent with practice in the late Renaissance. ____

   b) The Latin text suggests a secular composition. ______

c) The scale basis is G Dorian. ______

d) Imitative entries distributed among the three voices produce a unified relationship of parts which move rhythmically independently of each other. ______

e) Dissonances are generally unaccented and resolved by step. ______

4. This exercise is based on Example 14-3(d) by Claudin.

a) The harmonic style of the excerpt is clearly based on full-voiced triads. ______

b) The texture of the passage is essentially chordal, elaborated by occasional staggerings of parts, passing contrapuntal motion, and syncopation. ______

c) The composition establishes little feeling of tonality or key. ______

d) The two outer parts produce a clear, stable framework for the tonal organization and melodic details of the passage. ______

e) The changes of harmony occur in such a way as to reinforce the duple meter of the piece. ______

5. This exercise is based on Example 14-3(e) by Marenzio.

a) The overall tonal movement of the passage as exemplified by the opening and close of the excerpt suggests considerable variety of tonality. ______

b) Each vocal line is an effective, singable melodic part. ______

c) Little contrapuntal independence is present, since the voices move together in a texture that is mainly chordal. ______

d) Accented chords containing sevenths occur as the result of suspensions. ______

e) The principal tonalities of the passage are, in order of occurrence, G minor, B♭ major, E♭ major, and A♭ major. The close of the excerpt suggests a modulation to D♭ major. ______

Answers for Exercises 1 through 5

1. a) T	b) F	c) F	d) F	e) F
2. a) T	b) T	c) T	d) T	e) F
3. a) T	b) F	c) T	d) T	e) T
4. a) T	b) T	c) F	d) T	e) T
5. a) T	b) T	c) F	d) T	e) T

6. The Ritornello from Act II of *Orfeo* by Monteverdi, shown as part of Example 14-4(a), exemplifies early Baroque style in several ways. Cite three, being as specific as possible.

7. The organ composition by Frescobaldi shown in Example 14-4(b), while emanating from the early Baroque period, shows several features of style clearly carried over from Renaissance practice. Write or formulate a brief statement supporting this viewpoint. Give at least two illustrations from the music.

8. Contrast the tonal and harmonic materials of the Pachelbel *Courant* (Example 14-4c) with those of the Frescobaldi *Toccata* (Example 14-4b). Consider both keys and chord relations (functions).

9. Which of the eight summarizing statements about Baroque style given in the text are clearly applicable to the *Corrente* by Vivaldi (Example 14-4e)? List them by number and be prepared to substantiate your choices in a discussion.

10. The tonic-dominant relation is unquestionably the most significant tonal pattern in Baroque music. Pinpoint large-scale and detailed ways in which that relation is used in the Bach Fugue quoted in Example 14-4(d). Consider both keys and harmonic progressions, as well as melodic structure.

11. This exercise tests your knowledge of the stylistic characteristics associated with (but by no means limited to) works of the Viennese Classicists, particularly Haydn, Mozart, and Beethoven. Each item below consists of a formal or stylistic principle or treatment of material. Indicate which of the three pieces quoted in Example 14-6 best exemplifies each item. If more than one of the pieces applies, you need indicate only one. Where measure references are asked for, cite by measure numbers an occurrence of the item in the work that you name. See the sample in (a). It should be apparent that to complete this exercise you need a thorough acquaintance with the music quoted in the chapter.

Item	*Composition*
a) Melody based partly on recurring rhythmic pattern in common time (cite measures)	Haydn (Example 14-6a), measures 1-8
b) Melody and repeated chord accompaniment forming basis of homophonic texture	____________________
c) Symmetrical phrases organized into two-measure segments (cite measures)	____________________
d) Sectional form involving both *return* and *variation* principles	____________________
e) Chordal texture involving essentially conjunct voice leading (cite measures)	____________________
f) *Tonic-dominant-tonic* as main harmonic pattern of musical section	____________________
g) Sequence as basis for melodic statement	____________________

Item	*Composition*
h) Mutation to parallel minor key coinciding with texture change to set up formal contrast	____________________
i) Large section comprised harmonically of tonic and dominant functions only (cite measures)	____________________
j) Contrary motion predominant between outer parts for several measures (cite measures)	____________________

12. Account for the significance of each of the following in Example 14-8 by Debussy.

    a) Key

    b) Exploitation of instrumental (keyboard) color

    c) Melody

    d) Rhythm as an audible manifestation of meter

    e) Harmonic functions, particularly tonic and dominant

    f) Triads and extended tertian chords

    g) Planing

    h) Formal continuity

    i) Formal contrast

SUGGESTED READING

Willi Apel, *Harvard Dictionary of Music.* Cambridge, Mass.: Harvard University Press, 1944.

B. C. Cannon *et al., Art of Music.* New York: Thomas Y. Crowell, 1960.

William Christ *et al., Materials and Structure of Music.* Englewood Cliffs, N. J.: Prentice-Hall, 1966.

R. L. Crocker, *History of Musical Style.* New York: McGraw-Hill, 1966.

Archibald T. Davison and Willi Apel, *Historical Anthology of Music,* 2 vols. Vol. I: Oriental, Medieval, and Renaissance Music, rev. ed., 1949. Vol. II: Baroque, Rococo, and Preclassical Music, 1950. Cambridge, Mass.: Harvard University Press.

Curt Sachs, *Our Musical Heritage,* 2nd ed. Englewood Cliffs, N. J.: Prentice-Hall, 1955.

Homer Ulrich and Paul A. Pisk, *History of Music and Musical Style.* New York: Harcourt, Brace & World, 1963.

Chapter 15

THE TWENTIETH CENTURY IN BRIEF PERSPECTIVE

Despite a few provocative exceptions, twentieth-century composers have continued to deal with the same basic materials—melody, sonority, texture, rhythm, form, etc.—as their predecessors. It is in the *treatment* of such materials that current composers have departed most from previous practices. It goes without saying that some composers (such as Webern, Ives, Carter, and Stockhausen) have departed much more radically from time-established modes of organization than have others (such as Ravel, Hindemith, Copland, and Bartók). This can be seen by comparing the passages in Example 15-1(a) and (b). Example 15-1(a) reveals a style of writing comparable to traditional music, in contrast to the novel, if not perplexing, patterns of Example 15-1(b).

Example 15-1

a) Hindemith (1895-1963), *Sonata for Flute,* 2nd movement

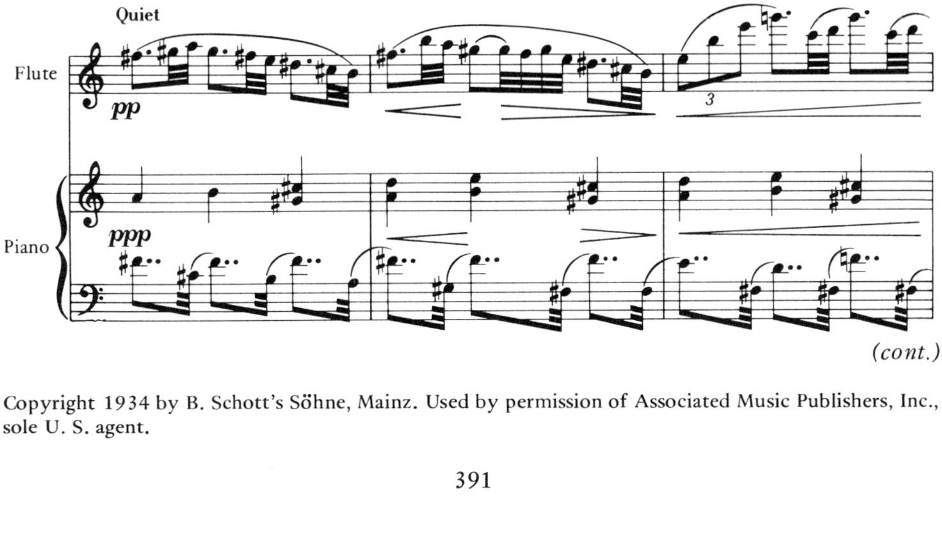

(cont.)

Example 15-1 (continued)

b) Webern (1883-1945), *Five Pieces for String Quartet,* Op. 5

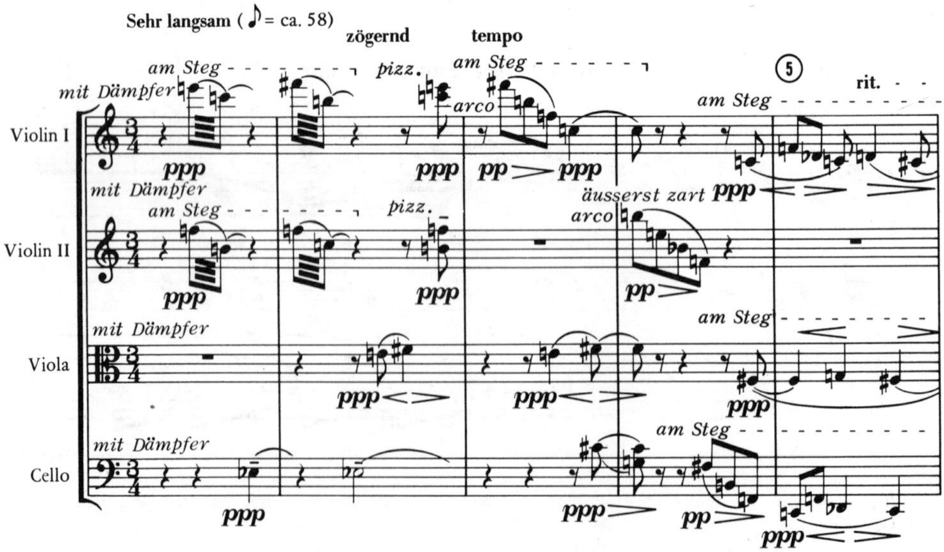

The Hindemith passage consists of a lyrical flute melody in B accompanied by the piano. The melodic patterns in the flute show no techniques of organization as unfamiliar as those of the Webern movement. The latter poses problems in comprehension, for its materials are less clearly defined than those of the Hindemith passage. This is neither good nor bad, but it is indicative of the degree to which some current music taxes both the intellect and the technique of contemporary musicians.

MELODY

In the hands of many twentieth-century composers, linear pitch relations and counterpoint have taken on the structural significance that harmony and tonality had in earlier music. That is to say, the structural logic and coherence of much current music depends more on melody (motivic relations, counterpoint, thematic design, etc.) than on functional chord progressions. Composers have found in melody a material whose form-building potential was to a great extent ignored by composers of the nineteenth century. Example 15-2 is a sampling of motives taken from Stravinsky's *Symphony of Psalms,* a work for chorus and orchestra based on psalms from the Vulgate. Note carefully the intervallic properties shared by the motives, ostinati, and chords shown here. Motivic relations such as these typify the contemporary composer's reliance on concise patterns rather than on prolonged songlike melodies as structural bases for compositions.

Example 15-2

Stravinsky (1882–), *Symphony of Psalms* (motives)

a) Ostinato Basis (two minor thirds separated by a minor second)

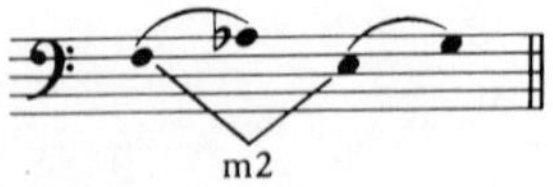

b) Superposed thirds

c) Successive thirds joined by seconds

d) The rhythm of (c), with thirds and seconds over a line of descending seconds

e) A melody consisting only of seconds

f) Seconds (symmetrical scale, alternate half-steps and whole steps)

Strict Scale Basis

g) Derivative of (a) and (f), a stepwise line of alternating major and minor seconds

h) An extension of the ostinato in (a)

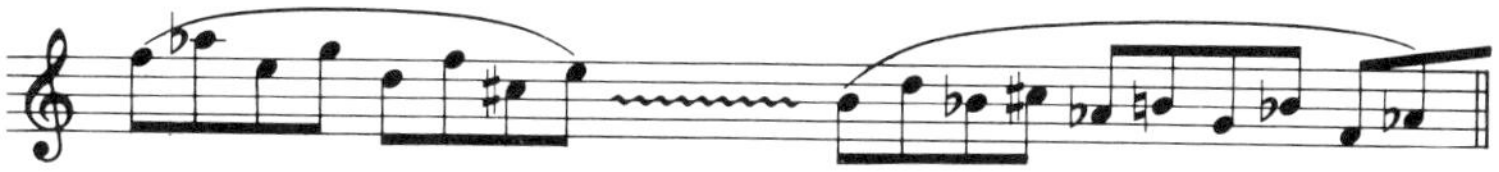

Wide leaps, producing angular contours, are a common feature of current melodic practice. Melodies like the one shown in Example 15-3 are typical of much twentieth-century writing. Such melodies are obviously better suited to instrumental than to vocal performance. However, melodies constructed along more conventional lines and paying homage to definite tonal centers are by no means rare; they occur in some works by composers such as Hindemith, Stravinsky (in works written before the late 1950's), Bartók, and Prokofiev, whose compositional styles depart less markedly from nineteenth-century practices than do those of the more progressive composers. Example 15-4 shows a smoothly flowing melody by Hindemith.

Example 15-3

Webern (1883-1945), "Wie Bin Ich Froh," Op. 25, No. 1

Example 15-4

Hindemith (1895-1963), *Second Piano Sonata,* 1st movement

During the 1930's and 1940's, many composers, Stravinsky and Hindemith among them, established a rather widespread but by no means clearly defined trend called Neoclassicism, which involved the patterning of compositions after formal models and techniques of the eighteenth century and earlier. Neoclassicism provided the composer with a ready-made model (in some cases a preexistent melody or formal basis) to be used for building compositions out of melodic and harmonic materials more complex than those of their eighteenth-century prototypes. The theme given in Example 15-5 exemplifies a Neoclassical melody. Note that the structure is quite uncomplicated and tonal, and the melodic patterns are not unlike those found in many eighteenth- or early nineteenth-century compositions.

Example 15-5

Stravinsky (1882–), *Sonata for Two Pianos,* 2nd movement

RHYTHM

Despite the flexibility, variety, and complexity of rhythm in much twentieth-century music, most twentieth-century melodies adhere to patterns of rhythmic organization found in earlier music. However, literal repetition is avoided in favor of varied rhythmic restatements, and strict observance of strong beats as a normal basis for rhythmic accent has been to a great degree replaced by the use of rhythms that are free of barline-based accents. The result of these practices in twentieth-century composition has been greater rhythmic freedom. A sense of rhythmic freedom also results from frequent meter changes, varied divisive patterns within the beat, reliance on irregular patterns of beat division and subdivision (quintolets, septolets, etc.), and the juxtaposition of

Example 15-6 Four excerpts illustrating twentieth-century rhythmic materials

a) Stravinsky (1882–), *L'Histoire du Soldat* (meter changes)

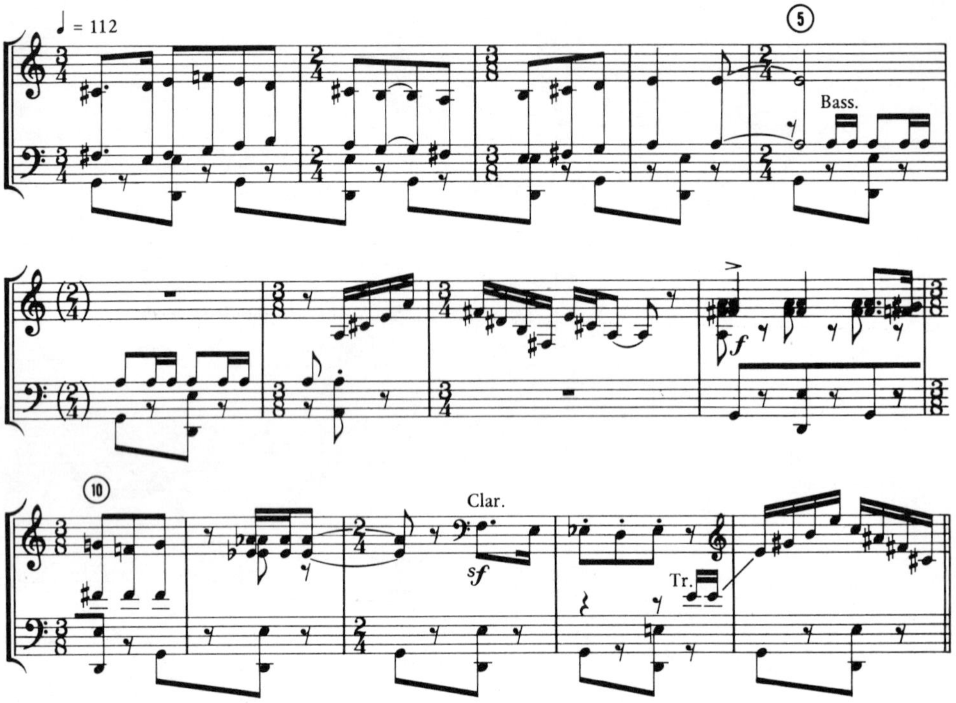

b) Webern (1883-1945), "Wie Bin Ich Froh," Op. 25, No. 1 (accents independent of bar-lines)

c) Messiaen (1908–), *Les corps glorieux* (nonmetric rhythm)

d) Kodaly (1882-1967), *Cello Sonata,* 1st movement (irregular beat divisions)

phrases and sections of highly contrasted lengths and rhythmic materials. Successions of symmetrical phrases of four or eight measures, unified by parallel or similar durations, are rare. Listen to the passages in Example 15-6 and note their rhythmic materials.

HARMONY

Tertian chord progressions have ceased to operate in much current music as functional bases for tonality. Furthermore, the traditional *interdependence* of melody and harmony, the one reflecting and seeming to evolve logically out of the other, is no longer a primary structural basis for most composition. This fact is reflected in the general abandonment of the major-minor key system. Harmony is treated differently and is given new meanings in the structure of current music; the most all-pervading feature of current harmonic styles is the abandonment of diatonic triads, dominant sevenths, diminished sevenths, and the like in favor of a more complex vocabulary including both extended tertian and nontertian chord types. Furthermore, twentieth-century compositions often reveal sonorities that are derived more from voice leading and counterpoint than from the use of chords reflecting consistent patterns of interval construction, such as triads or quartal chords.

In Chapter 6 (Example 6-3), several different chord types were shown, some of which are typically found in twentieth-century music. These included *quartal chords* (chords constructed primarily of stacked fourths), *heterogeneous chords* (chords constructed from a mixture of different intervals), *tone clusters* (chords built out of major and minor seconds), and *polychords* (chords consisting of two or more superposed combinations, such as two different triads or seventh chords). Example 15-7 gives several illustrations of contemporary harmonic practice. Study the excerpts, comparing them and using the piano to reinforce the aural impression that you form by reading the examples. Note the description given of their harmonic materials.

In summary, it may be said that the role of harmony in twentieth-century music is that of providing color rather than function; harmony is more often a product of converging melodies than a reservoir of melodic pitches.

Example 15-7 An overview of twentieth-century harmonic practice

a) Debussy (1862-1918), *Préludes,* Book II, "Canope" (planing, or parallelism, in triads)

b) Bartók (1881-1945), *Mikrokosmos,* "Variations on a Folk Tune" (consistent use of paired sixths to produce essentially tertian sonorities)

c) Stravinsky (1882–), *The Rite of Spring* (paired thirds in parallel motion, superposed to form a consistent chromatic conflict

(cont.)

Example 15-7 (continued)

d) Hindemith (1895-1963), *String Quartet No. 4 in E♭*, 1st movement (a mixture of mild and sharp dissonances, organized contrapuntally so as to produce both tertian and quartal chords)

e) Bartók (1881-1945), *Concerto for Orchestra* (five-part triads and seventh chords)

(cont.)

Example 15-7 (continued)

f) Bartók (1881-1945), *Four Hungarian Folk Settings* (chords constructed mainly of seconds—secundal harmony)

g) Schoenberg (1874-1951), *String Quartet No. 4,* Op. 37, 1st movement (serially derived tertian and nontertian chords showing a concentration of sevenths, tritones, fourths, and fifths; these chords, by virtue of their mixed interval content, are heterogeneous in construction)

h) Webern (1883-1945), *Variations for Piano,* Op. 27 (chords emphasizing major sevenths, tritones, thirds, and sixths)

(cont.)

Example 15-7 (continued)

i) Stravinsky (1882–), *Sonata for Two Pianos,* 2nd movement (triads, triads with added sixths, sevenths, and ninths, polychords, and chords of heterogeneous construction)

j) William Schuman (1910–), *Three Score Set for Piano* (polychords)

ATONALITY AND SERIAL COMPOSITION

Probably the most pervasive trend in twentieth-century composition is the abandonment of the major-minor key system and functional harmonic usage. Not all composers have abandoned all feeling for tonality or pitch focus. However, with the exception of certain types of composition, such as jazz, film music, pop music, and music written explicitly for teaching purposes, composers have on the whole turned to organizing schemes other than those demanding loyalty to the major and minor scales. The most important of these schemes is best known by the term *atonality.*

The expanding vocabulary of tonal relations in late nineteenth-century music was derived mainly from chromatic alteration of diatonic patterns. All the available twelve notes of the chromatic scale occur in the passage shown in Example 15-8, though the passage is clearly organized within the tonal

Example 15-8

Wagner (1813-1883), *Tristan und Isolde*

(cont.)

Example 15-8 (continued)

framework of A♭ major, the key in which it begins and ends. Example 15-9 is similar in that all twelve notes of the chromatic scale occur within brief spans of time. Unlike Example 15-8, this passage reveals no sense of key; it neither begins nor ends by establishing a key, nor do its melodic or harmonic materials allude to or suggest derivation from a diatonic scale. Such a passage is described as *atonal.* In an atonal composition the notes used do not reflect any particular key or tonal center. Each note is tonally independent, so to speak, of every other note. Instead of adhering to functionally oriented pre-established chord progressions, the notes are related to one another as a series.

Example 15-9

Schoenberg (1874-1951), *String Quartet No. 4,* Op. 37, 1st movement

Atonality represents the liberation of pitch from tonality; but composers such as Arnold Schoenberg and his followers, having discarded traditional tonality, felt keenly the need for a more positive basis for composition than the simple renunciation of traditional tonality. Schoenberg in particular searched for a compositional rationale that would provide a more systematic basis for organizing pitch. In other words, he felt an artistic need for a method of composition that would provide a basis for the continued composition of atonal works such as *Pierrot Lunaire* (1912), works whose artistic merit was apparent but which seemed arbitrary in their method. In the second decade of the current century Schoenberg perfected a solution to the problem posed by these earlier atonal works; the solution was contained in his *Twelve-Tone Technique.*

There were many historical precedents for twelve-tone serial* composition, but Schoenberg's method was the first carefully worked-out set of compositional principles premised on the use of all twelve notes. These principles may be summarized as follows:

1. The pitch materials of a given composition should be based on a tone row constituted of all twelve notes (of the chromatic scale) stated in any octave registration desired.
2. No member of the tone row should be restated until all other remaining notes have occurred.
3. The tone row may be stated in its original form, backwards, inverted, or inverted and backwards. Such row forms may occur successively or simultaneously, or in any of the eleven possible transpositions.
4. All melodic, harmonic, and subsidiary pitch materials are normally derived from the tone row.
5. Tonality, or semblances of key in the guise of triads, diatonic scale patterns, chord patterns suggesting functional relations, etc., must be generally avoided. Octaves, vertical or horizontal, are also avoided.
6. The treatment of dissonance is free of the limitations of traditional "rules" of composition or the inhibiting influence of key.

The tone row of a serially organized twelve-tone composition, followed by its alternate forms (permutations), is given in Example 15-10. One of the transpositions of the tone row is also included. It should be observed that the tone row amounts to a set of pitch materials, *not* a theme, whose order in a composition is largely determined prior to composition. However, the creation of *music* from a tone row requires the same problem solving and decision making that have always been a part of musical composition. Decisions regarding rhythm, texture, form, and to a great extent harmony are necessary for a tone row (or any abstract series of notes) to be transformed into music.

*"Serial" means adhering to a specific order.

Example 15-10 A tone row and its permutations

a) Untransposed

Original

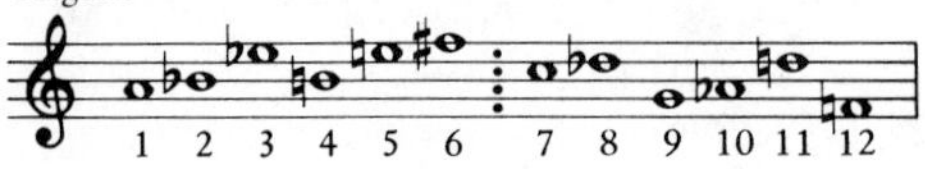

Original Backwards (Retrograde)

Inversion

Inversion Backwards (Retrograde Inversion)

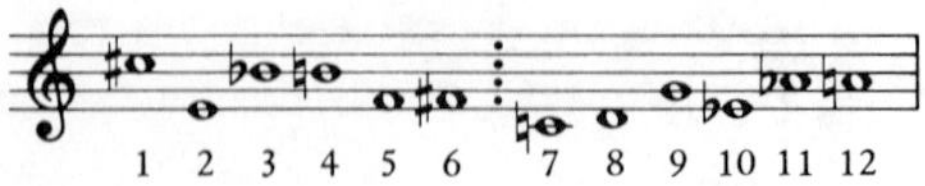

b) Transposed up a perfect fourth

Original

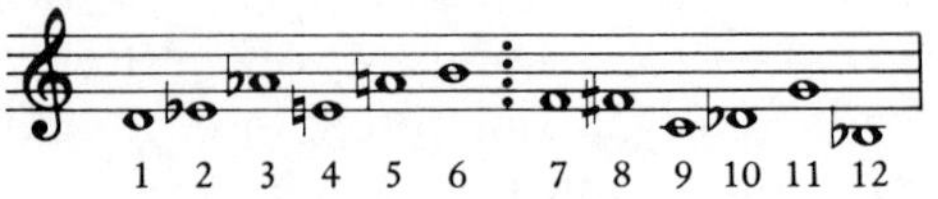

Original Backwards (Retrograde)

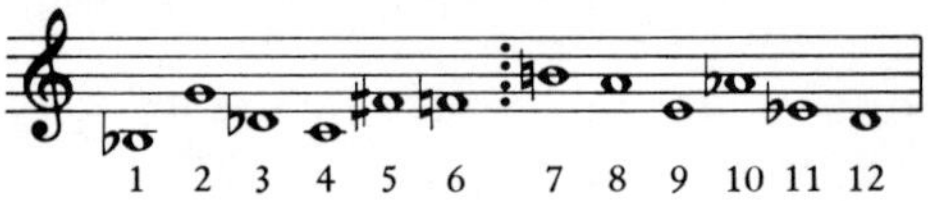

Inversion

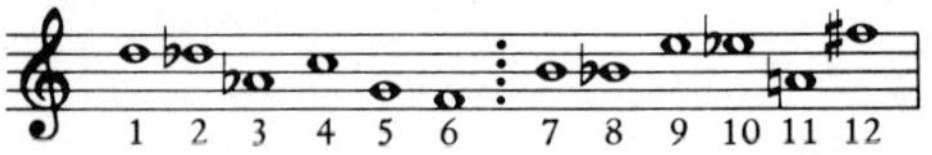

Inversion Backwards (Retrograde Inversion)

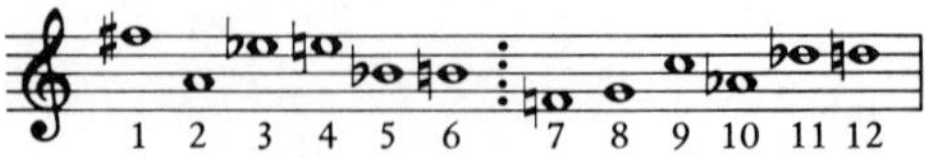

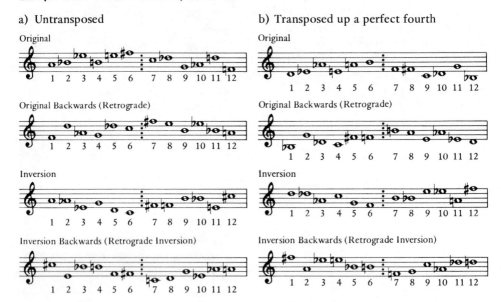

Note that the tone row's pitch order in Example 15-10 seems to rule out any definitive tonal center. Also note that patterns associated with tonality, such as triad outlines, octave leaps, and normal tritone resolutions, do *not* occur in either the original series or any of its permutations.

It is important to recognize that a tone row, in contrast to a melody, is not a series of specific, directed intervals. The interval between the first two notes of the tone row in Example 15-10 is a minor second as the row is notated here. However, in a composition, these two notes may be related in any of a number of different ways, including the following:

Each note in the original tone row is best regarded as a *pitch class.* The first note in the tone row of Example 15-10 represents a pitch class consisting of all notes, in all registers, having the pitch name *a,* the second note represents a pitch class consisting of all notes having the pitch name *b*♭, and so on. All possible intervals between the members of any two consecutive pitch classes are called an *interval class.* Thus all the intervals shown above belong to one interval class (note that both melodic and harmonic intervals are included). Viewed in this light, a tone row is simply an ordering of various interval classes to be at the composer's disposal. The precise intervals heard at any point in a composition are by no means predetermined.

The tone row of Example 15-10 is the basis of Schoenberg's *Violin Concerto,* the beginning of which is shown in Example 15-11. Before analyzing this passage as an example of serial composition, consider it in the same light as you would a piece by Mozart. Study the melodic organization and phrase structure, the rhythmic values, the texture, the accompaniment, and the use of repetition and contrast.

Example 15-11

Schoenberg (1874-1951), *Violin Concerto,* 1st movement

(cont.)

Example 15-11 (continued)

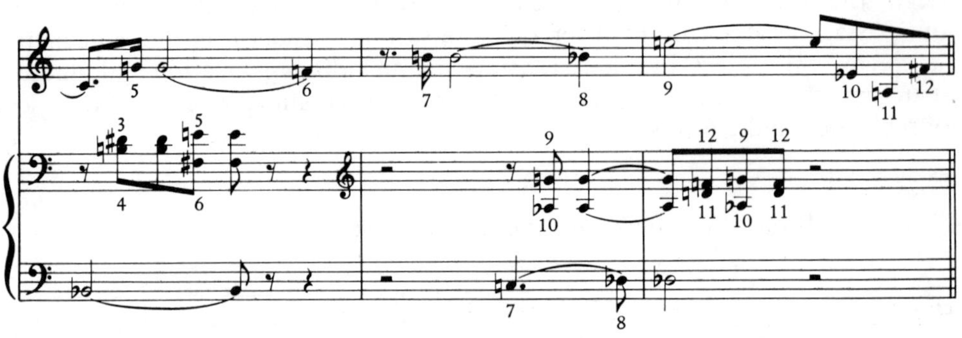

Each row form used in Example 15-11 is indicated by "Orig." or "Inv.," and each pitch is numbered. The work begins with the original row, untransposed, distributed between the violin and the orchestra. In measure 4 the inverted form of the row is introduced, transposed up a perfect fourth (or down a perfect fifth); this statement of the tone row is also shared by the violin and the orchestra. In measure 8 the soloist and the orchestra go their separate ways, the soloist reverting to the original form of the row while the orchestra restates the inverted and transposed form. In measure 11 the violinist and orchestra switch roles; the violinist takes over the inverted and transposed form of the row, and the orchestra restates the original form.

Despite the very simple pattern in which the tone row is deployed in this passage, the composer has built up an interesting and musically satisfying fabric. The row is stated in such a way as to project a motive, characterized by a long-short-long rhythmic pattern and ascending melodic half-steps. Both counterpoint and chords have been fashioned from the basic row. Note repetition has been used to add to the sense of rhythmic motion. The row is used flexibly enough for some notes to recur as members of reiterated figures, even after subsequent row members have been introduced. Despite the variety of notes in the row, the composer has clearly arranged them so as to emphasize the second as a characteristic melodic interval. Thirds, sixths, and sevenths are projected as the main harmonic materials of the passage. None of these ways of producing variety and unity is explicitly present in the tone row itself.

It should be clear that the tone row is musical raw material. Its use no more ensures artistic merit or effective music than does the use of any other type of raw material, such as a triad, scale, or interval. It is only through the manner in which the tone row is deployed and given structural significance that a serial composition is made intelligible and artistically acceptable.

Three illustrations of serial technique are shown in Example 15-12. These passages give some indication of the flexibility of the serial method of composition.

Example 15-12 Various aspects of tone-row treatment

a) Schoenberg (1874-1951), *Klavierstück,* Op. 33a (chord succession)

b) Schoenberg, *Violin Concerto,* 1st movement (a melody with chordal accompaniment)

c) Stravinsky (1882–), *In Memoriam Dylan Thomas* (non-twelve-tone serial technique, with all four permutations of a five-note row used as the basis for four-part counterpoint)

RECENT INNOVATIONS

Electronic Music

The creation of music by means of mechanical or electronic devices, as distinguished from instruments whose tone is produced by the physical activation of strings, air columns, or membranes, has been going on since the early part of the current century. Such innovators and experimenters as Lee de Forest, Leon Theremin, and Edgard Varèse began at that time to explore various ways of mechanically producing musical sounds and noise with electronic devices such as the vacuum tube and the theremin. The most prominent of these men, and the one whose work has apparently had the most lasting effect, was Edgard Varèse. In such works as *Ionisation,* for percussion and two sirens, and *Déserts,* for winds, percussion, and tape-recorded industrial sounds, Varèse brought about a unique merging of traditional sonorities with noise sounds. The acceptance of the latter as music necessitates some redefining of the term "music"; Varèse described his work as "organized sound."

Since the end of the Second World War, the musical scene has been enlivened by enormously varied kinds of musical composition. Not the least important of these has involved the use of electronically produced sounds, pitched and nonpitched, either as the sole basis for composition or in conjunction with traditionally produced musical materials.

The invention of instruments capable of producing a vastly enlarged spectrum of pitches and fine gradations of pitch, enormously varied timbres and colors, as well as durational patterns far exceeding in complexity those achievable by human performance, has resulted in a rapid expansion of the literature of electronic composition far in excess of the demand for it. The resulting surplus has in no way deterred the production of electronic music by composers at such centers as Princeton, Columbia, Yale, and the Universities of Illinois, California, and Toronto, to name only a few on this continent. Undoubtedly the foremost composer of electronic music is Karlheinz Stockhausen (born 1928), whose works represent a direct line of descent from the influence of Webern (for example, in Stockhausen's *Zeitmasse,* for wind quintet) to electronically composed works (such as *Electronic Study No. 1*). Other contemporary composers who have plunged into electronic composition include Pierre Boulez, John Cage, Milton Babbitt, Mel Powell, and Luciano Berio. Many others, such as Otto Luening and Vladimir Ussachevsky, had begun wrestling with the problems and possibilities of electronic music when Stockhausen was still a youngster.

Electronic music encompasses a wide variety of technical approaches to composing. Some composers have approached it by experimenting with new means of sound production *per se,* while others, such as Stockhausen and Babbitt, seem to have espoused electronic composition as a logical means for extending *serial* processes to mechanically and arithmetically determined music, at the same time eliminating the composer's dependence on human performance.

Electronic composition also involves an enormous array of electronic gadgetry, some of which is of questionable effectiveness. The basic electronic instrument is the tape recorder, which is used as an essential tool for storing and transmitting the sound patterns, whatever their source (electronically produced sound waves, adapted human voices, street noise, etc.). Equally important is the loudspeaker or speaker system, which projects the sounds transmitted by the recorder. The tape recorder is used in numerous ways:

for example, artificially produced pitches or pitch masses may be arranged in various dynamic and durational patterns; human-produced or artificially produced sound (music or noise) may be sped up or retarded as desired, for specific effects; and mixtures of sounds from different sources, recorded separately, may be superposed.

Perhaps the most significant result of such experimentation at this early stage is our recognition of the enormous capabilities of electronic media for exploring new gradations in pitch (microtones), new timbres, new durational patterns, and new, more complex combinations of these. An obvious result of using electronic media is the control capability extended to the composer through the elimination of human interpretation in performance. The composer may now, if he wishes, completely regulate all aspects of the composition and its performance. It is yet to be determined to what degree musicians and the musical public will accept such endeavors.

Aleatory Music

A countertrend to Stockhausen's attempt at total determination of the process and realization of musical composition is perhaps best exemplified by the *aleatory* or *indeterminate* compositions of John Cage. Cage's music, which on the whole allows for the inclusion of virtually any type of sound production including traditional instruments, prepared piano,* human voices (live or taped), and electronic media, as well as noises produced by household wares, street sounds, animal sounds, etc., reveals a trend toward the *absence* of planned or predetermined musical events. Random sound events, improvisation, and silence are some of the most provocative yet significant components of Cage's music. *Imaginary Landscape,* for 24 radios, exemplifies his partial abandonment of traditional instrumentation, as well as the significance of *chance* happenings as the basis for ordering sound events. Cage has been called the most influential composer alive in the United States today.

Many American composers, such as Earle Brown and Lucas Foss, have shown an indebtedness to Cage's use of random events and improvisation as part of the process of composition.

The Influence of Jazz

The rhythmic freedom, spontaneity, melodic invention, and ensemble intricacy of jazz have attracted many gifted composers of the current century. Obvious attempts at imitation of jazz clichés were made early in this century by such composers as Gershwin, Hindemith, Stravinsky, and Milhaud. Although such works as Milhaud's *Creation of the World* may have successfully alluded to jazz, they revealed little of the essence of it, the spontaneity of *improvisation.* Some more recent composers have similarly attempted to capture or

---

*A prepared piano is one that is mechanically adapted or altered to produce unusual effects.

allude to rhythmic patterns, figures, and even instrumental combinations associated with the jazz ensemble. Among the most successful in such ventures has been Gunther Schuller, in works constituting so-called Third Stream Music. The practicality of combining or juxtaposing concert orchestral music with small jazz ensembles is as yet doubtful.

On the other hand, composers steeped in the traditions of jazz by virtue of performance experience, and schooled in concert music as well, have in some instances successfully combined traditional concert ensembles with jazz and, furthermore, enriched jazz with such ingredients of traditional music as counterpoint, cantus firmus techniques, and highly complex harmonic patterns, metric schemes, and rhythms. The result of such ventures, undertaken by musicians such as Dave Brubeck, Lennie Tristano, John Lewis, Dizzy Gillespie, and Lalo Shiffrin, has been a many-faced contemporary jazz idiom that is complex yet essentially *spontaneous.* Perhaps the most significant contrast between contemporary composers trained in the traditions of classical music and those working in the jazz idiom is that the latter have continued to deal, however experimentally and individually, with traditional instruments and tonal materials, while their counterparts in electronic and aleatoric composition have, for all intents and purposes, discarded both tonality and the traditional media of performance.

TRENDS IN MUSIC NOTATION

Contemporary performers often encounter notational signs which are foreign to traditional music notation. The use of such unfamiliar symbols as **H** and **N**, employed by Schoenberg to denote principal and secondary melodic parts, respectively, is indicative of the desire of twentieth-century composers to control as much as possible the interpretation of their music.

Compositions for the piano sometimes call for the articulation of massed clusters of pitches, played by leaning on the keyboard with the forearm in order to activate all possible notes within a given span. The following is an example in which all the notes between *A* and f^2 are to be rolled in an ascending succession:

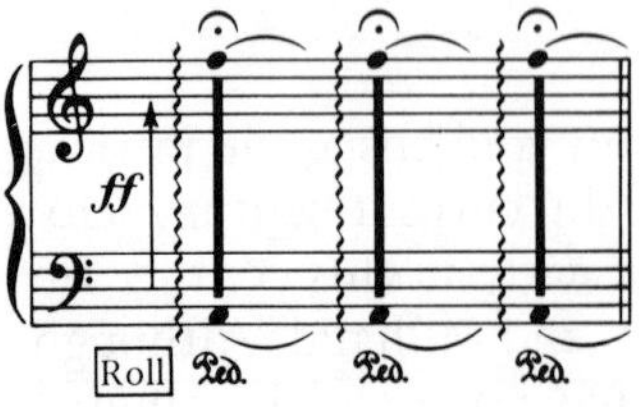

Many works reveal attempts to free rhythmic organization from the accentuation implied by meter signatures and barlines. Charles Ives's *Concord Sonata,* an excerpt from which is shown in Example 15-13, is an example.

Example 15-13

Ives (1874-1954), *Concord Sonata,* 1st movement

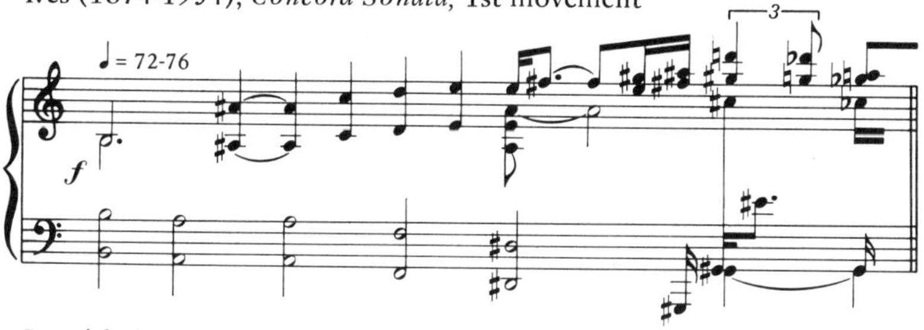

Note the tempo indication of MM 72 to 76 per quarter note, given without a specific meter signature. The player is to maintain a definite pace despite the irregularity of rhythmic accents and grouping.

Fractional meters are those which call for the addition to a common meter of a beat fraction, usually a half or quarter of the principal unit. In Example 15-14 rhythmic interest is heightened and an irregular beat grouping is produced by the addition of an eighth note, the equivalent of half a beat, to each measure.

Example 15-14

Chavez (1899–), *Sonata for Piano,* 1st movement

Example 15-15 shows the correlation of duration and dynamic level. The loudness of the pitches is roughly proportional to the lengths of the notes.

Example 15-15

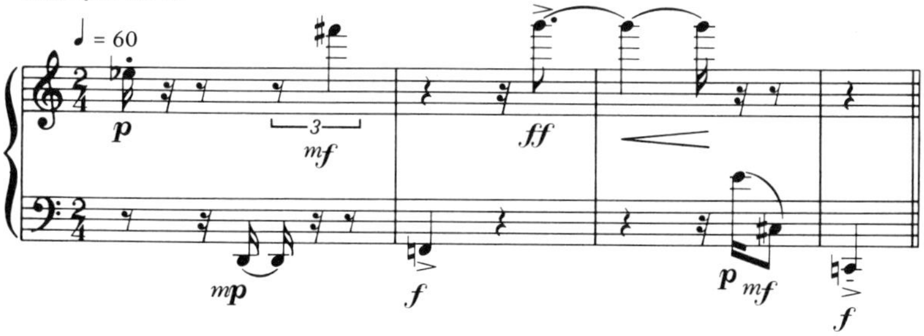

The use of an "x" affixed to the stem of a note to be performed by a singer, as in Example 15-16, indicates that the note is to be articulated in the style of "spoken singing" *(Sprechstimme).* There is considerable disagreement concerning the precise interpretation of this symbol. Some composers intend it to indicate the precise articulation of the indicated pitch, while others apparently prefer an approximation of the written pitch. Schoenberg, Webern, Berg, and more recently Pierre Boulez in his famous *Marteau sans Maître,* have used this device most effectively.

Example 15-16

Schoenberg (1874-1951), *Pierrot Lunaire,* Op. 21

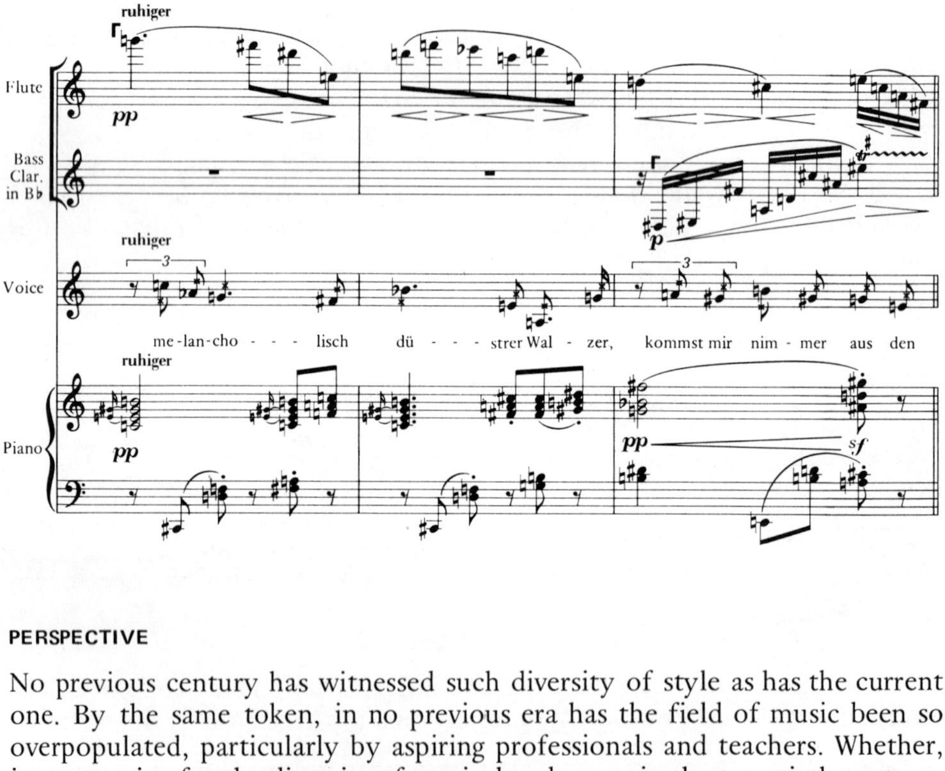

PERSPECTIVE

No previous century has witnessed such diversity of style as has the current one. By the same token, in no previous era has the field of music been so overpopulated, particularly by aspiring professionals and teachers. Whether, in accounting for the diversity of musical endeavors in the twentieth century, one points to the population explosion, revolutionized mass communication, skyrocketing technology, or simply a revitalization of interest in musical performance on various artistic levels (as seen, for instance, in the current craze for playing the guitar), he is taken by the innumerable *trends* that have constituted the history of music in the first 70 years of this century. Indeed, the diversity of music and musical practice is so great that any attempt at theoretical generalization can only be labeled as speculation.

It may be too early to appraise the significance and permanence of either the trends or the vast repertoire of recent composition—history has well documented man's past incapability either to discover or to project the significance of his own creativeness. However, most of the musical masters of past and current eras did not let such incapabilities deter their own pursuit of music. Nor should we. It is hoped that this book has helped to provide a store of basic information and thereby stimulate the curiosity that may lead the reader to deeper study and eventual mastery of one of the most rewarding of man's pursuits, the art of music.

EXERCISES

1. Define briefly each of the following terms.
    a) Neoclassicism
    b) Atonality
    c) Nontertian
    d) Serial
    e) Interval class
    f) Aleatory
    g) Sprechstimme
    h) Secundal
    i) Nonmetric rhythm
    j) Linear
2. Listen to recordings of Mozart's *Symphony No. 40 in G minor* and Stravinsky's *Symphony in Three Movements.* Then prepare an outline for a comparative discussion of the two pieces. Use the following main headings in your outline: (1) melody, (2) rhythm and meter, (3) tonality and harmony, (4) texture, and (5) form. Begin by formulating a series of general statements which summarize the characteristics of the two pieces with respect to each of the five main headings. Then select a number of subtopics under each heading which could profitably be discussed.
3. Turn to Example 15-1(b) by Webern. This movement is a study in the use of motivic detail as the unifying basis of a piece of music. Find five motives, chords, or figures derived from measures 1–2 and copy them below. Cite the measure in which each occurs. See the sample in (a).

a) 

(measure 3, Vln. I)

b)

c)

d)

e)

f)

(optional)

4. Invent a short piano composition (30 seconds to one minute long) with a homophonic texture in which the melody and chords are derived from the tone row given in Example 15-10.

SUGGESTED READING

William Austin, *Music in the Twentieth Century.* New York: Norton, 1966.

Leon Dallin, *Techniques of Twentieth Century Composition.* Dubuque, Iowa: William C. Brown, 1964.

Josef Rufer, *Composition with Twelve Tones Related Only to One Another.* London: Barrie and Rockliff, 1961 (revised ed.).

INDEX OF MUSICAL EXAMPLES

INDEX OF MUSICAL EXAMPLES

SUBJECT INDEX

SUBJECT INDEX

ABCDE79876543210